Studies in Education (new series) 13

Childminding and Day Nurseries
What Kind of Care?

Berry Mayall and Pat Petrie

HEINEMANN EDUCATIONAL BOOKS
for the Institute of Education, University of London

Heinemann Educational Books Ltd
22 Bedford Square, London WC1B 3HH

LONDON EDINBURGH MELBOURNE AUCKLAND
HONG KONG SINGAPORE KUALA LUMPUR NEW DELHI
IBADAN NAIROBI JOHANNESBURG
EXETER (NH) KINGSTON PORT OF SPAIN

ISBN 0 85473 160 1 ✓

British Library Cataloguing in Publication Data

Mayall, Berry
    Childminding and day nurseries.—
    (Studies in education; 13)
    1. Day care centers—Great Britain
    I. Title   II. Petrie, Pat   III. Series
    362.7'12'0941   HV861.G6

ISBN 0-85473-160-1 ·

0107009

362.71
MAY

119897

Printed in Great Britain by Biddles Ltd, Guildford

Childminding and Day Nurseries:
What Kind of Care?

Studies in Education ISSN 0458-2101

A series of monographs published by Heinemann Educational Books for the Institute of Education, University of London. Other titles in the series:

Further information about Institute of Education publications may be obtained from the Information Officer, Institute of Education, 20 Bedford Way, London WC1H 0AL; or from Heinemann Educational Books, 22 Bedford Square, London WC1B 3HH.

In memory of Jack Tizard

Contents

Acknowledgements

There are many people who helped us with our study and we should like to thank them here. Our greatest debt is to the late Jack Tizard, Director of the Thomas Coram Research Unit from 1973 to 1979, who offered us unfailing advice and encouragement. Without his support the study would not have been possible.

Katherine Schneider worked as our colleague throughout the work and made a much-valued contribution to the design, interviewing and analysis of data.

We are most grateful also to Professor Barbara Tizard, Professor Tessa Blackstone, Peter Moss, Ian Plewis and Charlie Owen for their advice and expertise, and to Jackie Lee, Lorraine Wilder and Olwen Davies for their patient secretarial backup. Responsibility for the content is, of course, our own.

Finally, we are most grateful for the help of local authority staff in several London boroughs, and for the cooperation and hospitality of minders, nursery staff and mothers, who gave up their time to help us.

B.M. P.P.
Thomas Coram Research Unit
March, 1983

Part One
The Study and its Setting

Chapter One
The Study

What sort of care do the youngest children get if they are away from their parents during the day? For most very young children day care means minding; and for a very few, day nurseries. We decided to study the service that they and their mothers get at minders' and nurseries, and we focused on children under two years old. There were two main reasons for this choice. First, minding is the only form of care that governments since 1975 have promoted for these children, although little was known about minders at this date, and what was known was disturbing. We wanted to provide information on the minding service, and on what it is like for mothers finding and using minding and day nurseries for these young children in the absence of any realistic alternative. Secondly, to say anything worthwhile in an observational study about relationships between children and adults it is desirable to narrow the children's age-range and focus on a particular stage of development. This narrow focus makes it easier to interpret findings. Many of the findings, however, apply to all under-fives and their mothers who use nurseries and minders. All are affected by day-care policy as it works in practice in these two services.

The kind of care children get depends a good deal on what policy-makers think and do. What do they think is best for families with young children? What proposals do they make towards appropriate provision? We have tried to set the research within a discussion of public policy towards day-care, to evaluate the consequences for families and to present proposals for improvement. Part I (Chapters 1 to 3) describes the study and provides a context in the history of day-care, the laws regulating it, and other research; Part II (Chapters 4 to 9) presents and discusses the findings; and Part III (Chapters 10 and 11) gives a summary of the services offered by childminding and day nurseries as revealed by the study, and outlines proposals for improving them.*

The forerunner of this study of under-twos in day care was a study of two-year-olds at minders' which we carried out as part of a programme of research at the Thomas Coram Research Unit (TCRU) on services for pre-school families. The report was published as *Minder, Mother and Child* (Mayall and Petrie 1977). It is perhaps appropriate to give a very brief account of the earlier study here, both because it led on to the under-twos study, and because our proposals for improving day-care services in Chapter 11 result from the findings of both studies and relate to children under three.

In this earlier research we studied the sort of service registered minders offered to mothers and children. We were interested in questions posed by existing research and by opposing views on childminding at the time. What was the day-to-day experience of the children? Were they offered motherly care? Were the mothers satisfied? If childminding had defects, how could it be improved? Unlike previous research we focused on minding in reasonably good circumstances, to study whether it could offer an acceptable service, or one that could readily be improved.

We focused on two-year-olds cared for by registered minders, drawn mainly from two inner London boroughs. We interviewed the minder and mother each at home (28 mother–minder pairs in all). We focused on what happened rather than on general practice, and collected information particularly on 'yesterday', the day before the interview. During the interview, observations were carried out of the child's interactions with his caregiver. A return visit was made to the minder to assess the child's language development.

By the standards of earlier descriptions of minders, these minders were probably a favoured sample. None lived in strikingly bad housing conditions. Nearly a third had had some previous work experience with children and 60 per cent had taken part in a local authority training scheme. The 28 mothers were probably representative of women who use registered minders, at least in inner London. Over half were born in the British Isles, and all but four lived with their husband. Three-quarters of the mothers were in non-manual work, and all worked full-time. The children's families lived in poor housing: nearly half shared or lacked basic amenities, a quarter were overcrowded and over half had no access to a garden.

---

* A note about style is necessary. We refer to the child throughout as 'he'. We are aware of the shortcomings of this, but it is a useful device which avoids ambiguity where the principal caregivers are all female.

The instability of day-care arrangements, noted with disquiet by earlier investigators, held good for these two-year-olds. As for the children's daily experiences at the minders', two-fifths were in groups of four children or more and for some of them their daily experience was impoverished and hazardous. A third had no access to a yard or garden, and half had not played outside 'yesterday'. More than a quarter were confined in too little space; more than half were subjected to safety hazards. Again more than half had not been out (off the premises) 'yesterday' and a third had not been out at all in the previous week.

The children's relationship with the minder, judged by the interview and observation, was in many cases rather distant. The child made few, in some cases no, advances to the minder during the visit, and significantly fewer than to his mother during the parallel observation at home. More than a third of the minders said they had not played with the child or told him a story 'yesterday'. Half did not touch the child during the observation, and a third did not speak to him. Only six did anything to encourage him to play during the visit. Given these findings, and the lack of stability in their day-care history, it is not surprising that all but four of the children scored below average on one or both scales of the language tests (Reynell), yet this was not a disadvantaged group of children: most of their parents were non-manual workers. In the light of this finding it was disturbing to find that health visitors had little contact with the minders.

We also assessed the minders' attitudes to their work. Most seemed well disposed towards the children and were able to focus on their needs, experiences and behaviour. Most were not punitive towards the child – although nearly a fifth were. But judging by their practice and what they said only 42 per cent seemed to see their job as in any way concerned with the child's development. A quarter of them were rated as generally hostile to mothers.

Perhaps it is not surprising that many of the mothers would have preferred other care for their child. About a third said they were satisfied with the present arrangement, half wanted to move their child to a nursery, and the rest wanted to supplement the minder's care with playgroup or nursery school.

What we found was disturbing, given that the minders were probably favoured in terms of their past child-care experience and local authority efforts to help them. Further, since the sample of children was weighted towards those who had been with their minder for at least ten months, there had been ample time for most of the children to settle in and form a relationship with her.

Our findings were consistent with those of earlier research which had reported unfavourably on minding. There was little evidence of 'motherly' qualities in the childminders towards their charges. The study identified and discussed some characteristics of childminding: the poor conditions in which minders work, the ineffective role of the local authority, the poor quality of the children's daily experience and the instability of placements. All these related to its being low-cost day care.

Questions addressed by the under-twos' study

This first study raised a number of questions which deserved further investigation and formed the basis for the present study:

1. *The quality of care.* We decided to study in more detail the environment in which minded children spent the day, their daily experience, and the kind of relationship they had with their caregiver. We thought it important to ask whether there were differences in the standards of care obtained by different groups in the community and whether the mother's social class or country of origin related to this.

2. To what extent is the minder a *mother substitute?* Did the findings of the first study hold good for younger children? There is little alternative provision to minders available for under-twos (see page 28). At the time (1976) minding was being recommended as especially suitable for babies and toddlers, in contrast to the day nursery, which it was suggested was unlikely to offer individual, affectionate care.

3. How *stable* is childminding for the youngest children and what factors relate to instability?

4. Was the children's *health* monitored regularly by the health services?

5. The *mother's side of the arrangement* needed more detailed study. What are the characteristics of mothers who work when their child is very young? How did they find day-care and how satisfied were they with the arrangement? How far did childminding meet the needs of a working mother? Did minders and mothers have a good working relationship on behalf of the child?

6. How did the experience of *the nursery child* compare with that of the minded child? We decided to make an additional study of local authority day nurseries, asking similar questions. Many assumptions have been made about nurseries and there has been very little research into them in this country, although with childminding they provide the main form of care for under-twos where standards can be affected directly by social policy.

7. How far did the *day nurseries meet the needs and wishes of the mothers who used them?*

The study's design and method

We decided to carry out a study of under-twos at minders' and to draw some comparisons with nursery children. The design and methods of the earlier study were retained to maintain comparability, and augmented. We intended to study childminders and day nurseries in each of four London boroughs, two inner and two outer boroughs. But this depended on cooperation at all levels from local authority staff. In the end we took our samples from five boroughs, two inner and three outer.

Collection and analysis of data
The pilot work for the study was carried out in 1977, and the main interviews and observations were done from October 1977 to December 1978. Three of us did this work, the authors of this report and a third research officer, Katherine Schneider.

Childminders and mothers – first round of interviews
We took a random sample of 208 registered minders from local authority lists in four London boroughs (two inner and two outer). Some had stopped minding (32), a few had no minded children at the time (9) and a few did not wish to be interviewed (8). We interviewed the remaining 159 minders.
Main sub-sample. Minders who were looking after at least one child under the age of two years, for at least six hours a day, were selected into this sample, up to a maximum of seventeen from each borough. The selection process was designed to get equal proportions of children aged under one year and over one year; these became the *focus children.* We interviewed each of the 66 minders for about an hour in most cases. Then we visited the mother of each focus child, and interviewed 64 of the mothers (two were not available for interview). We also carried out an observation of the child's interaction, first with his minder and then with his mother.
Secondary sub-sample. The 93 minders who had not been selected into the main sub-sample were given a short interview (10 to 20 minutes).

The interview schedule
The long interview with 66 minders (main sub-sample) covered the following

topics: data on the children cared for, including schoolchildren; the minder's own family; her work history and work intentions; the contractual arrangements made with parents; her contact with the health and social services for the children; any settling-in procedure adopted; the focus child's day at the minder's; her expenses, both at the outset and currently; her housing.

The questions emphasized the recent past. On child-care practice they related to 'yesterday' and to the previous week; on cooperation with parents, to the previous month; on events that might be less frequent, such as contacts with doctors, health visitors and local authority workers, to the previous six months.

The interview concentrated on events, rather than on attitudes, such as the child's day, the minder's contact with parents, and her use of health services.

The short interview with the other 93 minders (secondary sub-sample) covered some of the same topics. It was designed to take much less time, so that it could be carried out at first contact without disturbing the minder's day. Topics were mostly factual: data on the children cared for; the minder's own family; her work history and work intentions; her contact with the health and social services for the children; the charge made for one child – chosen at random; her housing.

The interview with the 64 mothers of the focus minded children covered family composition; the husband's work; the mother's education, work history and present work; the arrangements made for taking time off work for childbirth; her past caretaking arrangements for the child; her satisfaction with her working day and with the present minder; how she made the present arrangement with the minder; the child's health and use of services for him during his lifetime; her housing. The interview took an hour to an hour and a half.

Parts of the interview drew on questions used in the TCRU Social Survey (Bax, Moss and Plewis, 1979): in particular, questions on the child's behaviour and the mother's relationship with her child. Questions on the child's health and use of medical services were based on those used by the TCRU medical team (Bax, Hart and Jenkins, 1980) for their check-ups of under-fives in the three areas investigated by the Social Survey, and the coding of illnesses also followed that of the medical team. We discussed and agreed the rating of cases with the TCRU consultant paediatrician.

Observation

As in our earlier study, we carried out an observation of the focus child in two settings: with his minder and with his mother at home. The aim was to compare some aspects of the child's relationship with his two caregivers. Where the child was 'mobile' (able to get about by crawling or walking) we made an unobtrusive count of his interactions with his minder or mother during the first twenty minutes of the interview, using pre-coded observation categories, devised at the pilot stage and based on the earlier study. Where the child was not 'mobile', we noted interactions during a feed, again using pre-coded categories.

Parallel observations of the child and his two caregivers were carried out for 52 children. For the other twelve possible cases, we were unable to carry out the observations in one or other setting. This was either because the interview with the mother was abridged (because she spoke a foreign language), or the child was breast-fed at home, or he was not present, or was taken away by another adult (usually his father) during the observation period.

Day nurseries and mothers

We aimed to take a random sample of four day nurseries in each of the four boroughs used for the minding sample. One borough did not wish us to study its day nurseries, so we approached a fifth. In two boroughs we were able to take a random sample of nurseries; in the other two our choice was restricted by the local authority. In all we studied fifteen day nurseries.

At each nursery we chose randomly three children aged under two years, with a weighting towards children under twelve months, 44 children in all. We interviewed the fifteen nursery matrons, and we interviewed a nursery nurse about each child, in most cases a separate nurse for each child, so that in all 41 nurses were interviewed. Again, we approached the mothers of the children, and were able to interview 40 of them (four refused).

The interview carried out with the *40 mothers of the focus day-nursery children* was substantially the same as that for the mothers of the minded children. We adapted some questions to meet the different circumstances, and added some questions to cover the possibility that the mother might not be at work, and might have had specific problems that led her to obtain a day-nursery place for the child.

The interview with the *fifteen day-nursery matrons* collected data on the numbers of children at the nursery and how they were grouped; and the number and type of staff who cared for them. It also established what visitors (doctor, health visitors, social workers, and others) came to the nursery. The interview with the *41 nursery nurses* was designed to collect data comparable with that from the minder; but it was much shorter since we thought it inappropriate to ask the nurse to give more than twenty minutes to it. The data collected was on the nurse's family; her work history and intentions, and her satisfaction with the present job; the age, hours and length of placement of the children in her room; the day's activities, both in general and as regards the focus child yesterday; and the nurse's relationship with the child and his mother.

It is worth emphasizing that the study was designed to collect data on minders, mothers and minded children, following the methods used in the earlier study, and these methods could not be fully used in the day-nursery setting. The fact that the children were mostly cared for by two or more nurses meant that a nurse did not always have the precise information on the child's day, or on contact with his mother, that a minder would have. Most important, it was not possible to carry out comparable observations of the mobile children with the nurse, because of the number of nurses present during the interview/observation with whom he could interact. We did where possible observe feeds with non-mobile children but there were few. We accepted that these problems would limit comparisons between the nursery and minding data, but we opted to concentrate on a design comparable with the earlier study, so as to provide from the two studies the range of data on minding for under-threes, which seemed to be urgently needed.

Data collected from social services departments
In each borough we interviewed local authority administrative and executive staff to collect data on the minding and day-nursery services in the borough as a whole. The staff interviewed were those whom day-care management staff thought would be able to answer our questions. Their titles and responsibilities varied between boroughs.

Second interviews
Twelve months after the first round of interviews, we collected data on the stability of the child's placement. We had time to do this only with the inner London minders and nurseries. We asked minders whether they were still minding and whether the child was still attending; and matrons whether the nurses interviewed last year and the children in their care were still at the nursery.

Numbers of interviews and numbers of children
Appendix A gives a summary of the kinds and numbers of interviews, and of the children at minders' and nurseries on whom we collected data. These included both the focus children and all the other children in the care of the minder or nurse.

Weighting
A note on weighting is needed to explain the way we set out findings. The sample was not entirely representative of the general populations in the areas we studied, in that inner city minders and children under twelve months were, by design, over-represented. So we gave extra weight to some minders and children and their mothers, to restore to the sample their true proportions in the population. We have therefore presented the findings mostly as percentages rather than numbers, but in some cases, where the group is very small, we give numbers, and these are 'raw' or real numbers, not affected by weighting. Where statistical tests are used they have been performed on re-scaled, weighted numbers, not on percentages.

The children, their families and caregivers

We return now to the children with some information about the boroughs in which they lived, their families, and the childminders and nurses who looked after them. (More detail is given in Appendix F.)

The boroughs
The DHSS distinguishes three groups of local authorities, according to low, moderate and high need (DHSS, 1979, page vii). The four boroughs drawn on for the minding sample fall into the high need group, and three of these were used for the day-nursery sample too; the fourth nursery borough is in the low need group. Families living in high need boroughs compared with most other boroughs are more likely to be overcrowded, to live in privately rented rather than municipal accommodation, and to lack basic amenities. The proportion of mothers born abroad, of mothers working full-time and of lone-parent families is high.

The children and their families
The *minded children* were typically only children, who lived with their mother and father, both of whom worked. Almost half the children had

mothers who were born abroad, but for most mothers English was their main language. Most of the children had been looked after during working hours by someone other than their mother since before they were six months old. More than half of them were the children of non-manual workers (see Table 1). Almost a quarter of the children lived in overcrowded conditions, and nearly a fifth shared or lacked some basic housing amenity; two-fifths did not have access to a garden. Children living in the inner boroughs had poorer housing than those in the outer boroughs. (We discuss housing in more detail in Chapter 5.)

Table 1: Family characteristics – minded and day-nursery children's families

	Families of	
	minded children	*day-nursery children*
	(N = 64)	*(N = 40)*
	%	%
Number of children		
1	64	55
2	26	30
3 or more	10	15
Where mother born		
British Isles	52	60
West Indies	14	28
Indian-sub-continent	11	0
Europe	11	8
Elsewhere	12	5
Mother's work (RG)		
I,II, student	38	15
III non-manual	40	30
III manual or below	20	20
Not at work	2	35
Father's work (RG)		
I,II, student	48	7(1)*
III non-manual	13	7(1)
III manual or below	39	69(9)
Not at work	0	14(2)
No father in household	9	68

* The percentages are given for comparative purposes. The figures in brackets show the numbers of fathers in different kinds of work.

At the fifteen *day nurseries* there were 144 *children* under the age of two years, from whom we selected the 44 focus children. We were able to collect information from 40 of their mothers about the family background. Not unexpectedly, the nursery children's families differed in many ways from those of the minded children. They were children who had been judged to have a priority claim on a nursery place and this is reflected in their home circumstances. No attempt was made to pinpoint reasons why the mother got a place for her child, since a complex of factors was likely to determine this, but the mother was asked if she had had any problems since the time she became pregnant. Some of the most frequently reported problems were to do with housing and family relationships. Fifty-one per cent of the mothers said they had had problems to do with poor or unsuitable housing or with losing their housing. Forty-three per cent had had problems to do with their relatives or with their husbands; in a quarter of the households physical attacks on the mother and/or child were mentioned. Health was a major worry: 42 per cent had sought professional help for a psychiatric problem during the previous twelve months, and for 10 per cent this had included hospitalization. (By contrast, 19 per cent of minded children's mothers had sought help and none had been in hospital for a psychiatric condition.) In many cases the child's health was a serious problem: 38 per cent of the focus children had been admitted to hospital during their short lifetime. In addition to all this, most of the mothers (80 per cent) referred to difficulties in finding or keeping work, and 59 per cent to money problems. Taking all these difficulties into account, it seems reasonable to estimate that only about a fifth of the mothers were lone parents who needed to work, but had no other obvious problems – although two-thirds of all were lone parents.

Three-fifths of the mothers were born in the British Isles, and for almost all their main language was English. Of those in work at the time (65 per cent), the largest group did office work, followed by those in semi-skilled or unskilled jobs. Just over half lived in council or housing association accommodation and generally had more favourable housing than the mothers of minded children.

The minders and nurses

These were two very different groups of women who, from the mothers' point of view, performed the same task; that is, they looked after the children during the day. The minders were mostly older than the mothers whose children they cared for; they had more children of their own, but only a minority had child-care experience outside their own family. The nurses, on

Table 2: Characteristics of the childminders and nursery nurses

	Minders (N = 64) %	Nurses (N = 41) %
Age (years)		
under 21	0	29
21–25	5	39
26–30	28	22
31–40	25	7
41–50	33	2
51 +	10	0
Number of own children		
0	1	85
1,2,3	75	15
4 +	24	0
Country of birth		
UK and Eire	81	93
West Indies	8	5
Indian sub-continent	3	0
Europe	8	0
Africa	0	2
Training		
Child-related job/training	14 ⎫	5
Training for childminding/	⎬ 27*	
nursery nursing (NNEB)	18 ⎭	88
Nursing qualification	0	7
None	73	0
Years in work as minder/nurse		
Under 1 year	15	24
1 or 2 years	17	35
3 or 4 years	17	24
5 to 9 years	27	17
10 or more years	25	0

* These two groups overlapped.

the other hand, were mostly younger than the mothers of the children they cared for. They had nursery nurse training, and in some cases experience of working with children, but, given their age, this had rarely been for long. Few of them were mothers themselves and few had experience of work outside the child-care field. They were therefore less mature and experienced than the minders. Yet it is they who, as well as their child-care function, have the delicate task of interacting with mothers who are often facing considerable difficulties in their daily lives. It is considerations such as these, together with a dislike for institutional care, which may have led to the expressed preference by the DHSS for the childminder over the day nursery, even for priority category children (DHSS/DES 1978). This subject has some bearing on the findings about cooperation between mothers and nurses discussed in Chapter 9.

Summary

This first chapter has set out the background to the study, outlined the main research questions, and the study's design and methodology, and briefly described the sample. The rest of Part I covers the historical, legal and research background on day care. Readers who wish to look first at the findings should turn to Part II.

Chapter Two
Social Policy

What minding and day nurseries are like today depends on policy towards the provision of day care for children. This policy has its roots in the nineteenth century, when the needs of children for substitute care first became a pressing problem. It has barely changed since. Unlike other European countries which have responded with new policy initiatives to changing circumstances and new ideas, this country is still reluctant to intervene in what is widely seen as a private domestic matter. Policy-makers still emphasize risks to the health and welfare of children who are separated from their mothers, and voice indignation about mothers who 'neglect' their children by leaving them in other people's care.

There are several histories of day care[1] and it is unnecessary to go over the early development in detail. Broadly, with the Industrial Revolution and the concentration of work in factories, parents of the labouring classes could no longer look after their children during the working day as they had when they worked at home, in small workshops, or in the fields.[2] As a result a 'day nursing' system developed, mainly in industrial areas where young mothers from poor families had to go out to work (Hewitt, 1958). It was an early form of childminding, often carried out by the old or infirm, or by older children.

Manifestly, the system had shortcomings. Public concern focused on the children, whose health and safety were put at risk, and on the mothers who were seen as neglecting their children and households. But the state was unwilling to intervene in what was seen as a private family matter.[3] Intervention came first from charitable bodies which opened day nurseries (the first in 1850) as a healthier, safer alternative to childminding. By the 1870s there was an (unavailing) body of opinion that local authorities should provide nurseries and that minders should be regulated by law.[4] It was not until 1918 that local health authorities were empowered to provide day nurseries or to aid voluntary nurseries, as part of a package to improve health and welfare services for mothers and children. However, this proved ineffective; few nurseries were provided and by 1938 there were only 4000 places (Ferguson and Fitzgerald, 1954). Childminding up to this point was seen as a regrettable expedient in the absence of nursery places. It was during the Second World War that it was seen as a useful resource in the drive to get women back to work for the duration. An emergency scheme to recruit and subsidize minders was established (Riley, 1979).[5] It was attacked by women's organizations as a shoddy alternative to proper care in nurseries and except in the older industrial areas was not a success. At its peak it catered for only 4000 children.

Post-war legislation

In 1945 the new Labour government was faced with the continued need in some areas for women workers to help get peace-time production going. But it also wished to return mothers of under-twos to their homes. The Minister of Health made this clear:

> The right policy to pursue would be positively to discourage mothers of children under two from going out to work; to make provision for children between two and five by way of Nursery Schools and Nursery classes. (Ministry of Health Circular, 221/45).

Indeed the 1944 Education Act placed a duty on local authorities to consider the needs for nursery *education* of under-fives. So that when in 1946 some day nurseries began to close and others were transferred to the local education authority, the declared policy was for two distinct services: educational provision for children over two, and day-nursery provision for children with pressing needs (poor home conditions, 'inadequate' mothering, or a mother's urgent need to work). This represented a policy reversal. Until April 1946, nursery places were available *only* for the children of working mothers – other categories of need for day-care did not qualify. As it turned out, even from the point of view of the need for women's labour, the closing down of nurseries was too drastic, and two years later the Minister was reporting:

> Early in 1948, the Government decided it was necessary to take all practical steps to increase the labour force in the textile industries in order to meet the demand for exports and for home consumption. (Ministry of Health, Annual Report for 1948).

He believed it would be possible to attract trained young women back into the industry if they could make satisfactory arrangements for their children. In his annual report he said there was to be some small local expansion in day nurseries in the public sector, and that medical officers of health were to be encouraged to cooperate with any employer wishing to set up a factory crèche. Such cooperation would be limited to giving and receiving advice about adequate standards of care. While some employers welcomed such advice, others were less cooperative, and medical officers complained of crowded, ill-ventilated factory nurseries to which they had no right of access, and were powerless to improve.

It is clear from social histories, and from Hansard (see, for instance, the debate on day nurseries, 12 June 1947), that in the late 1940s government ministers had a vision of well regulated nursery schools for all two- to five-year-olds, and of under-twos safely at home with mother. But there were not enough schools, and they did not offer long enough hours (though they offered a full school day at this period), to meet the needs of working mothers. Day nurseries were being closed, private all-day nurseries were few, and minders were fast assuming a new importance as a main resource for working mothers. The government recognized the need for women's labour, was unwilling to provide nurseries for all the children, but did wish to regulate the remaining parts of the system – minding and private nurseries.

The regulation by law of private nurseries and childminders, 1948

The reduction in state day-nursery places, and the pressing need to regulate private nurseries and minders which replaced them, led to the Nurseries and Childminders Act, 1948, which first brought private day care under local authority control. In passing the act the state continued a responsibility assumed during the war when it opened nurseries and organized sponsored minding schemes for the children of working mothers. But other features of the post-war world may have contributed to the passing of the act.

In the immediate post-war period, the state began to assume more complete responsibility for the welfare of its people.[6] Education until the age of fifteen, health services and an insurance safety net for all – these measures resulted from a change in the way people saw the responsibilities of society.[7] Furthermore, the nation had over the war years

become sensitive to the emotional needs of children; to their right to the care and protection of a normal home; and to the responsibility of society to secure, by one means or another, the proper conditions under which these needs and rights might be met (Pinchbeck and Hewitt, 1973, chapter 21).

The contribution of the psycho-analytical view of child development, exemplified by Anna Freud and Dorothy Burlingham (1944) and their experiences of running a residential nursery during the war years, was an important influence. They focused attention on the problems of providing young children with substitutes for mothers whose lives had been disrupted by the war. Indeed the rise in the number of children needing substitute care imposed huge strains on the residential services for children and exposed their defects (Heywood, 1959). A campaign to improve child-care standards in residential and foster care led to the passing of the Children Act, 1948.[8] This activity on behalf of children in care spilled over into concern for children in day care (as it had in 1871).

The link between the child in day care and the child in care – that both are away from their family and need protection – was referred to in the debate on the proposed legislation for minders and private nurseries in the House of Commons in May 1948. The fact that children in day care needed protection was underlined by reference to instances of poor quality care at minders'.

In his opening speech for the second reading of the Nurseries and Childminders Bill (28 May 1948), John Edwards, then Parliamentary Secretary to the Ministry of Health, said that children at daily minders were the only children 'not properly cared for and supervised' (that is, by law). The government had considered including them under the legislation then before Parliament in the Children Bill, but had decided that children in day care should be dealt with under separate legislation. He saw childminders as forming only a small part of the service.

In the debate that followed, M Ps (mainly from industrial areas) discussed problems of private day care. In particular, they referred to poor accommodation, the use of untrained staff, and the difficulty of defining 'fit' premises and 'fit' persons. The problems of regulating childminding with its casual and shifting arrangements were noted. However, the bill was welcomed by all speakers, on the assumption that private nurseries, rather than minders, would be the main form of day care for children, and that it would be easier to regulate than the care of children by individuals in private houses.

The local authority's duties in respect of minders under the act are minimal. They are to register the person and premises if the person is looking after three or more children not related to her, unless they come from one household. The local authority is given certain powers. It may refuse to register the person if she or the premises are not fit, and may specify the number of children under five (including the minder's own) that a minder may care for. It may require precautions to be taken against exposing the children to infectious disease. It may cancel the registration if the person or premises are no longer fit or the person has contravened the permissive regulations. It may prosecute for an offence under the act. (see note 9 for the main provisions of the act concerning minders.)

In regard to minding, the 1948 Act did not work well. There are two outstanding reasons for this. First, the act offered the minder chances for evasion. She could argue that the children were there as a temporary one-off arrangement, or that no payment was involved, or that they were related to her. Secondly, the act imposed too few duties on the local authority. It could fulfil its duties with minimal regard to the fitness of the person or premises, and was obliged to condone large groups of children if they came from one household and/or if some of them were the minders' own. Scandals were bound to occur.[10] During the period 1948 to 1967 the subject of minding was not raised in the House of Commons, except for one inquiry by an MP about the numbers of registered minders (22 November 1965), and one about the working of the registration system (4 August 1965). However, by 1965 the Ministry of Health was so alarmed by the bad reports of minding that it initiated an inquiry in a sample of health authority areas, and followed this with Circular 5/65 to local authorities. This pointed to the need for closer supervision of private nurseries and minders, and asked local authorities to review and report on their registration and supervision procedures. This information provided a basis for the amendments and recommendations made in 1968.

Other factors also led to growing pressure for amendments to the 1948 Act. First and foremost was the steady increase in the numbers of mothers of under-fives going out to work. This appears to have been unexpected, and the available pre-school provision was unsuitable in quality and quantity. Secondly, as the numbers of day-nursery places provided by the local authority fell, the private sector responded to meet demand. Numbers of childminders increased rapidly. The contrast can be seen in the figures given in Table 3. Day nurseries took 11·6 children in every thousand in 1949, but only 5 in 1968. Registered childminders took 0·5 children in every thousand in 1949 and 11·3 in 1968. From being a minor part of the pattern

Table 3: Number of places/children (aged under five) at nurseries and child-minders in England and Wales, for the years 1949, 1968 and 1977

	Local authority day nurseries (places)	*Private nurseries (children)*	*Registered childminders (places)*	
1949				
places/children (in 1000s)	43	7	2	
places/children per 1000 children	11·6	1·9	·5	
1968				
places/children (in 1000s)	21	141	47	
places/children per 1000 children	5·0	33·9	11·3	
1977			full-time	part-time
places/children (in 1000s)	27	25	69	18
			87	
places/children per 1000 children	8·8	8·1	28·3	

Sources: For 1949: Yudkin (1967); Tizard, Moss and Perry (1976); for 1968: 1968 DHSS Annual Report; Tizard, Moss and Perry (1976); for 1977: DHSS Annual Statistics (as at 31 March 1977).

Note: The private nursery figures for 1968 include playgroups (then listed jointly in the annual returns). Playgroups grew rapidly in the 1960s and 1970s. In 1965 there were 500 groups, in 1975, 9100 groups. By 1977, 366 000 children attended (190 per 1000 children).

of pre-school services in 1949, minding now played an important part, and forced itself on public attention.

Thirdly, from the late 1950s the education authorities gradually introduced part-time provision (that is, morning or afternoon sessions) at nursery schools.[11] Working mothers who had somehow coped with the rather short school day and the long school holidays now found it difficult to use nursery schools at all. Two factors may be mentioned which featured in government pronouncements then, and since. Economic crises were blamed for the shortage of resources for nursery schools (for instance, in Circular 8/60 and the Annual Report for 1964 (Ministry of Education, 1964); providing part-time places could double the number of children attending nursery school at little extra cost. But the part-time place was becoming acceptable for another reason. The influence of John Bowlby became important in public utterances in the early 1950s. Policy-makers accepted his view that a child should not be parted from his mother at all until he was three, and after this only for short periods of the day (for example, Bowlby, 1964, page 101). The benefits of nursery-school education, therefore, could best be gained on a part-time basis. We turn later to evidence against Bowlby's theories (Chapter 3). However, they did influence, and still do, the hours offered at nursery schools and classes, and playgroups have since followed their lead.

The 1968 amendments

The 1968 amendments to the Nurseries and Childminders Act, 1948, were introduced in the House of Commons by Joan Lestor (24 April 1967) in terms which show that she was dissatisfied with them. She said they might 'help to assist in this very depressing and worrying situation'; but that 'the ultimate object of any solution to the problems of the under-fives is obviously an urgent expansion of the day-nursery service.' Since this could not be done all at once minding must be better regulated. She argued that the country must make up its mind about working mothers; as more and more of them were going out to work, proper provision must be made for their children. She referred to the desirability of the Department of Education and Science and the Ministry of Health having a joint responsibility for children over three, because so many children were not being catered for by the education service. And she pressed for a public inquiry into the problems of the under-fives.

The 1968 amendments tighten up existing legislation.[12] Anyone looking after even one child for two hours a day for reward must register. The applicant must state whether her fitness to care for a child has in the past been in question. The permissive powers of the local authority were extended to cover the quality of care offered, in terms of staff and premises. In fact the new powers over premises, equipment, staff qualification and experience were much the same as those set out for private nurseries in the 1948 Act. The local authority was given increased powers to control the numbers of children cared for, taking into account the minder's own older children.

The government's measures on minding in 1948 and 1968 left it the least well-regulated form of day care, and while the 1948 Act may be seen as a mopping-up measure offering some control over a small-scale operation, the same cannot be said of the 1968 amendments. By then it was clear that there was a huge demand for day care which was not being met by nurseries. And the government, not willing to expand nurseries to meet demand, offered a law which, because it was merely permissive, did not impose effective obligations. Indeed, the obligations under the act may be reduced to two: *the local authority* must either register or deny registration; the *minders* must not operate without registration.

The act made it likely that local authorities would condone illegal minding because of the difficulties in establishing that it took place. To hunt illegal minders takes up resources, and casts the local authority in a punitive rather than supportive role. Once located, it is difficult to prove either that a person looks after children for money, or that she is 'unfit' and should not be registered. The minder, for her part, may fail to apply for registration out of ignorance of the law, or because she dislikes interference in her way of life, or because she wants to take enough children to earn a reasonable living. Whatever the factors, prosecution for illegal minding is virtually unknown,[13] and it is impossible to say how many children are illegally minded.[14] Since 1968, minding has continued to grow to fill the gaps in state day-care, just as playgroups have filled in for nursery education.

Ministry of Health circulars published with the amendments

The Ministry of Health published two circulars with the amendments. Circular 36/68 offered guidance on the interpretation of the amendments. Circular 37/68 listed criteria for admission to day nurseries, noted the inadequate supply of places, and suggested the use of private nurseries and minders for some children on waiting lists. In these cases minders' fees could be partly or wholly paid by the local authority under Section 22 (as amended in 1968) of the National Health Service Act, 1946. A Memorandum enclosed with the Circular gave advice on standards of day care in the nurseries and at minders' registered under the 1948 Act, using as a reference point the recommended standards for day nurseries in the earlier Circular 5/65. The Memorandum suggests a maximum of three under-fives, including the minder's own. It explains the standards to be aimed at in accommodation, care of the children, health and diet, and training of staff. Recommendations on staff training are most rigorous for day-nursery staff, least rigorous for minders. Some implications of the recommendations are discussed in detail later, but a general point may be made here.

Circular 37/68 asked local authorities to improve standards at minders' in various ways. They might tighten their permissive regulations for registration to exclude unsuitable minders or unsuitable premises. Or they might exhort minders already registered to upgrade their standards by improving accommodation and equipment, and standards of care. Where these methods failed to produce a child-care service acceptable to the local authority, it could allocate resources to bring accommodation and equipment up to scratch and to turn minders into more effective child-care workers, either by recruiting more suitable people, or by training those who applied for registration. The amendments and recommendations were doomed to failure. Given that local authorities were concerned about the scandalously poor quality of care offered by some minders, registered and unregistered – which provided the main impetus for amending the 1948 Act – they were likely to register almost anyone who was minding, rather than drive them underground. Afterwards everything would depend on the willingness of the minder to be improved, and on the resources available to improve her. Resources were unlikely to be sufficient, since minding was being promoted explicitly as a cheap form of care. The circular presents an uncomfortable blend of pious hopes, recognition of some of the poor features of minding (poor diet, and under-occupation of the children are mentioned, for instance) and expediency.

Sunningdale conference

The 1970s saw cuts and restraints in public spending. Childminding placed little burden on the public purse and mothers turned increasingly to minders. There was increasing interest in the subject. More was published about it. It was more often the subject of meetings and conferences. This may be explained not only in the growing need for day care at a time of cuts in expenditure. At that time, responsibility for day care passed from health to social service departments, which needed to develop a policy for it. There was also increasing support then for the encouragement of service provision by the community (see, for a useful summary, Gilroy, 1982).

In 1976, in response to continuing concern about day-care services and the increasing demand, the Department of Health and Social Security and the Department of Education and Science called a conference at Sunningdale entitled 'Low Cost Day Care Provision for the Under Fives'. The then Minister of State, Dr David Owen, introduced the conference, explained why it had been called, and set it in the context of 'restraint in social expenditure' and concern for the under-fives.

We all know that the situation currently facing the 0–5 age group is deeply worrying, and that if we do not take every opportunity to improve existing provision, then a whole generation of children's futures could be unnecessarily blighted.

He concluded his address by stating a possible solution to the dilemma:

> We could improve the provision for 0–5s substantially by spreading the low-cost best practice which already exists, proven and documented, on the ground.

Most of the conference members argued that this 'low-cost best practice' was to be found among childminders and playgroups (DES/DHSS, 1976). Brian Jackson presented the main paper on childminding, and said that when it was bad it was part of the system which transmitted the 'cycle of deprivation' from one generation to the next. Nevertheless, he believed that at a relatively tiny cost – 'We don't want three-year courses at a Royal College of Childminding' – it could be supported, modestly subsidized, and thus improved. Part of his theme was that minding was essentially non-professional, and based on an extension of 'neighbourliness'.

Two other speakers, Lady Plowden and Dr Kellmer Pringle, put forward the minder as 'substitute' or 'proxy' mother, implying or stating her superiority over the nursery.

There were also critical and cautionary voices raised both on childminding and the possibility for improvement. Alan Little dealt especially with the problems faced by ethnic minorities. He pointed out that while minding offered certain advantages, being cheap, community-based and having flexible hours, nevertheless in poor, badly-housed communities the care given by minders was equivalently impoverished, and was difficult to regulate. Jack Tizard said that very few mothers would make a childminder their first choice.

> Those who do use them are far less satisfied than mothers using other services (Bone, 1977). Even where the physical environment is fairly satisfactory, the minders rarely offer a close mothering relationship to the child . . . Most minders do the job for their own convenience – and often short term – because it fits with their domestic commitments, not out of an informed caring interest in children. The very poor rates of pay are an indication of their low and exploited status . . . So training schemes are unlikely to affect the attitudes of those currently minding who have nothing to gain by improving the way they mind.

He referred to the high turnover among minded children, and foresaw only a minor part for minding (and that professional) in a properly organized pre-school service. He based his statements on the findings (from his own research unit, TCRU) in our earlier study of two-year-olds.

Joint Letters from DHSS/DES

Another government circular followed the Sunningdale Conference. It was a Joint Letter from DHSS/DES to social service departments and education authorities (DHSS/DES, 1976). It urged them to cooperate in making the best possible use, in the present economic difficulties, of resources for the care and education of under-fives, and suggested how they might do this. It was reinforced in 1978 by another more detailed Joint Letter (DHSS/DES, 1978) which discussed how to achieve coordination. This letter indicated that resources must be concentrated in areas of social and educational disadvantage, and pointed to the particular disadvantages suffered by newly arrived ethnic minority groups. Many of the proposals were concerned with including education in forms of care where staff did not necessarily have an educational training (minding, day nurseries, playgroups). It proposed that day-nursery children should attend nursery school for part of the day, or that a teacher should be employed in the day nursery (para. 18). It noted (para. 13) that socially and economically disadvantaged families were more likely than others to use minders and suggested that these children should have high priority for nursery-class places or other help from the education service. It also urged local authorities to review their support and advice services, including in-service training for minders (para. 25). It asked for links with the health service to be set up so that children's health needs were not neglected, and went on:

> Because children who are merely minded are more likely than other children to be denied the social and intellectual stimulation that is important to their development, the Department attach great importance to fostering links between child-minders and nursery schools, classes and teachers, with child health clinics and with voluntary groups working in this field – pre-school playgroups and toy libraries for example.

The Joint Letter accepted that children who attended minders were likely to be deprived, both at home and at the minders'. It proposed that minders should cooperate with schemes to link minding with education and health services. The implications of these proposals are discussed later.

The 1948 Act with its 1968 amendments, the circulars and two joint letters represent official policy to date on private day care, and that policy is echoed by government ministers from time to time. The message essentially is that standards may be set low in order that supply may meet demand. Where problems are located, make-do-and-mend patchwork may be applied. The government will not take responsibility for ensuring adequate minimum standards. Using day care remains a private decision by parents and a private responsibility.

Day-care services for under-fives today

Since the Second World War private and voluntary services have made up for the inadequate supply of places in day nurseries and nursery schools and classes run by the local authorities, and as we saw, there was a huge growth in the numbers of children attending registered childminders and play-groups.

In 1977, the year we began the study, DHSS and DES statistics show that under-fives attended the various forms of day care as given in Figure 1 (Hughes et al., 1980).

The smallest group (16 per cent) attended schools and day nurseries provided by local authorities. The second group were provided for on a private or voluntary basis (mainly in playgroups), but regulated by the local authority. The largest group of children do not appear in the statistics of any service provided by local authorities or registered with them. Many of these

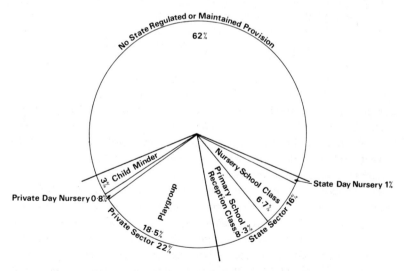

Fig. 1: Percentage of children under five years attending different types of pre-school provision, England and Wales, 1977

children are at home, in the care of a parent, a nanny or au pair; some are looked after in the homes of unpaid relatives or friends; a few accompany their mothers to work, and a very small percentage go to private schools.[15] Others are in the charge of unregistered childminders.

That is the general picture. But different kinds of provision impose different barriers to use and have different clients. In the state sector, *education services* are offered mainly on a part-time basis and only in term-time. When these places are scarce, they are taken by older rather than younger children – 35 per cent of four-year-olds, but only 9 per cent of three-year-olds had places in classes and schools in 1977 (Hughes et al., 1980, Fig. 5). The *day-nursery service* on the other hand offers full-day care, all the year round, and this reflects its history as a form of care for the working mother. But places are offered only to those children deemed to be in need of a place (see below), and an acute shortage means that even 'priority' cases may have to wait for a place, or never get one (see, for example, Jackson and Jackson, 1979, Chapter 4). In 1977 there were in England 27 000 places and another 10 000 children on waiting lists; the figures for London were 9400 and 4400 respectively (DHSS, 1979). Nationally places are provided for only one in every hundred children, and provision varies widely: for instance, one London borough provides nine day-nursery places per hundred, while some authorities provide none. There is evidence too that there are few places for the youngest children. Indeed, in our study, we found proportionately few under-twos, and still fewer under-ones in nurseries (see Appendix A).

In the private and voluntary sectors, playgroups predominate. More children attend these than all state provisions put together. About half are run by parents' committees (Pre-School Playgroups Association, 1978), others by children's charities or community groups, and some are owned and run privately. They offer short hours, perhaps on only one, two or three days a week, and places are mainly for children aged three and upwards. There are no places for under-twos.

Private nurseries, on the other hand, offer full-day care, but places are available for less than one per cent of under-fives and very few cater for under-twos. In the five boroughs in our study, there were only four private nurseries that took such children, and of these only two took babies under twelve months; altogether they offered about 55 places for under-twos. (Garland and White (1980) in their study of nine nurseries in London found a similar picture.) Social workers told us that local authority requirements for nurseries taking under-twos may be commercially prohibitive. They may include a higher staff – child ratio, more space and equipment, and extra facilities (such as a kitchen used only for preparing babies' feeds). Thus, apart from relatives and unpaid friends, *childminders* are the main providers of care for children under two. According to Bone (1977) minders (paid relatives or non-relatives, in her terms) provide day-care for 2 per cent of children under one, and 3 per cent of children aged one to two. This percentage (3 per cent) remains constant for children aged two, three and four years, and is of course small. Nevertheless, there were in England in 1977, 86 706 places for children at registered childminders, three times the number of places at local authority day nurseries. In addition, some children were with unregistered minders. While there are places for only 3 per cent of children at any one time, many more children are likely to have been minded during their pre-school career. Some start with minders and move on to nursery school or playgroup, others leave minders if their mothers stop work (perhaps for another birth), to be cared for at home.

Day-nursery children
The Ministry of Health Circular 37/68 (paras 5 and 6) gives guidance to local authorities on criteria for the selection of children for day-nursery places. It recommends that priority be given to children with only one parent

> who has no option but to go out to work and who cannot arrange for the child to be looked after satisfactorily. Other children who may need day care, some for the whole day, others part-time, will include those:–
> a) who need temporary day care on account of the mother's illness;
> b) whose mothers are unable to look after them adequately because they are incapable of giving young children the care they need;
> c) for whom day care might prevent the breakdown of the mother or the break-up of the family;
> d) whose home conditions (e.g. because of gross overcrowding) constitute a hazard to their health and welfare; and
> e) whose health and welfare are seriously affected by a lack of opportunity for playing with others.
> It may sometimes be appropriate to admit selected handicapped children to a local authority day nursery, i.e. children who are suffering from some continuing disability of body, intellect or personality likely to interfere with their normal growth, development or capacity to learn.

There are tremendous problems about the meaning of the words used in the circular. For instance, what is meant by having 'no option' but to work;

and having a child looked after 'satisfactorily'? What constitutes being unable to give children the care they need? The reader may pick and choose and, according to interpretation, the criteria may cover a large or minute proportion of children. It seems likely that over the years, with growing demand and a slow rise in the number of places, local authorities have used ever more stringent interpretations. Essentially day-nursery care today is intended to prevent children being harmed by inadequate homes or parents, and to avoid the last resort of residential care. It is *not* provided to help working mothers in general. A sample of day-nursery children, therefore, will contain a concentration of children from difficult family backgrounds, as well as children from one-parent households, and some handicapped children.

Minded children and working mothers
Children who go to minders on the other hand are mainly the children of mothers who work full-time. Although the single working mother is listed as having some claim on a day-nursery place, in practice few get one. In Bone's study, a tenth of these mothers used a day nursery, a third used a nursery school or playgroup, two-fifths made informal arrangements with relatives and friends and a fifth left their children with paid minders (Bone, 1977, Table 4·5). The pattern was much the same for full-time working mothers from two-parent families, but part-time working mothers from two-parent families used minders and day nurseries less; more of them (54 per cent) relied on informal arrangements.

In general, minders are used *only* by working mothers (this is indicated by Bone's table and by studies of mothers who use minders (Gregory, 1969; Bryant et al; 1980, Mayall and Petrie, 1977), and minding is seen as a cost of employment rather than as something good in itself. This is in contrast with nursery facilities, such as the private nursery school or playgroup, which parents may choose to pay for, even when one parent is available to look after the child at home.

Mothers who work when they have a child aged under five years are in a minority, but both the numbers and proportions of these mothers have grown steadily over the last decade. This was shown in a recent study of day-care services for children of working mothers (Central Policy Review Staff, 1978, Tables 2 and 3). The number of under-fives with working mothers rose from 700 000 to 850 000 between 1971 and 1977, and the proportion of these children rose from 16 per cent to 24 per cent. Most of these mothers (about four-fifths) work part-time; and this is true for each year-band of children. This was shown too by the Office of Population Censuses and Surveys data for 1978 – see Table 4, which also shows that while 36 per cent of four-year-olds had a working mother, only 21 per cent of one-year-olds and 14 per cent of under-ones did.

Table 4: Working mothers of under-fives (OPCS data for 1978)

	Proportion of employed mothers working		Proportion of mothers who work	Sample number
	full-time	*part-time*		
	%	%	%	
Child's age (years)				
0	24	76	13·5	334
1	20	80	20·9	377
2	22	78	25·4	426
3	22	78	24·8	416
4	17	83	36·3	430

Source: OPCS (unpublished data for 1978)

Other evidence from two large-scale studies shows a dramatic increase during the last twenty years in the numbers of mothers who work at some stage before their child is five. In the 1950s, 26 per cent of them did (Douglas and Blomfield, 1958); in the 1970s the proportion had risen to 55 per cent (Child Health and Education in the Seventies study (Butler, forthcoming); see also Moss, 1980).

All in all, we may say, using the OPCS data quoted above, that the number of all children under two years who had a working mother in 1978 nationally was about 200 000. Most of these mothers worked part-time. Of children with a working mother, only about a quarter of the under-ones, and a fifth of the under-twos, had a full-time working mother: about 47 000 children in all.

Which mothers of under-fives go out to work is a big question, and a comprehensive guide to the topic is given by Moss (1980). Briefly, in the past, working-class mothers have been more likely than middle-class mothers to work; but the gap is now small and there is some evidence that more highly educated mothers are more likely to work than the rest. In general, mothers born abroad have higher rates of employment than native-born mothers, but the ethnic minority groups vary. Mothers of West Indian origin work more and Muslim Asian mothers, much less. Women in urban areas work more than in rural areas; but there is wide variation between urban areas, with London, Manchester, Birmingham and Leeds having the highest rates. There are also some differences between groups as to full-time versus part-time work, and lone mothers and ethnic minority mothers are more likely than others to work full-time.

Bone (1977, Table 3.3) shows proportionately greater use of day care by non-manual than by manual workers for all age bands under five. Since day-care provision for children under two is mainly confined to minders (with a very few children cared for in nurseries and by in-home help) it can be inferred that most of these children were with minders. For all ages of under-fives, Bone (Table 2.7) shows that 4 per cent of parents in Class I and 3 per cent in Class II use minders, compared with 2 per cent of other non-manual workers and manual workers.[16] This is a remarkable change. Until recently it could be assumed that minders were used only by working-class mothers. Now mothers from a wider social range (and from varied ethnic groups) used them.

Regional differences should be noted, too. The number of mothers using registered minders depends not only on how many mothers work, but on other local factors. In areas where shift work is available and relatives and friends are willing to help, there may be less use of registered minders. Some local authorities are probably more active than others in registering minders. Some areas, such as Lancashire and Shropshire, have a long-established tradition of minding (Ferguson and Fitzgerald, 1954, Chapter 6). Certainly the DHSS returns indicate wide variations in the number of minding places per thousand children across the country. For 1977 (DHSS, 1979), they indicate that of the 69 000 full-day places, almost a quarter were in Greater London. The number of places varied from less than one per thousand children to over 70. Areas with the highest proportion of places to children (three or more per hundred) were most of the London boroughs, some industrial areas (Leeds, Oldham and Coventry) and some counties (Shropshire, Staffordshire and Leicestershire). Areas with the lowest proportion of places (less than one per cent) were some northern and Midland non-metropolitan counties and some metropolitan county districts (Gateshead, North and South Tyneside, Sunderland, Rotherham, Wakefield, Knowsley, Dudley, Wolverhampton).

Attitudes to working mothers

Although governments halted the decline of day nurseries for priority children, after the late 1960s legislation did little to *ensure* an acceptable standard of care for children with registered minders. It gave local authorities powers, merely. Underlying this neglect of the children of working mothers are attitudes and phenomena that emerged in the nineteenth century and still persist.

Concern about the child's physical health, paramount in the nineteenth century when it was claimed that minded children had a particularly high death rate because of neglect, unclean milk and the use of pacifying drugs, has shifted to concern about emotional well-being and the critical nature of the mother–child relationship. The influence of psychoanalysis and in particular of Bowlby was important here. Politicians urged mothers of young children to stay at home, and later suggested that the minder was the best alternative on the assumption that she offered motherly care. These psychological theories also provided a justification for giving nursery education only to over-threes and only part-time.

Then there is the long-established idea that women's role is to service their men and children as wives, mothers and housekeepers. There can be no doubt, as Elizabeth Wilson (1977) forcefully indicates, that this is at the heart of much welfare provision established since the Second World War. Central to this are the social security provisions initiated by the National Insurance Act, 1946. The Beveridge Report (1942), which outlined the programme, makes its attitudes to women's role explicit.

> That attitude of the housewife to gainful employment outside the home is not and should not be the same as that of the single woman. She has other duties . . . In the next 30 years, housewives as mothers have vital work to do in ensuring the adequate continuance of the British Race and British Ideals in the world. (p. 52)

These attitudes are also displayed in many other pronouncements, notably in government-sponsored reports such as Crowther, Newsom and Plowden, which Wilson argues both reflect public opinion and influence it for the future.

There is also the view, persisting since the nineteenth century, that finding and using child care is essentially a private family matter and not one for public policy. We have argued the weakness of this standpoint and drawn attention to other European countries who manage things differently (Hughes et al, 1980). There has been some official recognition (limited, it is true) of women's changing role in society. The rights of women to equal opportunity have recently been ratified in law (the Equal Pay Act, 1970 and the Sex Discrimination Act, 1970), and a limited right to return to her job after childbirth has been guaranteed under the Employment Protection Act,

1975. While these measures may have been achieved by the governments concerned at no great cost, they have gone some way to respond to changing behaviour and expectations and have probably had an effect on the aspirations of some women. But governments have not accepted that women will not have equality with men until children are seen as the responsibility of both parents, and unless adequate day care is provided to meet parents' needs (see Hughes et al, 1980). Clarke (1979, Chapter 10) argues that the provision of day-care facilities is a 'mechanism through which the state could intervene to change the balance between women's two functions.' There is in fact no consistent thorough-going policy towards equal opportunity for mothers to work. This is reflected in the way successive governments have shifted the balance of decision-making from central to local government, with regard to the provision and allocation of nursery places, and also the regulation and support of childminders (Rein, 1976, Chapter 1). It is assumed that working mothers must generally take responsibility for paying for day care and for satisfying themselves as to its adequacy.

In brief, long-standing attitudes and beliefs inform the provision and regulation of day care in this country. Essentially public policy is to provide for children who are socially disadvantaged, and in many cases at risk of being taken into residential care. In the private sector, a weakly regulated childminding service provides for the needs of working mothers.

Notes

1. Tizard, Moss and Perry (1976) and van der Eyken (1977) cover 'education' and 'care'. The history of pre-school education is covered by Whitbread (1972) and Blackstone (1971). See also David (1980) for an analysis of the relationship of the family to the education system and of family issues within the education system.
2. See especially Hobsbawm (1969) for an analysis of the changes brought about by the Industrial Revolution as they affected the labouring classes, the new working classes. Laslett (1965) charts the changes from the small human-scale way of the agricultural worker and producer of goods, to a way of life dictated by centralized units of production.
3. Pinchbeck and Hewitt (1973) are a good source of quotations. Two may give the flavour of contemporary views and indicate the extent to which social reformers could be controlled by a belief:

   > I would far rather see even a high rate of infant mortality prevailing than has ever yet been proved against the factory districts or elsewhere . . . than intrude one iota further on the sanctity of the domestic hearth, and the decent seclusion of private life . . . That unit, the family, is the unit upon which a constitutional Government has been raised which is the admiration and envy of mankind. (Whateley Cooke Taylor).

Early attempts by the Society for the Prevention of Cruelty to Animals to canvass support against cruelty by parents to children at home led to this response by Lord Shaftesbury (1871):

The evils you state are enormous and indisputable, but they are of so private, internal and domestic a character as to be beyond the reach of legislation, and the subject, indeed, would not, I think, be entertained in either House of Parliament.

4. Pressure for public provision of nurseries came from those who were concerned with high infant mortality. Hewitt (1958) quotes from *The Lancet* (2 February 1867), and from the *Public Health Magazine* at about the same time. Public response was similar to that of today: mothers should be discouraged from working when their children were young; providing nurseries might encourage women to desert the hearth for the factory; factories themselves, as originators of the problem, should provide nurseries.

In 1871 a bill to control the activities of baby-farmers, who took children for longer than a day, included clauses to regulate day-nurses, and to make it an offence for parents to hand over a child for the day, or for longer, to unregistered persons. The clauses on day-care were dropped from the act passed in 1872 on the grounds that they encroached on the rights of parents; and that attempts to control day care would result in an underground illegal market (Owen, 1979).

The idea of providing part-time pre-school provision had not yet been widely canvassed in local authority day nurseries and nursery schools. Margaret McMillan (1930, Chapter 4) justified the long nursery day in terms of the children's need for long unbroken periods of time to engage in the 'great process' of maturation in the best possible environment, with trained guidance. For slum children she argued, too, that to return them to their streets and homes for half the day would undo the work done at the school. By 1938, Cusden could describe without questioning the all-day routine at nursery schools. She assumes a day that starts at 8.30–9 a.m. and ends at between 4 and 5 p.m., during which the children will have had dinner, tea and, in some cases, breakfast. She does not discuss the working mother in detail, but says that the day may start as early as 7.30 in areas 'where the employment of mothers makes it necessary' and arrangements for keeping the children at the end of the day may be similarly necessary.

5. The report of the committee set up to develop the scheme for the Ministry of Labour commented by way of caveat: 'It has to be stressed that the scheme is not designed as a measure of social progress, but as an emergency method . . .' (i.e. of increasing the supply of women workers) (quoted in Ferguson and Fitzgerald, 1954, Chapter 6).

6. A good example of the gradual acceptance of responsibility by the State for the welfare of its citizens is to be found in the history of child and maternal welfare measures (see Ferguson and Fitzgerald, 1954, Chapter 5). Concern about mortality rates grew during the first years of this century, and in 1918 the Maternity and Child Welfare Act gave local authorities permissive powers to provide for the health of mothers and young children. This formalized and brought together voluntary and charitable agencies which had been working in the field. But these powers were converted into a duty only after the Second World War, under the National Health Service Act, 1946. Margery Spring-Rice (1939) shows in her accounts of the lives of working-class women what it meant to have no freely available health service; at that time only working people were covered by health insurance.

7. Titmuss (1950) points to the effects of the Second World War in changing people's

attitudes. During the War it was seen as fair that if dangers were to be shared, resources should be shared too. He argues that this mood persisted after the War; people should be given a more equal start in life, and this implied that the State should take responsibility for ensuring reasonable standards in what was on offer.

8. The campaign was spearheaded by Lady Allen of Hurtwood, who in the 1960s joined the campaign to improve day care for under-fives – see Chapter 3 for an account of Yudkin's work on this. (See also Heywood, 1959, for a full account of the events leading up to the Children Act 1948.)

9. The main provisions of the Nuseries and Childminders Act 1948 (II and 12 Geo 6 Ch. 53) as regards minders are:

> The local authority *must* keep a register of persons in their area who for reward receive into their homes children under the age of five to be looked after for the day or for a substantial part of it (Section 1(1) (b)).

> A person contravenes the Act if he/she is receiving for reward for the day or a substantial part of it children of whom he is not a relative and the number of children exceeds two and the children come from more than one household (Section 4(2)).

> A person guilty of an offence under the above section is liable to a fine of not more than £25 for the first offence, and for later offences to a fine of not more than £25 or imprisonment for up to one month or both (Section 4(4)).

> The local authority must issue a certificate of registration to a person minding under Section 1 with the name and address of the person on it. If the person moves house, an amended certificate must be issued (Section 3 (1 and 2)).

10. See Yudkin and Holme, 1963 and Yudkin 1967 to be discussed in Chapter 3.

11. Until the 1950s nursery schools, like primary schools, provided a full day. (See note 4.)

12. The 1948 Nuseries and Childminders Act 1948 was amended under the Health Service and Public Health Act 1968 (Chapter 46). The main amendments are as follows:

> A person must register with the local authority if he/she is looking after a child who is not a relative. This applies if the child is cared for, for two or more hours a day. (Section 60(2) and (3)).

> When a person applies for registration, he/she must declare whether he/she has had any disqualification from fostering or adoption, any conviction for maltreating a child, or the loss of a child into care. (Section 60(7)).

> Maximum fines are raised to £50 for the first offence, and £100 for subsequent offences under the Act, and the maximum imprisonment term to 6 months.

Permissive powers are tightened too:

> The local authority may refuse registration if the equipment of the home or the situation, size or construction of the home is not acceptable (Section 60(5)).

> In considering the number of children it may take into account the number of any other children who may from time to time be in the home (Section 60(8)).*

> It may impose requirements for securing various provisions: adequate qualifications or

experience in the staff; safe, adequately maintained premises, and equipment adequately maintained; adequate arrangements for feeding the children, and a suitable diet; record-keeping by the minder about the children (Section 60(9)).

* Circular 36/67 (para. 14) explains that formerly local authorities were required to include the minder's own school-age children in the number permitted, which allowed the minder to take on extra under-fives while her own were out of the house. The amendment allows the local authority to take them into account, but to exclude them if their presence after school and in the holidays will not place an extra burden on the minder.

13. In answer to a question in the House of Commons (21 December 1971), the following information on prosecutions for illegal minding was given: before 1964 figures 'were not readily available'; for the years 1964 to 1970, numbers of prosecutions were respectively 3, 1, 1, 2, 2, 0, 2. We have been unable to find any later reference in Hansard or elsewhere to figures for later years.

14. Estimates for numbers of children illegally minded have been set at about 100 000 (Community Relations Commission, 1975; Jackson and Jackson, 1979). Other estimates have put the figure at not more than half that, using Office of Population Censuses and Surveys (1977) data (van der Eyken, 1977; Hughes et al., 1980).

15. Where a private school takes both under-fives and over-fives, the under-fives do not appear in the DES statistics. Private establishments calling themselves schools, but catering exclusively for under-fives, are registered with the local authority social service department, and the children appear in the DHSS 'private nursery' statistics.

16. Again, we must remember that for Bone 'minder' means a paid person, whether a relative or not, at the child's home or not. And Bone's definition of 'day care' excludes care by unpaid relatives, friends and neighbours.

Chapter Three
Research about Day Care

Because the study was set in the context of social policy in this country, the research reviewed here is mainly British and about working mothers, child-minders and day nurseries. An exception is research about the possible effects of day care on the mother-child relationship; there is no British work in this area.

Research about working mothers

We have described how in the nineteenth century day care was provided, mainly by women in their own homes, in response to the needs of working mothers. Voluntary bodies intervened to provide better care in nurseries and the state began to take responsibility if the standard of care in the children's homes was unacceptable. Over the last thirty years the number of working mothers has increased but policy has not changed. It is still assumed that mothers must take all the responsibility for the care of their children, including, if they so choose, that of finding and paying for day care.

In this connection some studies in the first two decades after the Second World War are interesting, as much for the attitudes of the researchers as for the data collected. Studies by Jephcott (1962),[1] Myrdal and Klein (1956)[2] and Klein (1965)[3] were concerned, as Titmuss says in his Foreword to Jephcott's study, with the implications for 'family life, for the woman herself, for employers, and for society in general' of some women's attempts to carry out a dual role as housewife/mother and worker. Douglas and Blomfield (1958)[4] also dealt with this issue, though their central concern was with the health and welfare of young children. These studies found that married women worked to earn money, but also because they had been partially freed from home-based tasks by social and demographic changes:

the fall in family size, and of the age at which a woman had her last baby, better health, better housing, more labour-saving devices. Most working women coped with their two roles by doing part-time jobs, and relying on older female relatives and neighbours to care for pre-school children. It was pointed out (for instance by Klein, 1965) that if employers wanted to make use of this last reserve of labour (married women) they would do well to offer reasonable employment conditions which made concessions to women's role as housewife. The studies noted that the supply of older women available as caregivers for under-fives might well dry up if it became usual for women to return to work when their children became independent.

The authors of these studies were interested in the trend for mothers to work, but their main concern was with the dual role. They did not consider any implications for change in social policy towards child care, if women expected to work on equal terms with men. A speech given by Titmuss in 1952 (Titmuss, 1963) shows clearly how different then were the preoccupations of an acute observer of social trends. He pointed out that compared with 50 years before, women had longer life-expectancy, more compressed years of child-bearing and child-rearing, and longer-lasting marriages. These changes raised new, untackled problems about the re-entry of women, into work *after* the period of child-rearing. But he did not foresee that some women might wish or need to work during their child-rearing years. Nor did he consider whether men's role in the family (and at work) might or should change if women's role changed.

However, as the number of mothers in work continued to grow, investigations began which took as a central issue the amount and quality of day care available for the children. Yudkin and Holme (1963)[5] analysed data on 243 working mothers of under-fives. They found, like earlier researchers, that relatives were the main caregivers, although day nurseries and non-relatives were used more where mothers worked full-time. The main strength of their book lies in its discussion of the merits and demerits of different forms of care and in its perception that blanket comments on the desirability or not of mothers of under-fives working must be modified by consideration of the mother's situation and of what different forms of day care could offer to the child. This work was continued by Yudkin. When amendments to the 1948 Nurseries and Childminders Act were being considered, he reported on behalf of a working party set up by the National Society of Children's Nurseries to study pre-school provision in order to campaign for action. Yudkin pointed to the totally inadequate numbers of places in day nurseries and nursery schools by comparison with the demand. Like Joan Lestor in the same year (1967), he called for a review of the needs of mothers and their under-fives, and the formulation of social policy to meet them.

Yudkin's views were confirmed by Hunt's study (1968) of women's work. In a nationwide study of 6500 women she found high demand for state day nurseries and nursery schools, but little for private provision. Two-fifths of non-working mothers of under-fives said they would work if a day-care place were available. Most day care was by relations and friends, but minders and nurseries played a larger part where the mother worked full-time. There was a huge gap between existing provision and the potential demand for places, especially for day-nursery places. The Ministry of Health added a note, defending its position: that it provided day care on health and welfare grounds, and not to meet the demands of working women generally. This is still policy today.

Hunt carried out a second, smaller study of the circumstances and needs of one-parent, compared with two-parent, families in five areas (Hunt, 1973). She showed that there were wide variations in the use of different kinds of provision between areas but that lone parents used day nurseries more, wanted all-day care. Their rates of employment were higher than other mothers, in some areas twice as high or more. Further, Hunt found poverty in some two-parent families, in many where there was no mother and in nearly all where there was no father.

Later evidence of the gap between provision and desire for provision was given by Bone (1977). Her national study of 2500 children under five years showed that day care was used by 32 per cent of children and desired for a further 33 per cent, the highest unmet demand being for two- and three-year-olds. Like Hunt, Bone found that many mothers would return to work earlier if they could find acceptable day care (Bone, 1977, 4·3). She also confirmed that parents were still dissatisfied with private care. Of parents using various forms of day care, those using childminders were the least satisfied (Bone, Table 3·5).

During the 1960s and 1970s, studies were revealing great social changes. Women, even those with young children, worked, and more wanted to. Day care by private individuals was not greatly liked by mothers; they preferred state provision of which there was little. It was also becoming clear that the reasons why women worked were many. One important reason was poverty, which had not, as had been hoped after the war, been conquered, and not only lone-parent families, but many two-parent families were poor.

The demand, especially for all-day care, was far greater than had been foreseen, and provision in day nurseries and in nursery education had not grown as planned in the early 1940s. In fact social changes had not been matched by a response from policy-makers. As Yudkin and Lestor said in

1967, a reformulation of policy was needed to take account of the changes. Ten years later, when we began this study, demand was still growing but policy had not altered. Calls for change have been many, ranging from those of the National Child-Care Campaign, the Equal Opportunities Commission and the Trade Union Congress to that of the Central Policy Review Staff, in its 1978 review of services for the young children of working mothers.

Research on childminding

Research on use of day care showed that while many children spent the day with relatives or minders, mothers often preferred nursery care. When Yudkin was assembling evidence from medical officers and local authorities about day care, and the Ministry of Health was inquiring into the working of the 1948 Act, the first studies of childminding were undertaken. This research began to provide data on childminding as a service to mothers and children. It was also a response to current concern for the well-being of ethnic minorities. At this time the Political and Economic Planning *Report on Racial Discrimination in Britain* (1967) appeared, and the Institute of Race Relations began to produce a series of studies on problems facing ethnic minorities. The children of West Indian immigrants were studied by doctors, whose professional experience of local communities led them to think that some children were at risk (Stewart Prince, 1967; Stroud, 1967; Pollak, 1972).[6] Possible factors were thought to be: poverty and poor housing; the high proportion of mothers who worked and left their under-fives in unsuitable care; the poor mental health of many of the mothers; and inadequate attention-giving by the parents. None of the three studies referred to here was methodologically rigorous and all took place in deprived areas, but they did offer evidence of disadvantage among West Indian families compared with indigenous families, and pointed to factors that cried out for more systematic investigation. Among these was the care given by childminders.

Interest in the disadvantages suffered by ethnic minorities was matched by a new interest in disadvantage in general. The anti-poverty campaign, represented most powerfully by the Child Poverty Action Group (founded in 1965), was given strength and purpose by the documentation of the extent of poverty in Britain set out by Abel-Smith and Townsend (1965).[7] Until recently studies of day care have followed this lead and tended to focus on ethnic minorities and the poor.

At the political level, too, there was debate on poverty from the late 1960s onwards. The fears of Sir Keith Joseph that disadvantage might be inherited put emphasis on the characteristics of individual families. The Labour Party, by contrast, emphasized the economic and social forces that created poverty. But as Bruner (1980, Chapter 1) suggests, one effect of these discussions was to make it appear that alleviating poverty would solve the problems of young families. It was assumed that those not in poverty were not in need of help. In this respect, public debate on poverty diverted attention from the need to provide adequate day care for the increasing numbers of working mothers' children.

The first studies on minding, then, focused on samples of poor mothers and mothers from ethnic minority groups. Hood's 1965 study (Hood et al., 1970) was concerned mainly with the health and development of 101 one-year-old children, of West Indian families living in Paddington. A control sample of non-West Indian children was drawn from the same area. The study found that half the West Indian mothers compared with less than one-fifth of the control mothers worked; more of them lived in overcrowded conditions, and many more were lone parents. The day-care arrangements of the two groups were roughly similar: 44 per cent of the West Indian mothers and 52 per cent of the other mothers used minders and neighbours.

In 1967, Gregory (1969) interviewed most of the same sample of West Indian mothers, whose children were by now about two-and-a-half years old. Again, a high proportion (over a half) were at work, and three-quarters of these worked full-time. Two-fifths making day-care arrangements used minders, almost all unregistered. Twenty-two per cent of the mothers had moved their child from a minder in the last year, usually because of dissatisfaction with standards of care. Gregory also interviewed all the minders, registered and unregistered, used by a random sample of 49 West Indian mothers in the same area. She found that, compared with the registered minders, more unregistered minders were West Indian and their housing was poorer. They also charged less and tended to take more children. In term of quality of care, she found no clear differences between the two groups. No doubt, she comments, the local authority was unwilling to enforce high standards in an area lacking enough child-care facilities.

The studies by Hood and Gregory had well-defined objectives and methodology to match. They provided data on some of childminding's most accessible characteristics, such as poor housing and instability, but did not provide good data on quality of care. Hood commented that 'most of the private care-taking arrangements seemed, from the mothers' descriptions, to be grossly inadequate both in terms of meeting the infants' needs and financial cost to the mothers'. Some minding situations observed first-hand led to the comment that there seemed to be little stimulation or activity for the children, and little interaction between child and minder; ten of the 56 minders said they did not play with the children. Gregory pointed to the casual nature of some of the arrangements: minders who did not know how to contact the mother during the day; and others who left children unattended while they went out. It seems from these researchers' accounts, that it was enough for them that the standard of child care was way below that offered by a day nursery in terms of physical conditions, attitudes and equipment. There was little need to look further. The view that minding might be a good thing in spite of such drawbacks had not yet gained currency.

The Community Relations Commission study (CRC, 1975)[8] provided perhaps the firmest evidence up to then of the deficiencies of minding. Like earlier studies it was interested in the problems of day care from the point of view of ethnic minorities, as well as the wider problems posed by limited provision. The study deliberately took areas thought to be disadvantaged. It can be argued that the report presents a special case, and that no conclusions can be drawn generally about mothers, minders and day care even in the social service areas concerned. But the report does focus in detail on some of the problems faced by the poor, and by ethnic minorities. Nearly three-quarters of the working mothers' children were cared for by private individuals, including almost a third with registered or unregistered minders. Almost half the white children, but only 7 per cent of the Asian and 17 per cent of the black children, were at nursery school or day nursery. Mothers disliked leaving their children with relatives; minders were popular when registered, otherwise not. Those using day nursery or nursery school were the most satisfied. Asian mothers had the most difficulty in getting the day care they wanted. Of the children currently with minders, almost a quarter had had three or more placements with minders.

The CRC recommended developing the existing childminding service. It saw minding as a flexible, local service that could be expanded and made acceptable at less cost than nursery care. It recommended that government should take responsibility for meeting the needs of under-fives, with particular attention to the language and social needs of ethnic minority children. It proposed that minders should be employed by the local authority and that the service should be free to mothers, or offered at a low flat rate, or on a means-tested basis.

The study described some of the problems faced by poor mothers in making arrangements for child-care. It also gave pointers to particular problems of day care in the inner city. Because demand was high (and pay low), minders took on large numbers of under-fives, so the children were unlikely to get much individual attention. Minders expressed the need for more facilities – parks, playgrounds, playgroups, and for assistance towards making their houses safe, and providing toys and books. Finally the study described some of the particular disadvantages of ethnic minority mothers in getting acceptable child care; they were less successful in getting places at state nursery schools and day nurseries; they had less choice at minders' because some refused to take ethnic minority children. And the language needs of their children were not being met.

Brian and Sonia Jackson's work has also been concerned with childminding in cities, but it has focused on the working class as provider and user of minding. Sonia Jackson was perhaps the first to claim (in *The Illegal Childminders*) that minders, unlike day nurseries, could offer the 'continuous care of a single mother-figure'; she also drew a parallel between minders and foster mothers (S. Jackson, 1972). (The anti-institutional element and notion of the minder as a mother-substitute which Sonia Jackson reintroduced have their roots in the work of John Bowlby (1951, 1958).)

The Jacksons suggested that minding is a response by working-class communities to the need for day care (B. Jackson, 1976) and that these communities 'nurture' minders (Jackson and Jackson, 1979, p. 251). The Jacksons' 1979 book is a record of work carried out for three or four years from about 1973. It covers studies of the gaps between the amount of day care *provided* and the needs of parents, working or not working, in inner-city areas. One study took a day-nursery waiting list and interviewed most of the parents about their work situation and use of pre-school provision. A second study analysed the number of under-fives in an area of Huddersfield and the extent of the demand over supply for pre-school provision. A third took volunteer women from a factory to establish their working and day-care arrangements. All these studies found, like Gregory (1969) and the CRC (1975), in similarly poor districts, high levels of working by mothers of under-fives, using relatives and friends as the main providers of day care. Care by mother and father working different shifts was important too. The use of day nurseries was negligible. The book also describes improvement schemes: the setting up of drop-in centres and training schemes for minders; experiments with toy kits, advice kits, and advice on the radio; and the part played by the Jacksons in the BBC television training series for minders (first televised in 1977).

The Jacksons' findings are consistent with those of earlier studies. Their improvement schemes were unfortunately not monitored, so no assessment can be made as to their value. The one exception is discussed with other improvement schemes in Chapter 11. Their work was extensively publicized as it proceeded, and was probably influential in persuading policy-makers to support minding. Meacher referred to their work when he promoted minding in the House of Commons in 1975.[9] The CPRS (1978) quotes with approval one of their improvement schemes.

A major difficulty faced by the reader of the Jacksons' book is the unresolved conflict it presents. By its dramatic presentation of individual cases, it exposes the totally unacceptable problems faced by parents who have to use child care which is unsatisfactory as to housing, safety, equipment, range of experience, and interaction with adults. But the book's message is also that minders can offer acceptable care if they are supported by modest, low-cost schemes, such as drop-in centres and short training courses. It offers no firm evidence that these measures will improve the lot of the parent seeking day care, or the daily experience of the children. Furthermore, the schemes outlined were chronically under-financed and insecure, and depended for their impetus on the enthusiasm of a few people.

However, the Jacksons (like Yudkin, 1967, Gregory, 1969 and Tizard, Moss and Perry, 1976) end up by recommending a unified approach to pre-school provision. They argue in favour of a minister responsible for children, to promote their interests. They also recommend that full registration of a minder should take place only when she has taken a training course provided by the local authority. They are also in favour of a salaried minding service, to run alongside the registered minder. In this respect they go some way with the CRC (1975) and with other similar proposals (Mayall and Petrie, 1977) as well as with the views of the TUC (1978a) and the EOC (1978).

The studies up to this point described two widely differing views of childminders: that many of them offer a poor quality service in poor surroundings; and that they offer the best form of care for young children, because they are motherly figures. Neither view was supported by much evidence at the time we were first considering studying the topic in 1975. Our study of two-year-olds, whose findings are described briefly in Chapter 1, did not make for optimism.

Following this earlier study a research team under Jerome Bruner at the Oxford Pre-school Research Group conducted a study of a one-in-five random sample of registered minders in Oxfordshire (Bryant, Harris and Newton, 1980), following basically the same methods we used (and have used again in the present study) – interviews with minders and mothers about one particular child, and observations of interactions between the child and his two caregivers.[10] Because of these similarities, useful comparisons can be made between minding in Oxfordshire and London. In general, the researchers found that the minders were well-meaning and caring people, who offered good physical conditions to the children but, in many cases, insufficient attention. They found a majority of the children were 'quiet' and 'detached' at the minders'; nearly a quarter were judged to be disturbed, or distressed, or to have language retardation. The authors argued that home difficulties may have accounted for some of this quiet and detached behaviour, but they also identified factors at the minders' which may have played a part. These were: that there had been little or no settling-in period for the child; that he had to face a new set of rules when he started at a minder's; that unlike the minder's own child he had no rights in the minder's home; that minders might encourage quietness because it is easier to live with; that minders might not tolerate troublesome, active or protest-ing children; and that minding a child on a daily basis does not involve com-mitment to the child and his future and might inhibit the formation of close relationships. The authors concluded that the myth of the minder as mother-substitute was seriously challenged by their findings. They accepted that minding would continue and proposed the setting up of far more careful and expensive support systems to encourage a better service.

This small group of studies represents minding research in this country. Most of the studies focused on poor neighbourhoods and especially on ethnic minority mothers or minders. More recently, first in the Mayall and Petrie (1977) study and later in the Oxford Study (1980), minding has been considered as a system operating in the wider community. It was with these studies too that the first attempts were made to collect data on the relation-ships between the people involved: the minder, the mother and the child, and especially on the child's relationship with his minder. The evidence is not encouraging for those who claim that minders are motherly to minded children. Improvement in the quality of child care demands either voluntary effort by minders, or incentives to attract suitable minders, or tougher legislation to cut out unsuitable minders. Improvement in the minders' housing and equipment would be expensive. Proposals for reform have had much in common. They include recommendations for much greater participation by the local authority in controlling standards, and changes in the law to back this. Like observers of the whole day-care scene, researchers into minding have called for the formulation and implementation of policy on day care at government level.

Day-nursery research

Very little research has been carried out in local authority day nurseries, and still less relating to the under-twos. In 1970 Parry and Archer (1974) studied various forms of pre-school services. They were concerned to define 'good nursery practice', and visited fifteen day nurseries in three areas of England, recommended to them by various official bodies as exemplars. They used self-completion questionnaires for nursery staff, filled in observation schedules to assess the children's activities, nursery premises and equipment, and held informal group discussions to establish how the role of the day nursery was perceived by the staff. There were few under-ones and one-year-olds at the fifteen nurseries; the proportions of children in each age band – 0, 1, 2, 3, 4 years – was 7, 15, 23, 30 and 25 per cent respectively. The largest group of children were those of lone working mothers. While the staff stressed the physical care of the children, they were also concerned with the educational opportunities they could offer them. However, the children's play was often static or repetitive. The authors believed that the National Nursery Examination Board qualification was not sufficient preparation for working with children from a disadvantaged background. The study is descriptive rather than analytic, and its interest lies in the issues it raises (for example, how staff should be trained) rather than in the questions it poses or answers.

A later study was carried out by Garland and White (1980) as part of the Oxford Pre-school Research Group's work. They visited nine nurseries in London, offering all-day care, including three local authority day nurseries and six private nurseries. The day nurseries were recommended to the research team as 'good practice' nurseries; the rest were selected according to no firm criterion. Six of the nurseries took no under-twos. Two day nurseries took them only in exceptional cases. Only one, a hospital nursery, saw taking babies and toddlers as routine. The book is a thoughtful introduction to the study of nurseries, offering useful consideration of pertinent topics: the relationship between the adults and children and the effects of the purposes of the nursery on this; the job of caring for the children; the contract between the parents and the nursery.

Four studies have reported on intervention in the day nursery. Coleman et al. (1975) withdrew an experimental group of children for special language work. At the end of six weeks the language test scores of these children had improved, but so had those of a control group. It appeared that the staff had copied the intervention methods and this resulted in closer staff–child interaction. Another piece of research by Coleman, this time with Laishley

(1978) was concerned to improve the way in which staff related to children. Three different programmes were used in six nurseries. The first used a development assessment form to be completed for each child in order to encourage staff to focus on children as individuals; the second was a series of discussions on children's behaviour problems; and the third was a series of workshops on language development and the role of nursery staff. The first two programmes were popular with staff but the third was not welcomed. There was no study of possible outcomes of the programmes.

A different sort of intervention was carried out by Pinkerton (Hughes et al., 1980). She studied one day nursery and seven nursery classes and found that most parents had friendly conversations with staff but these were mostly social rather than about the children. Interviews with day-nursery staff and parents revealed that both wanted better communication about the children. Parents were invited to an evening meeting to see a video-recording of a nursery day. One or both parents of every child attended, to the surprise of the nursery staff. The opportunity was used to explain nursery activities. This small intervention demonstrated the interest of the parents and also showed a way of achieving better communication.

The fourth intervention study is from the Tavistock Institute (Bain and Barnett, 1980). This was a study of twelve children and all ten staff at one day nursery in London, over a period of two and a half years. The research team claims that most of the children were unwanted by their mothers, had experienced painful separations from them and were unable to form good relationships. They locate the basis of the children's problems in inadequate care by their mothers and nursery nurses, and consider that the amount of aggressive behaviour observed in the children was related to the length of exposure to the nursery. In order to improve the care given at the nursery the research team initiated changes in the grouping of children: family groups were abandoned in favour of age-band groups, and a nursery teacher was employed to help with the older children. Nurses were given responsibility for individual children, instead of caring for the group as a whole. Nurses and parents were encouraged to work together for the children's benefit.

At the end of the study period the children were tested. Most were thought to be still disturbed, their language development was not commensurate with their intelligence, they had poor concentration and were immature. The authors argue that the nursery had not compensated for the poor mothering and separation experiences suffered by the children.

The report offers judgements and interpretations based on psychoanalytic theory, and much therefore depends on readers' sympathy with this, and whether they think it valid and useful. However, the authors' suggestions for more individualized care of the children, work with parents and more direct teaching of the children are sensible – and are indeed in operation in some day nurseries and combined nursery centres.

Another study of nursery care was a small-scale observation in one day nursery over one week, carried out to consider whether group care in a day nursery could meet the needs of under-twos (Marshall, 1982). The author concludes that it can not. Unfortunately the methodology was not systematic and only adverse findings are reported. Generalizations are made on the basis of what may well have been a poor nursery group.

Finally, a study of combined nursery centres must be mentioned here (Ferri et al, 1981). The four centres were financed jointly by education and social service departments with the aim of providing care and education under one roof. They differed from each other in numbers and grouping of children, and the children's ages. The layout of the buildings was also different and affected grouping and activities. The study focused mainly on three and four-year-olds. (There were few places for under-threes and almost none for under-ones.) Where 'education' was offered, there was little difference in cognitive development between children at the centres and at local nursery schools and day nurseries; there was more concern for the social and emotional behaviour of the centre children. Staff attitudes and the larger numbers of children at the centres were possible factors here. The researchers carried out an observational study of two-year-olds at the four centres and three local day nurseries, and found adequate emotional and physical care in both settings, but a more stimulating environment in the centres. Staff-child interaction was poor in both, however, especially in verbal interaction. The two-year-olds who were grouped with older children interacted with their nurse less than children in baby rooms did. The great value of this report is in showing how the divisions between the departments responsible for education and care are highlighted when integration is tried out. They also show that, for two-year-olds, how best to provide good care remains an open question.

This small number of research studies has each considered only a small part of the day-nursery service, and each a different one. Research effort has been sparse and fragmented in approach. The exception is Garland and White's (1980) wider-ranging discussion of ideologies influencing nursery practice. There is no study of the service as a whole, or any systematic study of children's activities, or the effects of attendance on children.[11] In our study, which was designed as a comparison with childminding, we have focused on the service to mothers, and some aspects of what nurseries offer to under-twos.

The consequences of day care for the mother-child relationship

While we considered aspects of the minders' and nurses' relationships with children, we did not choose to study the consequences of day care for the mother-child relationship. We did not think it the most urgent question. However, this topic is fundamental for many people, as discussion with mothers and professionals reveals. In essence what people often say is: day care is bad for the mother-child relationship, so it is not worth studying day care; what we need to study is how to return the mothers to their homes full-time with their children. So we decided to describe what research has suggested on this issue.[12]

We noted in Chapter 2 that policy-makers accepted Bowlby's view that children under three should not be separated from their mothers on a daily basis, and that for three-year-olds separation should be limited to a few hours a day. His views became prominent when his report on maternal deprivation (1951) was taken up by the WHO Expert Committee in its 1951 report. They have been forcefully and convincingly criticized, however, by a number of eminent psychologists, notably Schaffer (1977) and Rutter (1972). In particular, Rutter criticized Bowlby's reliance on data on children separated from their mother for long periods in hospitals or large impersonal institutions, and his extrapolation from this (sometimes dubious) evidence to day care. Secondly, Rutter criticized his view that a baby's attachment to his mother will be weaker or will not form securely (thus endangering, in Bowlby's view, his future emotional maturity) if he spends time away from her. He refers to evidence (notably Schaffer's) which indicates that children may make attachments to several mother-figures. He concludes that children will not be harmed in day care providing it enables the child to form secure, stable relationships with the substitute caregiver(s). (Stability of care is further discussed in Chapter 4.)

There have been many recent studies investigating the possible consequences of day care with especial reference to the mother-child relationship. None was carried out in the UK, however, and the dangers of attempting to generalize from them to day care within the context of British social policy should be borne in mind. Day nurseries in this country are provided specifically for children who might otherwise need to be taken into care, and the regulation of childminding varies from country to country, and in the United States, from state to state. It would be unwise to seek parallels between English day care and its counterparts abroad – quite apart from any other effects which might result from cultural differences.

Much of the work on the subject has investigated effects of day care on the attachment between mother and child. Studies have frequently used 'strange situation' experiments to investigate this. The child is subjected to treatment which is assumed to be stressful for him. He is separated from his mother, and/or a strange adult is introduced (Ainsworth and Wittig, 1969). A rating of the attachment between mother and child is made, based on his protest (or otherwise) when she leaves, his exploratory behaviour in the stranger's presence, and the extent of his proximity to his mother, and other positive reactions to her.

The validity of the 'strange situation' technique has been questioned (see, for example, Belsky and Steinberg, 1978). The grounds for questioning it are broadly that it is unwise to generalize from the laboratory to real-life settings; that there is a wide range of individual variation in the children's response to separation from their mothers which cannot be explained solely by the strength or quality of attachment; and that separation reactions are related to cognitive rather than emotional development. However, many studies have used the technique or variations of it, and have found no differences or no consistent differences, between children in day care and other children (for instance, Brookhart and Hock (1976), Ricciuti (1974) and Kagan et al. (1978)). A problem with these and other studies is that they have been carried out in university-based centres where the quality of care may be higher than that available to most parents. So the findings may not be typical of less exemplary situations.

The study by Kagan et al. (1978) is a case in point. It is especially relevant to the present study because the children entered day care early in their first year. Kagan set up a centre in Boston to which he admitted Caucasian and Chinese children from working- and middle-class families. A control group consisted of 67 infants, of whom 32 were matched for ethnicity, age, sex, and social class with the centre children. The child's attachment to his mother was measured in two situations. In the first, when the child was twenty months old, his mother, a familiar woman (either from the centre or a family friend), and an unfamiliar woman were present. The authors noted whom the child went to for comfort when he was bored, tired, or apprehensive, and his proximity to the different adults during a 45-minute period.

The children spent more time near their mothers than near the familiar woman, and rarely played near the stranger. The Caucasian day-care children and home controls behaved similarly throughout. The Chinese day-care children, however, spent more time near their mothers and less near the familiar woman than their home-based counterparts. A possible interpretation is that the Chinese centre group tended to be less secure than their fellows. All the children preferred their mother when they were bored, tired or distressed – seven times more than the other familiar adults.

A second set of procedures involved the mother leaving her child alone in a strange room for two minutes; the occurrence and duration of fretting and crying was noted. The children were observed at two monthly intervals, from age 3·5 months through 29 months. Again differences were found between Chinese children (who showed more distress, and at an earlier age) and the rest. However, there was no difference between day-care children and home control children within the two ethnic groups at any age.

Only one investigation using the 'strange situation' technique (Blehar, 1974) suggests that children who experience day care from the first years of life may develop less than optimal attachment to their mothers – that is, judged against the experiment's criteria. This finding has not been replicated and may have resulted from the nature of the sample, which was small, and included a disproportionate number of first-born children. Later work suggests that Blehar's findings may also result from her sample having spent a relatively short time (four to five months) in day care. Blanchard and Main (1979), observing one- and two-year-olds both in the laboratory and in the nursery, found they avoided their mothers progressively less as months went by. Portnoy and Simmons (1978) also point to a 'transient period' during which children's early distress in experiencing day care decreases.

We turn now to a study which has the advantage of dealing with child care in the community rather than in an exemplary setting. Again the findings may have been affected by the length of time the subjects had spent in day care. Clarke-Stewart (1980) studied 150 children distributed among different forms of care, including children cared for at home, part-time and full-time nursery children, and a group in family day care (childminding). Half the children were two years old, and half three when they entered the study. The day-care children had entered care for the most part within the preceding six months. Research procedures included a rating of interaction between mother and child after a contrived separation. The full-time centre children showed less interaction with their mothers than the other groups, including the family day-care children. But other findings in the same study point to a relationship between home variables and the 'attachment' shown in the experimental situation, whichever care group the children belonged to. Children rated as ambivalently attached, interacted with peers during the observation of an evening meal at home four times more than other children. Clarke-Stewart suggests that the 'ambivalent' children were not receiving enough attention from adults at home and that this was reflected in the experimental situation, irrespective of whether they were looked after by substitute caregivers. Again, as with Kagan et al. (1978), the children's behaviour in the separation experiment related to factors other than whether they received day care.

Unfortunately, Clarke-Stewart's study has limitations with regard to the method of selecting subjects. No sampling procedure was used; subjects were located through paediatricians, churches, day-care agencies, a child-care task force, and a mailing list. Non-English speaking families, single-parent families, and the lowest socio-economic groups were excluded. Caution should be exercised therefore in generalizing from the findings.

A study by Vaughn et al. (1980) also considered day care in the community. The children studied came from impoverished, often single-parent families. The care was typically unstable, and few were looked after in licensed nurseries. Their attachment relations were studied at twelve and eighteen months. Half the children whose mothers had returned to work before they were one year old had attachments which the authors describe as 'anxious avoidant'; the rest had established secure attachments by the time they were eighteen months old. This study points to a possible interaction between adverse conditions in the child's home background and features of his day care (lack of regulation and unstable placements) which may have deleterious effects on the mother–child relationship.

To sum up: while empirical findings to date do not suggest that the mother-child relationship is affected by day-care separation in itself, what the child brings to the situation – his temperament and/or his experience at home – may have an effect. The research shows how complex a matter it is to study children's relationships and day care. Day care cannot be considered as a unitary experience for all groups of children (Kagan et al., 1978). Other factors in the children's lives may have a greater effect than day care on their attachment to their mothers (Clarke-Stewart, 1980). Some disruption of their attachment may be a passing phase while they settle-in to their day-care placement (for example, Blanchard and Main, 1979); and poor quality unstable arrangements in the first year of a child's life may increase the likelihood of disturbed attachment (Vaughn et al., 1980).

Notes

1. Jephcott (1962) studied working women in Bermondsey. One sample was of women at Peak Frean's factory; a second was taken from the electoral register. She found that one-fifth of under-fives had working mothers; most of these worked part-time. In most cases day care was given by relatives, most often a grandmother. Jephcott concluded that the

existence of part-time work and the close-knit, stable character of the area allowed women to carry out the dual role of worker and mother successfully and without harm to the children.

2. Myrdal and Klein (1956) discuss changes in the part played by women in Western society; the emancipation of women; their increased labour force participation and their wish to pursue two aims – to participate in adult social and economic life and to have a home and family. They point to the economic and psychological advantages of these changes and consider measures needed to enable women to fulfil both aims. They recommend reform of working hours to allow men to take a fuller part in family life, but they assume that mothers should remain responsible for their children's upbringing.

3. Klein (1965) reports on two studies. The first was based on a 1957 sample of 2030 people, including 837 married women, representative as to age, class, sex, town size and regional distribution, and as to the proportion of employed and non-employed married women. One in three of the married women were at work, but only one in six married women with an under-five worked. Informal day-care arrangements with relatives and friends predominated. Klein's second study was based on a postal questionnaire (1960) to employers. Though the response rate was poor, the sample covered was large: 27 000 married women throughout the country. Klein concluded from this survey of employers' practices and views that they disliked women as workers and did not make concessions to them nor offer them good career prospects.

4. Douglas and Blomfield (1958) reported on the national longitudinal study of 5386 children born in the first week of March 1946. Their concern was with the health and welfare of the children during their first eight years. The highest proportion of mothers of under-fives in work at any one time was 14 per cent, but at some point in the child's first five years, 26 per cent of the mothers had worked. Most day care was given by relatives. There were large regional variations in the proportions of mothers working: the highest levels were in the county boroughs of the North and Midlands, and in London, also in the county areas of the Eastern counties.

5. Yudkin and Holme's study (1963) was based on a sample of 1209 working mothers with children under fifteen. Of these mothers 243 had at least one child under five. The sample was assembled by a variety of methods, and by different teams in various parts of England (and one group of mothers came from Scotland), and included some mothers living on housing estates. The largest group of women were those working for three reputable firms. The sample may well have under-represented the most hard-pressed and the poorest mothers, and the day care they used. The sample is probably biased towards mothers who were coping well. Yudkin suggests, for instance, that Marks and Spencer (for whom one-third of the mothers worked) checked that mothers could provide adequately for their children before taking them on.

6. Stewart Prince (1967) found common characteristics among West Indian children under five seen at his child guidance clinic: 'They were aloof, apathetic, withdrawn, scarcely speaking or not speaking at all'. He thought that separation from their mothers, and grossly inadequate substitute care, might help to account for this. Stroud (1967) found that two-thirds of a sample of West Indian mothers of under-fives went to work, and three-quarters of them used minders. The childminding arrangements were unstable. He also found evidence of poverty, and especially of poor housing. Pollak (1972), a GP in Brixton, studied all the three-year-olds in her practice. She too found high rates of employment and high use of childminders among West Indian mothers, compared to the English mothers.

She found that the children were developmentally retarded compared to the English children, and blamed this on poor housing and inadequate attention from the parents. However, the measures she used were of doubtful value.

7. Abel-Smith and Townsend's study (1965) of data on expenditure for 1960 indicated that about 18 per cent of households had incomes below 140 per cent of the basic National Assistance scale. This represented nearly 7·5 million people, of whom 2·25 million were children under sixteen (17 per cent of children in the UK). Of the people in low income households, therefore, 30 per cent were children, 20 per cent aged five and over, and 10 per cent under five. This finding challenged current assumptions that such poverty as existed was overwhelmingly among the aged; and that a trend towards greater equality has accompanied the trend towards greater affluence.

8. The CRC study was carried out in 1975 in three social service areas: Manchester, Lambeth and Leicester. Local authority officials were interviewed. Women were contacted at factories and service industries; 340 were interviewed, and of these 126 had at least one under-five. The selection was weighted towards Asian women, in order to collect data on this under-researched group. Details of selection procedures and refusal rates are not given. A short interview was carried out at the work-place.

Registered minders were contacted using local authority lists (including an extra sample from Slough) with a deliberate weighting towards ethnic minority minders: in one area more of these were selected; in another more minders were selected from a multiracial district. There was also a sample of minders from an area where support services were 'most developed'. Interviewers made up to two attempts to contact the minder. Lists were out of date, even where the local authority had checked them.

9. On 8 July 1975. This was the first time it was argued in the House of Commons that minding had intrinsic merits: the home-like surroundings, and 'the opportunity to form the close continuing relationship with one adult that most research has shown to be so important for [the child's] development'. Minding should not be seen as second-best to day nurseries, but should be recognized and developed as a service in its own right.

10. The Oxford study sample was drawn randomly from the local authority list for Oxfordshire of registered minders. The 182 minders chosen were a one-in-five sample. In all, four refused and thirteen were not contacted. A sample of 165 minders was interviewed, including 66 active minders (that is, currently minding a child), 73 inactive minders (not currently minding a child) and 26 ex-minders (who had given up minding). At each active minder's a child was chosen at random to be the main focus of questions. Sixty-three mothers of the focus child were also interviewed.

Data was collected by means of questionnaires, and included a 'diary of yesterday' for both minder and mother. Observations were carried out of the child's approaches to the minder and his mother. (These observations were used in the Mayall and Petrie (1977) study (see Chapter 1), with one extra measure: coming within one yard and looking at the minder/mother.) A set of ratings was made immediately after the interview of the child's behaviour during the observation period (the first twenty minutes of the interview) and of the minder's or mother's behaviour to the child. An assessment was also made of the toys in each setting.

The Oxford study described demographic characteristics of minders and mothers, and noted contrasts and similarities between the two groups of women (Chapter 3). It gave an account of the process by which the minding arrangements had been made and how it had continued (Chapter 4). The daily life of the minder and the mother were described

(Chapters 5 and 6). Chapter 7 discussed the children's experiences at the minders': past placements, and the present placement in terms of play-space, toys, outings and the day's activities. Chapter 8 considered the child's relationships at the minder's and at home with his mother.

11. A research study at the Thomas Coram Research Unit is currently (1982) examining the effects of three kinds of day care on children: nurseries, childminders and relatives. The study is longitudinal, covering children in their first three years.

12. See also Hughes et al. (1980, Chapter 2) for a full discussion of this topic.

Part Two
Findings of the Study

Chapter Four
Availability and Stability

This chapter is about how and when mothers found a day-care place, and whether the child stayed put or moved on. The emphasis is on mothers, rather than mothers and fathers, or fathers only, because we assumed – rightly, as it turned out! – that families see the father's working life as unaffected by the arrival of a child, whereas they consider that if the mother wants to do anything that conflicts with looking after her child full-time herself, she will have to make arrangements for this.

We also knew that many mothers of children at day nurseries would be lone heads of the family – two-thirds of them were. For these mothers, having a safe place to leave their children meant that they could work – although the place was probably not explicitly, or specifically, or wholly offered for this purpose. Most of the nursery mothers took all the responsibility for taking their children to the nursery and fetching them at the end of the day. A few had some help from husbands, their own mothers, or other relatives and friends.

The minded children's families – where mostly there was both a mother and a father – gave interesting information on how some working parents today view their responsibilities. We collected facts and opinions from mothers only, not from fathers, so we have only mothers' picture of daily life and responsibilities, but the picture strongly suggests that the mothers take the main responsibility for child care.[1] It was the mothers who had searched for day care – following up advertisements for minders in shop windows, visiting libraries and local authority offices for lists of minders and nurseries, negotiating with minders and nursery staff. And it was the mother's return to work, not the father's, that depended on finding day care. At most the fathers took a week or two off when the baby was born. For these households an important daily job was taking the child to the minder and collecting him. Sixty-four per cent of the mothers regularly did both trips; only one father did. In the rest of the households the task was shared. It is worth noting, too, that mothers who use minders are likely to work a full day, to make it worth while employing a minder, but one that falls within 'sociable' hours. All the mothers except one worked under 43 hours a week, and all worked within the hours of 8 a.m. to 6 p.m. Most children arrived at the minder's after 8 a.m. and none left later than 6 p.m. By contrast, only two-fifths of the fathers worked regular, reasonably short hours; the rest worked for over 45 hours a week, or did varying hours, or did paid or unpaid overtime.[2]

·We asked the mothers who did the shopping, housework and child care. Just over half the fathers were reported as doing some work in all three areas; where they participated in less than all three, child care was slightly more popular than housework, and shopping least popular. There was a slight tendency (but not statistically significant) for the fathers who did all three to be in non-manual work.

It seems reasonable to conclude that for these families, responsibility for the child rested with the mother. The father was seen as the main wage-earner. The mother's working hours were geared to fit in with reasonable day-care hours. The fathers varied in the extent to which they helped at home.

Many studies confirm this picture. Oakley, in a small study of forty wives, found only a minority of husbands gave the kind of help that assertions of equality in modern marriage imply. Even then responsibility for household tasks rested with the wife. 'There is a long way to go before equality even appears on the horizon' (Oakley, 1974). Similarly Gronseth (1978), in a Norwegian study of sixteen couples who chose to do part-time paid work and share household and child-care work, found that in only nine households were all tasks shared equally; in the rest the overload was always on the woman. Yet these parents were committed to equal opportunity.

This is not to say, of course, that things have not changed. Most studies nowadays suggest some participation by most husbands, and in some cases commitment by both sexes to the equal shouldering of household and child-care tasks. About a fifth of our mothers mentioned that all jobs were shared equally. Young and Willmott (1973) may be right to suggest (though not to emphasize, as they do) that there has been some shift in the behaviour and attitude of men and women since the Second World War – since, for instance, 1939 when Margery Spring-Rice wrote about the hard lives of working-class wives, or since the first two decades after the war when Jephcott (1962) and Klein (1965) studied working wives. All three researchers found that women took full responsibility for housework and child care, and the researchers did not question the appropriateness of this, even where the women had paid jobs. It would seem that in general nowadays mothers and fathers take a more equal part in running the home and caring for the children, at least where the mother works too. But responsibility still rests with the mother. It is against this background that we set the mothers' search for day care and her experience of using it.

The discussion in this and following chapters is about whether mothers' and children's needs are met by the minding and day-nursery services, and whether the standards laid down by the government department responsible are met. A mother needs a dependable, high-quality day-care service where she will be happy to leave her child. The service should also meet her own needs, be responsive to her situation and her wishes for herself and her child. As a basis for discussion we have used the standards laid down by the DHSS for the care of children at minders' and nurseries, and we also refer (mainly in Chapter 9) to standards laid down for the education service for underfives. In addition, we rely on generally accepted opinion about what is desirable. For instance, most people think that children need their day-care placement to be stable, because stability offers an opportunity for the child to form a constructive, interactive relationship with their caregiver. And people assume that children need the opportunity to play outdoors. However, there are few certainties about how important for children such things as stability or outdoor play-space are, and even fewer about how relatively important they are. Rather than make judgements, we have tried to describe whether minding and day nurseries meet suggested standards and conform to generally held opinions.

So the discussion centres on norms – what is normally, nowadays, thought acceptable and desirable. But in this study mothers were also asked what they wanted, and what they had chosen. For instance, did mothers want a minder or a nursery place? What had they done about it a year later? Here the emphasis is on felt need, what people say they want; and on expressed need, how they translate that feeling into action (Bradshaw, 1972). What people say they want is important. If mothers want playgroups and not nursery schools, policy-makers would do well to take this into account. Otherwise resources will be wasted and people will be dissatisfied. Furthermore, mothers are on the whole good judges of what suits their children, probably the best judges, and their opinions should be respected and taken note of.

A recurring topic in the discussion is whether day care is or should be a 'complement' or a 'supplement' to parental care. Both words suggest an incompleteness in the care provided at home, but there is a difference in common usage. 'Supplementary' is usually used to refer to a lack or deficiency to be remedied, while 'complementary' indicates a broadly satisfactory situation which may be improved or enhanced by some addition. The day nursery has traditionally been seen as a supplementary service – one which offered what a deficient home could not, in particular, good physical surroundings and careful attention to health and hygiene. The earliest day nurseries were established on this principle and it is still influential, although more weight would now be put on the child's psychological health. Some of the earliest nursery schools for poor children, such as the one set up in Deptford in 1913 by the McMillan sisters, had similar purposes, together with explicit educational aims. Children were rescued from their unsatisfactory homes and offered opportunities to develop in spacious, airy, clean, well-equipped surroundings, with trained guidance.

Running alongside this tradition was that of the nursery school, seen as a complement to the home. The Froebel-trained teacher offered specialist skills to promote the child's development. From the 1870s, middle-class parents began to send their children to nursery school, and by the 1920s it was suggested that every child could benefit from nursery education, guided by trained teachers in his exploration and questioning of the physical world (Isaacs, 1929; Russell, 1926; Whitbread, 1972). The nursery school could be seen, as it is today, as an extension downwards of the education system, providing a specialist service few homes could match.

Childminding has developed as a service with other functions. It is used almost exclusively by mothers who need a place for the child while they work, not primarily to rescue the child from home, or to promote his development. Yet childminding comes under the DHSS, which has a long tradition of regulating services to supplement the home. In 1918 when local authorities were empowered to provide for the health care of mothers and their under-fives, by providing clinics, day nurseries and health visitors, a central aim was to improve mothers' child-care and housekeeping practices (Riley, 1979; Bruce, 1961, Chapter 5). Recent circulars issued by the Ministry of Health (later the DHSS) seem still to reflect the long-held belief that children in day care (as opposed perhaps to those in nursery schools) come from deficient homes. The Memorandum to Circular 37/68, which remains the fullest Departmental guide to good practice, suggests that parents of minded children may fail to meet their child's health and dietary needs, and if so the minder should strive to remedy this, if possible with the mother's cooperation. (Yet the same Memorandum notes that minders may be deficient in child-care practice and need supervision. This paradox is discussed in Chapter 10.) It would seem that the mother who leaves her child with a minder is cast by the Department in the same mould as the traditional day-nursery mother – she may be a 'poor' mother. This view may be held especially strongly where the child is under three years old. The idea that under-threes need their mother with them continuously probably accounts in part for the emphasis the DHSS gives to the importance for the young child in day care of an opportunity to form a close lasting relationship with his caregiver. The minder is seen as more likely than the nursery nurse to provide this opportunity, and perhaps she is seen too as supplementing the mother's care, by offering what he most needs, but is deprived of, if she goes out to work.

The first topic to be considered here is availability – was there a day-care place when and where mothers needed it, offering reasonable hours, and available to all comers.

Availability

Available at the right time

The first problem for the mother is to find a day-care place for the time that suits her. She may find a job that starts in a week or two and need to settle her child in advance. She may know she is to go into hospital and needs to book a place for him. Or she may wish to plan for a longer period ahead – for instance, a pregnant woman may wish to arrange to return to work six months hence. The number of women who wish to plan ahead may increase as a result of the provisions of the Employment Protection Act 1975.[3] A recent study (Daniel, 1980) showed that though the rate of return to work did not vary according to whether a mother was entitled or not to return to her job under the 1975 Act, those who were entitled deferred their return longer than those not entitled.

So mothers need a day-care service that both responds to immediate need and allows for planning ahead. Some people may argue that these needs are personal whims, and not ones to which society should respond. However, given the establishment in law of the principle of equality of opportunity and of the right of mothers to keep their jobs after childbirth, it is reasonable to suggest that day-care services should be structured to allow them to do so. The working mother's needs can be described as functional, they must be satisfied if she is to work (Benn and Peters, 1959, Chapter 6).

In addition, mothers should be able to choose at what age their child is to be placed. This is implied by the Employment Protection Act which protects a mother's income only up to a maximum of six weeks after the birth.

How then did our mothers and children fare – was there a day-care place for them? First of all, the mothers whose children were minded. By comparison with the general population, a high proportion of these mothers were well qualified and in high status jobs, and many were born and brought up abroad (see Chapter 1). All of them had, by definition, gone back to work before the child was two (all the focus children were aged under two years); and most had gone back when he was very young. Sixty-four per cent of mothers of under-ones and 53 per cent of mothers of one-year-olds had returned to work when the child was under six months old. Most (73 per cent) had decided in advance of the birth to go back to work. Many (70 per cent) were entitled to maternity leave, having worked for two years in their job.[4] And most of those entitled (72 per cent of them) took it.

Of those who had decided in advance to return to work, just under half (25 mothers) had tried to find a day-care place before the birth. Only twelve of them managed to do this, and only one of these made an arrangement, through the local authority, with a childminder. All the other successful mothers secured a place through a personal contact. These were minders they knew already, or relatives or friends. Mothers living in the outer boroughs were more successful than those in the inner boroughs.[5]

These mothers were people who wanted to make an orderly arrangement for their child, often well in advance, so that they could be sure the working day and the child's day would fit satisfactorily together. But mothers who wish to plan ahead are particularly badly served by minding. Minding is a private, casual arrangement which requires each side to trust the other: the minder must trust the mother to pay; the mother must trust the minder to take, care for and keep the child. This can be hazardous enough when the arrangement is due to start immediately, but where the mother wishes to book a place and defer using it, difficulties are likely to be insuperable. Either the mother would have to pay for the intervening period, or the minder would have to forego payment and trust the mother to turn up on the appointed day. The problem is likely to increase if more mothers take up maternity leave.

The data indicate that mothers in high status jobs were more likely to take maternity leave[6] and more likely to plan ahead[7] than the rest. This combination of characteristics is relatively new. As far as availability goes, minding may suit people who can take a more casual attitude to work, and go back when a minder turns up. It is not suitable for the career woman who wishes to plan, nor for the woman who must return to work soon after the birth to contribute to the family income.

Many mothers mentioned problems in finding a minder. Local authority officials told them there were no places available, or none for babies, or that the mother should stay at home with her child until he was older. Some mothers set off with a list given by the local authority, and found only minders who said they had no vacancy, or did not take babies; or the mother considered what she saw at the minder's unacceptable for her child. A few mothers made temporary arrangements to tide them over: they took the child to work, or left him with a relative or friend. Some mothers found a minder but soon removed their child because they were dissatisfied with the care given, or because the minder gave up minding. Seventy-five per cent of inner London mothers and 38 per cent of outer London mothers had one or more of these problems.

Day-nursery mothers were not as well placed as the minded children's mothers to plan ahead, and to benefit from the Employment Protection Act. Smaller proportions of them were eligible for maternity leave; even fewer took it; fewer of them planned before the birth to go back to work (see Table 5). This reflects the instability of their work history, and the difficulties of their circumstances, such as illness, and marital, financial and housing problems. A high proportion of them were lone parents (68 per cent), and many mentioned the need to work. Half of them did plan before the birth to go back to work. Most (65 per cent) were in work at the time of the interview, and a further 18 per cent were actively seeking work or about to start a new job. Most (88 per cent) had worked at some time since the birth. So while many of these mothers had other reasons for wanting a day-nursery place, the need to work was important too.

Table 5: Mothers' plans to return to work (minding and day-nursery samples)

	Mothers of:	
	minded children	*day-nursery children*
Proportion of mothers:	%	%
eligible for maternity leave	70	30
who took maternity leave	54	18
who planned before the birth to return to work	73	53
Number of mothers	56	40

But day-nursery places are hard to get, and even children put on a waiting list may have to wait some time. While 24 per cent of the mothers got a place for their child within a month, 38 per cent had to wait four or more months, and of these half waited for over eight months. On average the waiting time was nearly four months. Like the mothers of the minded children, the day-nursery mothers used temporary arrangements before getting the present placement. Of the 22 past arrangements made fourteen were seen as stopgaps, allowing the mother to work while she waited for a day-nursery place.

These findings suggest a shortage of both minding and day-nursery places. Some mothers resorted to more informal kinds of care, friends and relatives or paid help at home – and it might be claimed that these were a good option. But many mothers had looked in the first place for more formal day care, such as nurseries, and had in some cases seen informal care as a stopgap measure. For them minding was second-best.

The shortage of places reflects the fact that local authorities do not see themselves as providing for mothers who work. Minding is not a planned service; it is a system regulated by the local authority. There is no reason therefore why there should be a place for each child whose mother seeks it, whether for immediate or deferred use. The day-nursery service is designed to meet the needs of parents who cannot manage to find day care for themselves, or where the family is in some danger. The disadvantages for mother and child of the shortage of places hardly need emphasizing. For the child, short-term and stopgap arrangements are likely to be distressing, and to preclude the formation of trusting relationships with the caregiver. For the mother, the child's distress adds to her own worries, and a shortage of places restricts her ability to make reasonable plans and choices about combining work and being a mother.

Available in the right place

Mothers need day care within reasonable access of their home, otherwise the day may be unacceptably long for both mother and child. If the mother works, she may spend long periods travelling to the day-care place and then on to work. Some working mothers prefer the child to be near their workplace: this reduces travelling, gives mother and child more time together, and allows the mother to get to the child quickly in an emergency. But probably most mothers prefer day care to be near home. In Denmark, a country with wide experience of planning various types of provision (the factory crèche, city-centre nursery, neighbourhood nursery and minders), local provision is widely recognized as preferable, especially because it allows for easier coordination with health and social services for children (Wagner and Wagner, 1976).

At the time of the interview, most mothers were using a minder or day nursery within reasonable distance from home. About four-fifths of both samples lived within a fifteen-minute journey. Some mothers of minded children (27 per cent) travelled for twenty minutes or more, or by car for ten minutes or more. They had either been forced by shortage of places to look further afield, or had chosen a more distant minder. Use of a car gave some mothers more freedom of choice. Day-nursery mothers with longer journeys tended to be in the outer boroughs where nurseries are scattered more thinly.

Mothers are unlikely to use for long a placement which involves an hour's travelling or more, especially if they then have to travel on to work. It cannot be inferred from the data that minders and nurseries are conveniently placed, but only that those who use them will mostly only tolerate fairly short travelling times.

Available for the right hours
If the working mother is to compete on equal terms with other workers, she has to conform to the standard working day, with its inflexible hours, and demand for regular attendance. The structure of most jobs takes no account of parental responsibilities, so the working mother needs a day-care place that allows her to conform. This is true too of mothers who are students. Ideally mothers should have a major say in what hours are right for them and their children (for a full discussion, see Hughes et al, 1980). This happens at a very few nurseries (such as Coram Children's Centre and some community nurseries). But with most provision for under-fives the staff or the local authority decide on hours – as at playgroups and nursery schools. Day nurseries have traditionally offered a full-day service, but only within set hours; minders offer the longest and most flexible hours.

The current minding arrangements were working reasonably well, as regards hours. No mother had been dissatisfied with the initial arrangement, nor did minders complain about the length of time they had the children. According to minders, two-thirds of the mothers sometimes arrived late in the evening. This is presumably a big-city problem: mothers commented that they got held up in the rush-hour. Most minders understood this and tolerated it. Only 9 per cent expressed dissatisfaction, and only 7 per cent charged extra for lateness.

It may be thought remarkable that minders should be willing to take responsibility for children for such long hours. The 66 minders (main sub-sample) worked on average for 47 hours a week. The children came and went at different hours, and most of them stayed for a long day. On average the 361 under-fives at the 159 minders spent 37 hours a week with their minder; most of the children (86 per cent) attended for five days a week, and most (86 per cent) attended for regular hours. These figures confirm that most mothers who use minders work full-time. And minders respond to their needs: they offer long hours with various starting and ending times, within reasonable limits – in practice very few children came before 7·30 in the morning or left after 6·30 in the evening.

The day nurseries were open from 7·30 or 8·00 a.m. to 5·30 or 6 p.m., but for some mothers working full-time even this presented difficulties. A quarter of the working mothers, had found problems in working and meeting the hours offered. Mostly the problem was in getting to the nursery to time in the evening, but one nursery also imposed a deadline in the morning, after which children were not accepted. It is strange that day nurseries are not more responsive and flexible about hours. Of course there are problems – arranging for staff to cover the last half hour, coping with mothers who are often late apparently for no good reason – but some nurseries seemed to have responded to these problems rather harshly.

Available to all comers
Mothers need a service which will accept their child regardless of his nationality, creed or colour. Such distinctions are illegal in public places, and in establishments such as schools and nurseries, under the Race Relations Act, 1976 (Section 17–21). But the Act excludes actions within a family or where a person is treated as a member of a family (Section 23), and childminders are not covered by this Act.

Some minders are registered for different age-groups. The local authority may consider the premises unsuitable for babies, or may rule out toddlers if the minder has one or two of her own. We decided to ask the sample of minders (159) whether they had any preferences. In the question we used broad, standardized prompts, which minders could interpret as they pleased:

Are there any children you prefer not to take? . . . What about babies . . . older children . . . children from other countries/cultures . . . children who speak a foreign language . . . handicapped children?

The minders showed clear preferences. Only 34 per cent said they were willing to take any of the first four groups of children mentioned in the question; 18 per cent were unwilling to take children from two or more of these groups, and 70 per cent were against taking handicapped children. The reasons given suggest some of the practical difficulties of childminding, and cast doubt on a day-care policy which allows for discrimination.

Babies
Thirty-eight per cent of the minders said they preferred not to take babies. Their arguments were understandable and reasonable. Some thought their housing was unsuitable – prams are hard to manoeuvre up and down stairs and into lifts. Babies are a great responsibility; caring for them involves many more jobs than for a toddler, yet minders did not think they could charge more for a baby. Babies are restrictive; they have to be changed and fed regularly and frequently; outings with babies on public transport, and especially with one or two other under-fives, are almost impossible.

Two main points emerged. First, caring for babies in flats is difficult – yet there is virtually no alternative form of care for babies, and in cities, where demand is likely to be high, many minders live in flats. Secondly, caring for a baby is expensive, because it is virtually a full-time job and difficult to combine with caring for other children too. Minders need a reasonable return for the hours they put in, so they may either refuse to take babies, or try to manage other children too. However you look at it, the chances of a mother of finding good care for her baby at a city minder's are poor.

Older children
Only a small proportion of minders (12 per cent) were against taking older children. They said that forming a relationship with older children was more difficult, and it was more satisfying to see a child through from babyhood than to take him on at two or three. Older children were also seen as more likely to present management problems. Again, this seems reasonable, especially if minders found that older children had had other placements before coming to them, and if the children had little opportunity to settle in gradually (see below, page 82).

Children from a different country or culture, or with a foreign language
The proportion of minders who were against taking foreign or ethnic minority children was 24 per cent, and of those against taking children who spoke a foreign language (or whose family did), 23 per cent. Thirty-four per cent of the minders fell into one or both categories. This is probably a

minimum score; some minders might not admit prejudice to an interviewer, but would discriminate against a mother. Minders said that caring for a foreign-speaking child was too difficult; that various ethnic minority or national groups were unwilling to pay or haggled about the price; or that the children were dirty; or that the parents made unreasonable demands, especially about food and cooking methods; or that their own family or neighbours would be hostile. It is not surprising that minders should hold such views. Very many people do, as surveys of attitudes and practices (especially in housing and employment) have regularly shown.[8]

So mothers from various minority or national groups were likely to face prejudice against them and their children at about a third of the minders. Later we show that foreign-born mothers got a poorer service from their minders than mothers born in the British Isles; this may have been partly because they had a smaller range of choice and had to settle for second-best. Discrimination on grounds of nationality or ethnic group is clearly deplorable. We discuss policy options to deal with it in the last chapter. Meanwhile, given minders' freedom to discriminate, was anything being done to protect mothers and children from this loophole in the Race Relations Act? The local authority is responsible for registering minders, though they have no further legal responsibility. Were they taking on the task of protecting families?

Local authority staff were not complacent about their contact with parents. In three of the four boroughs, when asked what improvements they would like to carry out in childminding, staff said they would like to interview all parents and provide a matching-up service. In the fourth borough they claimed to do this already. In practice, most mothers thought that little help was being given. Seventy-five per cent of the mothers had been in touch with local authority staff in connection with the child, but of these only 15 per cent had found staff helpful. Most (65 per cent) had only been given the name of one or more minders. Sixteen per cent thought staff unhelpful. Many mothers (48 per cent) had found their present minder through personal, informal contacts. The rest found her through official sources – the local authority, health visitor or child health clinic. It was interesting that this second group was less likely than those who found the minder through local networks to have been given some information about the minder to help them judge whether she would be suitable for their child.[9] There seems to be a need, recognized by both local authority staff and mothers, for better information.

Handicapped children

Few of the minders (30 per cent) were willing to consider taking a handicapped child. Some felt they did not have enough expertise, or did not wish to take on so serious a responsibility. Others said they would not be able to look after more than just the one handicapped child, so that the presence of their own children, or the desire to take more minded children would rule this out. However, if minding is the only day care available apart from the day nursery, and if, as seems likely, governments increasingly promote voluntary and private day-care rather than expand state provision, this would probably result in the small number of day-nursery places being reserved for families in even greater need than at present. It is questionable whether it is desirable for handicapped children and children with severe social disabilities to be concentrated at nurseries.

Two further points should be made here. There is evidence that mothers are not all willing to accept that they stay at home full-time with their handicapped child, yet providers of services continue to assume that they do and will. Secondly, it is widely accepted that 'normalization' (the Swedish term) is desirable: children, except the most severely handicapped, should be integrated within the range of pre-school services; and an essential condition of this is an expansion of day-care provision with trained staff.[10]

Data on the minders' stated preference not to take some categories of children, raises important general questions which we consider later. Should we condone as a major form of pre-school care a system which allows staff to discriminate? Can the system be improved to an acceptable standard within the present policy framework? How far do the data suggest the need for a local authority to plan for the needs of their area?

Selection of the children at the day nursery

The day-nursery service is provided for children who fall within the priority groups described in the Ministry of Health Circular 37/68 (see Chapter 2). Interpretation of the advice rests with the local authority, but shortage of places means that even those accepted in principle by the local authority do not all get a place. People who fall within the broad categories may not even be put on the waiting list. For instance, of the sample mothers using minders, 9 per cent were lone mothers, and 22 per cent living in over-crowded conditions, both categories listed by the Circular as constituting need for day-care. In three of the sample boroughs, day-care management staff said that children at risk, especially of violence, were given top priority; in the fourth borough all decision-making was decentralized to area office level and no information was available at the central office. The sample day-nursery mothers typically had many needs, any one of which would qualify them for membership of a priority group.

Clearly there was a shortage of places at the day nurseries and some mothers had to wait a long time for a place. But boroughs vary widely in the number of places they provide. Information on the sample boroughs is given in Table 6. The waiting list numbers are high seen as a proportion of the number of places, and vary considerably between boroughs. This may reflect variations in expressed demand, and more or less screening by local authority staff; some of the families may no longer need or want a place. Day-nursery provision was high in the four boroughs by comparison with the national figure of 0·9 per cent in 1977, but notably higher in the two inner London boroughs: 6·3 per cent and 5·5 per cent, compared with 1·8 per cent and 1·4 per cent in the outer boroughs.

Table 6: Numbers of day-nursery places in the sample boroughs

	Number of under-fives June 1976 (a)	Number of day-nursery places 1978 (b)	Number on waiting list 1978 (c)	(b) as % of (a)	(c) as % of (b)	Social need category*
Inner	7,900	500	114	6·3	22·8	high need
boroughs	6,500	360	142	5·5	39·4	high need
Outer	19,700	354	280	1·8	79·1	high need
boroughs	18,700	263	97	1·4	36·9	low need

* As defined by DHSS (A/F77/6) 1979 (see page 000).
Sources: Local authority management staff, 1978; DHSS returns (A/F/77/6) 1979 for under-five populations (latest figures available).

It may be that some children have a better chance than others of getting a place. One factor is borough policy. There were few children under one year old on the registers in the sample nurseries. In all there were 36 under-ones, compared with 108 one-year-olds. Management staff for each of the four boroughs were asked if they had a minimum age for entry to day nurseries. All four reported differently: that policy was to take a baby no younger than six weeks old; that there was no lower limit but that nursery staff considered six months a desirable minimum age; that policy was to aim for no younger than six months; that possibly three months was a desirable minimum age (see also Chapter 2). There was thus considerable variation between boroughs, but it seems that older children are more likely than younger ones to get a place.

Another possible factor is that some mothers get a place because they try harder. Half the mothers (20 of 40) said they had taken the initiative. They asked the matron at the nearest nursery, a health visitor or social worker for a place. Some of these might have been offered a place anyway, but it also seems likely that persistence, making a case and being visible to the local authority may push the claims of some mothers. Speaking English may be useful too – all but two of the day-nursery mothers spoke English. Probably local authorities do not systematically seek out need in their areas, and may not in all cases be meeting the greatest need. One ethnic minority group, West Indian mothers, was disproportionately represented in the sample. Of the 40 sample mothers, sixteen were born abroad, including eleven from the West Indies. It may be that the needs thought to be characteristic of West Indian families have been defined and are met, while those of other minorities, such as Asian families, have not been.

Stability

Childminding was promoted in the House of Commons in 1975, as offering home-like surroundings, and 'the opportunity to form the close continuing relationship with one adult that most research has shown to be so important for his development'. This claim is echoed in the DHSS/DES Joint Letters of 1976 and 1978. It implies that a minder's care is superior to group care in offering this opportunity. In Chapter 6 we will discuss how close and personal the minder's care was. But first we consider the continuity of the relationships between minders and children, because it is on stability that close, personal relationships are built.

The Departmental view presumably originates in the well-established body of opinion that the relationship of child and caregiver must be stable, so that the child feels secure and confident, and so that both parties have time to learn to respond sensitively to each other. The child's learning during his first years depends to a large extent on his interactions with people. The good caregiver will provide opportunities for the child to learn. She will know him well enough to interpret what he does and to respond with what he needs.[11]

The implication is that the caregiver needs to acquire sensitivity to the child, to spend time concentrating on his needs and behaviour in order to learn how best to respond to them. The child can feel secure with an adult only when he can predict how that adult is likely to behave, and when he feels he can influence that behaviour. Again this takes time. The introduction of a child to a new caregiver needs to be gradual, so that the child may become accustomed to interacting with the new person in the reassuring presence of a more familiar one, usually his mother or father.

How far were the sample children offered the opportunity for continuing relationships with their minders and nurses?

Children who moved on

The study provides information on children's day-care placements in the 'present' (at the time of the interview with minders, nurses and mothers), in the past (before the interviews), and a year after the interviews (from a brief return visit to some of the minders). Some of the difficulties mothers had in getting a day-care place for their child have been described. While for a majority of the children their present placement was their first, a substantial minority had spent time with other caregivers in the past. Thirty-two per cent of the mothers of minded children had made one or more arrangements for their child in the past. These included friends, minders,[12] relatives, nannies, one day nursery, and taking the child to work. As for the day-nursery mothers, many of whom had to wait a long time for the nursery place, 45 per cent of them had made one or more arrangements for the child beforehand.

A year after the first interviews, we asked the first half of the minding and day-nursery samples (those in the inner boroughs) whether the children were still attending. Sixty-two per cent of the under-twos and 88 per cent of the over-twos who had been at minders' a year earlier had moved on, but only 33 per cent of the day-nursery under-twos had moved.[13] So why do placements end and are there factors that make some placements less stable than others?

Why do placements end?

One reason why children are moved about is the shortage of adequate day-care places. Mothers made stopgap arrangements to tide them over. Another reason is that mothers made arrangements which proved unsatisfactory and so they removed the child; or in some cases a minder had asked for the child to be removed. Between them the minded children had had 15 past placements with minders. All but two of these ended because of dissatisfaction. For the day-nursery sample, most of the previous placements had been seen as stopgap arrangements while waiting for the day-nursery place (64 per cent or 14 of 22 past arrangements). The rest ended because the mother's circumstances changed – her housing, her work or day-care needs.

Mothers' dissatisfaction with the quality of minders' care was closely paralleled by our own assessment. We assessed the minders' child-care practice at the first interview (see Chapter 7). Where it was assessed as good few children had been removed a year later. But where it was assessed as poor almost all the children had been removed (see Table 7). There was no relationship between the child being removed and his mother's social class or country of birth. There may have been other reasons why mothers removed their child, such as moving house or giving up work, but it seems likely that the mother's level of satisfaction plays a part, and that the mother and the interviewer arrived at similar conclusions about the standard of child care.[14]

Table 7: Whether child is still attending minder, according to her child-care practice (return visits)

	Assessment of minder's child-care practice			Row
	good	less satisfactory	poor	%
Situation one year after first interview:				
child attending	64	27	9	44 (11)
child left	7	36	57	56 (14)
Total %	32	32	36	100

N of children = 25

Kendall's tau c* = ·68; p < ·001 one-tailed test

* Kendall's tau c is a non-parametric measure of association using ranked scores which can vary between plus and minus one. It compares cases by their rank order on two sets of scores.

A closely related reason why mothers removed their children from minders is that they preferred other kinds of care. Some evidence on this comes from the return visit to the minders. We asked why the child had left her. The minders' opinion may have differed from the mothers', and it was not always easy to distinguish between cases where the child left because the minder stopped minding and where the child left before that. But the largest proportion of children (42 per cent) had left to go on to other kinds of care, including 26 per cent who had gone to 'nursery' or playgroup.

Another indication of mothers' preferences is that many had tried at some point in their search for day care to get a nursery place: 80 per cent of inner

London and 40 per cent of outer London mothers.[15] When mothers were asked whether they would prefer a nursery to their current minder, if it offered the same hours, 41 per cent said they would prefer a nursery now or later; 18 per cent said they would like to supplement the minder's care with a playgroup or nursery school, 11 per cent were unsure, and only 31 per cent said they were content for their child to continue with the minder as at present.[16] (These answers are virtually identical to those mothers gave in our earlier study of two-year-olds at minders'.)

The other major reason why placements at minders' end is that some minders stay for only a short time in minding. Two-fifths of the sample had been in the job for less than three years. On the other hand, half the minders had minded for five years or more, including 28 per cent for ten years or more. Some women settle down to minding and provide a stable form of care, but within quite a short space of time a high proportion may move out of the job. For instance, 15 per cent of those on the list of 208 minders given to us by the local authorities (and checked by them) were not minding by the time we contacted them within a few weeks. And the return visits to inner London minders showed that 25 per cent had stopped minding since our first visit a year earlier.

The reasons minders gave for both taking up minding and giving it up are worth considering. Asked what led them to take up minding, 35 per cent of the minders mentioned wanting to be at home for their children, and another 41 per cent gave other family reasons (Table 8). Of those who said they were not settled in the job, but intended to go back to work in the future, 67 per cent gave a reason connected with their own young children becoming less dependent. So it seems that for these young women minding was a job they did while it suited them to stay at home with their family. It was not seen as a long-term occupation. This was borne out by the fact that, of the inner London minders, those who had an under-five at the first interview were more likely to have stopped minding a year later than those who had no under-fives: 42 per cent compared with 18 per cent (see Table 9). It seems that women with young children are less likely to provide a stable day-care service.

The nursery nurses were also an unstable work-force. Fifty-nine per cent of them had less than three years' experience. Of the twenty nurses interviewed in inner London, six had left a year later (two of these had been employed temporarily because of staff shortages). By contrast with the minders, their stated reasons for taking up nursery nursing were mainly to do with an interest in child care (see Table 8). But they were at an earlier stage in their lives: 68 per cent were aged under 25 years and only three had

Table 8: Minders' and nurses' reasons for taking up their present job

	Minders		Nurses	
	% of	*% of*	*% of*	*% of*
Category mentioned by caregiver	*responses*	*cases*	*responses*	*cases*
Love of/interest in children	12	17	53	61
Already in child-care job	–	–	13	15
Experience in child care	–	–	15	17
At home with own under-five	23	35	–	–
Other family reason	28	41	8	10
Physically ill	6	8	–	–
Lonely/bored/depressed	16	23	–	–
Needed money/had left job	16	24	–	–
No qualifications for other job	–	–	8	10
Teacher/parent suggested	–	–	4	5
	N of minders = 56		N of nurses = 41	
	N of responses = 83		N of responses = 47	

Note: Since some caregivers gave more than one category of response, the totals under '% of cases' sum to more than 100%.

Table 9: Whether minder had stopped minding a year after the first interview according to whether she had a child of her own under five (return visits)

	Minder has own child under 5 years	Minder has no own child under 5 years	Total number
Number of minders:			
who had stopped minding	10 (42%)	9 (18%)	19 (25%)
who were still minding	14 (58%)	42 (82%)	56 (75%)
Number of minders	24 (100%)	51 (100%)	75 (100%)
		Kendall's tau c = ·23; p < ·01	

children of their own. Where they had left, it was either to go to another job, to move away or to have a baby.

So staff turnover was high among both minders and nurses. It is not surprising that young women should seek other employment, perhaps with better pay and conditions of work. Minding is poorly paid, has long hours, and no security. Nursery nursing in day nurseries is poorly paid too, and has few prospects beyond the small career structure through deputy matron to matron.

Finally, yet another factor led to instability for the child. This is that young families tend to move house. From the return visits we learned that 10 per cent of the minders, 12 per cent of minded children's families, and 13 per cent of the nursery families had moved house in the intervening year. We showed earlier that many mothers and minders lived in poor housing, especially as regards bringing up children. Young families are likely to prefer a house and garden to a flat or rooms, and will move to achieve this.[17]

The study showed that several factors may lead to instability for the child. There is a shortage of adequate day-care places; mothers are dissatisfied with the care at some minders'; some mothers prefer other forms of care, such as nurseries, nursery schools and playgroups; some childminders and many nursery nurses stay in the work for only a short time; and young families are mobile.

How long do placements last?

Mothers have to find their way around the complicated day-care system, each one more or less on her own in uncharted territory. For many of them, finding a day-care place they considered good enough for their child was a matter of trial and error. This was shown earlier: 32 per cent of minded children and 45 per cent of day-nursery children had had some sort of past placement. Most of these had been either unsatisfactory or seen as a stopgap arrangement. In particular, it was the past placements with minders that mothers had been dissatisfied with. Most of the past arrangements, whether with minders, relatives or friends, had lasted for less than four months. So these young children and their mothers were caught up in a system which resulted in instability, and added to the mothers' worry for their children while they were also going through the difficult business of re-establishing themselves at work.

We asked the minders how many children had left them during the year, and how long each child had been with them. Minders varied a lot on this. Some had had many children through their hands, often for short periods only – to help a mother through a crisis, or because of dissatisfaction on one side or the other. Other minders had had no changes to their group of children. On average 1·5 children had left the minder's during the previous year, and of these 108 children, 42 per cent had been with her for a year or more, 26 per cent for six to eleven months and 33 per cent for under six months.[18]

In addition we asked about all the under-fives currently at the minders' and all the under-twos at the nurseries – 361 minded children and 144 nursery children. How long had they been going to the minder or nursery? Over half the over-twos (56 per cent) had been with their minder for ten months or more, including 31 per cent who had been there for two years or more. Of the under-twos, 27 per cent were similarly settled – they had been there for ten months or more. At the other end of the scale, many children had been there for under six months – 32 per cent of over-twos and 50 per cent of under-twos. And many of these children were in their first two months (19 per cent and 30 per cent respectively). As for the day-nursery under-twos, 24 per cent had been there for ten months or more, and most (60 per cent) were in their first six months, including 36 per cent in their first two months.

The return visits a year later to the inner London minders gave information on how long placements had lasted altogether for those children who left minders' or day nurseries during the intervening year. Over half the over-twos had stayed with their minder for over two years, and 35 per cent had stayed for less than a year. The completed placements for the younger children were, of course, shorter, but more minded children (34 per cent) had very short placements (under six months) compared to only 10 per cent of nursery children (Table 10).

Table 10: Duration of completed placements – minding and day-nursery samples (return visits)

Completed placements	Minding sample under-2s	over-2s	Day-nursery sample under-2s
	%	%	%
Under 6 months	34	10	10
6–11 months	17	25	50
12–23 months	43	10	35
24 months or more	3	55	5
Number of children	29	20	21

Note: 'Under-twos' – those who were under two years old at the time of the first interview; similarly for 'over-twos'.

What does all this information tell us about stability for children at minders' and in nurseries? It seems that in many cases minder and mother are happy with the arrangement and the child is able to settle down and stay put. In other cases children move for reasons unconnected with the adults' satisfaction with the arrangement: parents or minders move house; the mother stops work to have another baby; a few children are taken on by minders for a short time only, in an emergency; the minder decides to take up better paid work; the child leaves to go to primary school. In other cases, mothers prefer different kinds of care, especially as their child gets older – a nursery where he has more indoor and outdoor space, trained staff, a larger group of children to mix with. This may be not so much dissatisfaction with the minder as a feeling that the child has grown out of the minder's – he has different needs. But a high proportion of the placements, both past and present, were short, and this suggests that mothers quickly move their children if they are dissatisfied. To start with a mother may not be able to assess what makes for good minding. They may learn through experience and it is while they are learning that their children will be moved about. Dissatisfaction is likely to be with the physical conditions at the minder's, the care offered to the child or the terms of the contractual arrangement. Minders too may find conflicts with parents too much to bear and may ask for a child to be removed. In later chapters we look at these aspects of minding.

The data on day nurseries presents a different picture. Few children under the age of six months get a place, and this probably accounts for some of the short placements. But once there, most children stay put. In three of the four boroughs we studied few children lost a place each year. No doubt the principle is that once a child has a place, his need for stability overrides the needs of children on the waiting list. So in those boroughs there was no instability arising from the provider's side.[19] And the mothers were almost unanimous in wishing the child to stay on. For them the advantages outweighed any disadvantages. The advantages they tended to stress were the good physical conditions, the trained staff, the fact that it was cheap, and that the nursery could be relied on to be there and to take your child each day. For it cannot too often be repeated that for mothers finding a satisfactory place for their child to spend the day is at best nerve-racking and for many a nightmare of trial and error. Many mothers breathe a huge sigh of relief when their child finally gets settled into his day nursery. For the mother of the minded child, of course, there are no such certainties.

Finally, one of the principal causes of instability for children is that there are not enough day-care places, and that many of them are unacceptable to mothers. Policy-makers are unwilling to recognize the needs of mothers and children for a high quality, reliable day-care service. So children are shifted from pillar to post while waiting for a day-nursery place, or until their mother finds a minder she is willing to settle for.

Which mothers and children got the least stable care?
Two groups of mothers of minded children had greater difficulties than the rest in getting a stable placement for their child. These were mothers from inner London, and mothers born and brought up abroad. Inner London children were more likely than outer London children to have had a past placement (47 per cent against 26 per cent). They were much more likely to have had an informal past placement (with a relative, friend or nanny) or to have accompanied their mother to work); there were twelve of these arrangements in inner London compared with three in outer London. Mothers were more likely to have tried, unsuccessfully, for a nursery place (80 per cent against 40 per cent). All the mothers who were unsuccessful in arranging day-care before the birth came from inner London.

Similarly, children of mothers born abroad (and there were equal proportions of these in inner and outer London) were more likely than the rest to have had a past placement (40 per cent against 25 per cent). This may have been because they tended to get worse minders (see Chapter 7). It may be that tension is higher between minders and mothers born abroad (see Chapter 9). Furthermore some minders preferred not to take foreign or ethnic minority children, and so mothers had a more restricted choice.

Both these groups also got a poorer service from their current minders than the rest. This will be discussed in later chapters. The difficulties experienced by these two groups of mothers highlight some of the disadvantages of an unplanned system. In areas where demand is high some people will be disappointed, and the ones who suffer most will be those least able to negotiate a passage through the system.

Stability within the day nursery
So far we have discussed stability in terms of children leaving their placement. But what are the opportunities for a close continuous relationship *within* the placement? Both nursery and minded children may have many contacts with adults and children during their day, and we have noted that the turnover of children at minders' may be high. While for the minded child, the minder herself is the main, usually the sole, caregiver responsible for the child during the whole day, at the nursery a child may have more than one caregiver both concurrently and successively. In general the focus children were cared for jointly by two or more nurses, and, in some cases, also by students. Where the child was cared for by one nurse only (16 per cent of children) this was mostly not as a matter of policy, but because he happened to be in a small group led by one adult. Successively too he might

have to learn to relate to more than one caregiver. There are two reasons for this. The first is that nurses move from one group of children to another. Twenty-one of the 41 nurses had been with their present group for less than a year; yet two-thirds of these had worked in the nursery longer than that. Staff move about to meet their own needs and requests as well as the staffing needs of the nursery groups. The second reason is that the children themselves move on. All the nurseries grouped babies and in some cases toddlers apart from the rest, and if a child starts young he may have one or two moves ahead of him. In all, 17 per cent of the 144 under-twos studied had moved from one group to another since they started at the nursery; for many others a change was forthcoming (see Chapter 7).

At the day nurseries in the study it seems that children, once there, are likely to stay, but within the day nursery they will probably have several different caregivers. It is often said that day-nursery staff undervalue children's need for continuity of care by one caregiver, and claim instead that joint care by two or three nurses of a group of children obviates their distress when a nurse leaves. Bain and Barnett (1980) argue that nursery staff often work under stress and that they arrange for their relationship with children to be impersonal as a defence. In our study over half the staff said they needed extra nurses to allow for more flexible and individual care of the children and to reduce stress on staff. There is no certainty, of course, that a child will be happier with one rather than a few caregivers; but it did seem that the nursery children had to learn to live with many. It would seem desirable, as is done in some nurseries, to decrease the numbers of staff each child has to relate to, and to increase staff responsibility for individual children (see also Chapter 11).

Settling-in

It is generally accepted that children who are given the chance to settle in gradually will be happier with their new caregivers and will find it easier to form secure relationships with them. Although the study was not designed to study the child's introduction to his placement, it is worth noting what we found on this.

We decided to ask the mother and minder about settling-in only if the child had been with the minder for less than a month, since questions on events further back in time may not produce reliable information. As it turned out only six children had been with the minder for under a month at the time of interview. For these children settling-in procedures were minimal. Only one mother made several visits with her baby and left him for gradually lengthening periods of time with the minder. There were few preliminary visits with the child (two mothers went three times, three went once, and one not at all). In four cases the child stayed for a full day on his first day. Only one child stayed for more than one short day. The Oxford Study (1980, Chapter 4) found a similar picture. Data were collected on all the focus children (all ages) at their 66 minders. Of the 40 children who did not already know the minder in advance, almost all went only once to see her before starting, and one-fifth met her for the first time on the day they started, for real, at the minder's. Less than a quarter of the minders thought mothers should settle the children in; half definitely preferred the mother to leave the child and go straight off; the rest were unsure.

At the day nurseries, there were ten children in their first month and they attended six of the nurseries. Two of the nurseries had encouraged the mother and child to come and spend several sessions getting to know the nursery, with the child being left for short periods (four children). Another new child's mother was routinely spending time at the nursery each day for other reasons. In the other five cases, there was no settling-in: the mother went for an interview one day and left the child for a full day on the first day in order to go to work.

From the limited data, it would seem that settling-in procedures at both minders' and day nurseries need study. It might be useful to consider how best to introduce a child to a new placement; what practices are followed, and how these might be improved.

Summary

As far as availability and stability go, childminding has many of the defects one might expect of a system which is not planned to meet need, but which is the only available source of day care for many mothers. One problem is that there is a shortage of places. Mothers cannot find a place when they want it. Furthermore some children (babies, handicapped, and foreign or ethnic minority children) are more difficult to place. Another problem is that the system does not allow for the orderly placing of children – for planning in advance, getting to know the caregiver, settling in the child. Minders do not all offer reliable and acceptable standards – this will be discussed in more detail later, but it is clear from the data referred to here that some mothers are dissatisfied with the care offered; and some prefer nursery care. An additional cause of instability is that the minder may stay in the work for only a short time – while it suits her, or while her children are young.

Finally, there is the mobility of young families – the placement may end when either the child's family or the minder moves house.

The day-nursery service is planned to meet extreme need; historically to help working mothers, more recently to prevent the break-up of families. But it does not meet even the needs it recognizes, as waiting lists and stopgap arrangements testify. Day-nursery hours too are not structured to meet the needs of full-time, working mothers. For staff it is an unattractive job; and the rapid staff turnover creates some instability for the children. Within the day nursery children are likely to be cared for by several nurses, both concurrently, and successively as children and staff move from group to group.

Notes

1. These data relate to 49 households from the under-two study minding sample, where there was a working mother and father, and where data could be collected in full (that is, where there were no language problems).

   (a) *Mothers' working hours*
   Ninety-two per cent (45) of the mothers worked only within the hours of 8 a.m. and 6 p.m., five days a week. Only one mother worked for more than 43 hours a week. Two mothers worked extra hours at the weekend, and two mothers started work before 8 a.m., but finished before 5.30 p.m.

   (b) *Fathers' working hours*
   Thirty-eight per cent (19) of the fathers worked within the hours of 8 a.m. and 6 p.m.; for not more than 45 hours a week. Thirty-eight per cent (19) worked for over 45 hours a week, including some extra hours on one or more days a week in alternate weeks; this overtime was paid or unpaid, voluntary or compulsory. Twenty-four per cent (11) worked varying hours, or worked extra hours less frequently than the second group, or they worked some unsociable hours (outside the 8 a.m. to 6 p.m. limits).

   (c) *Focus child's hours at the minder's*
   Eighty-one per cent (41) of the children were minded within the hours of 8 a.m. and 6 p.m. Eight children arrived earlier, between 7 and 8 a.m. No child was minded after 6 p.m.

   (d) *Daily trips to the minder's*
   Sixty-four per cent (30) of the mothers regularly did the two daily trips to the minder's. Only one father did this. In the rest of the cases, 34 per cent (18), father and mother shared the taking and collecting.

   (e) *Participation by fathers in household tasks*
   Fifty-three per cent (26) of the fathers did some work in all three categories: housework, shopping and child care. These fathers were drawn slightly more proportionately from the non-manual classes than from the manual classes (not significant). Their participation was not related to the three types of work-hours noted above in (b); nor was their social class related to the type of work-hours. Twenty-one per cent (10) of the mothers said that father and mother shared out the tasks between them.

2. A recent Office of Population Censuses and Surveys study (Marsh, 1979) presents data from areas with a high proportion of women in manual work. This shows that few working wives work overtime, or do double-day shifts or night shifts. It may be assumed that this

relates both to employment practices and domestic responsibilities. On the other hand, a high proportion of working wives with under-fives work evening shifts; this no doubt relates to the availability of relatives to take on child care in the evenings. By contrast, high proportions of husbands of working wives work long or unsociable hours. Other studies add detail to this point. Moss (1980) quotes from Young and Willmott (1973) and from a DHSS analysis of FES data (1975) to show that fathers of dependent children are more likely than non-fathers to work long hours. When there are dependent children, wives are less likely to be at work, and fathers may be attracted to working longer hours to make up the financial loss.

3. The Employment Protection Act (1975) gives three new rights to pregnant women (Department of Employment, 1976).

   1. The right not to lose her job on the grounds of pregnancy. This right depends on the woman having worked for her employer for at least six months.

   2. The right to return to the job at any time up to 29 weeks after the birth of the baby, or, if the actual job is no longer available, to a similar job, provided that the terms, conditions and location are the same. This right depends on her having worked for her employer for at least two years.

   Both these rights were effective from 1 June 1976. They apply to all women, provided they work at least sixteen hours a week for the employer, or eight hours if they have worked for him for more than five years.

   3. The right to maternity pay. This right depends on the woman having worked for her employer for at least two years. This right became effective from 6 April 1977. Maternity pay covers the first six weeks the woman is away from work, and is to be paid at the rate of nine-tenths of her normal weekly pay, less the amount of the standard social security maternity allowance.

   A useful discussion of the progress of the Employment Protection Bill through Parliament in 1975 is given by Fonda (1980). She shows that the original generous provisions which would have brought Britain into line with Europe were gradually abandoned. She also indicates that there is already evidence from some firms that more women are returning to work after maternity leave. She suggests that some groups of women are more likely to do this: working-class women in the north-west, Midlands and London, women from some ethnic minority groups, and professional women in London. Also that rates of return are likely to be higher where employers make information readily available and are supportive.

   The Act was amended in 1980. Small firms (employing fewer than six people) are exempted from the duty to reinstate the mother. And mothers must give more precise information about the expected date of the confinement and of their intention to return to work. As Fonda says, these measures are not likely to affect women's legal rights significantly. But the new requirements should be accompanied by publicity to employers and to women, so that both sides are fully aware of their rights and duties.

4. In all but two cases where the mother had worked for two years in the job, the child was born after the provision of the Employment Protection Act came into force (see Note 3).

5. Under 'tried for a day-care place before the birth' were included those who had made an approach to an official or agency, such as a health visitor or social services department; or had gone more directly to the providers of the services by using lists from libraries of nurseries and approaching the nurseries direct. Also included were those who made a private arrangement with a minder (registered or unregistered) or with a relative. Outer London mothers were significantly more successful than inner London mothers at

arranging day care before the birth (tau = $-\cdot61$; p < $\cdot001$).

6. The likelihood of entitled mothers taking maternity leave was related to their job status. Sixty-six per cent of mothers in Class I or II jobs (Registrar General's classification), 43 per cent of those in III non-manual jobs, and only 28 per cent of those in manual jobs, took maternity leave (tau = $\cdot28$; p < $\cdot02$).

7. Ninety-three per cent of mothers in jobs classed RG I and II (or student) had decided before the child was born that they would return to work, compared with 70 per cent of those in III non-manual work, and 26 per cent of those in manual work (tau = $\cdot46$; p < $\cdot001$). This tendency was present too in relation to the mother's husband's job (tau = $\cdot37$; p < $\cdot003$). But it was not significantly related to her marital status, nor to where she was born and brought up (British Isles or abroad), nor to the number of years she had spent in this country.

8. Studies on racial prejudice include: Daniel, 1968; Deakin, 1970; Richmond, 1973; Miles and Phizacklea, 1979.

9. Sixty-two per cent of mothers who found their minder through personal informal contacts, compared with 30 per cent of those who found her through official sources, were given information about the minder, beyond that she was 'good'. (X^2 = 8·26; 2 d.f.; p < $\cdot02$).

10. See for discussion of these points: Hewett, 1970; Carr, 1975; Anderson and Spain, 1977; Wilkin, 1979; Warnock, 1978; Loring and Burn, 1975.

11. See Rutter, 1972; Schaffer, 1977; Dunn, 1977; Clarke-Stewart, 1977; Bruner, 1974; Ryan, 1974.

12. On past placements we asked the mothers if the caregiver was unrelated to her and had been paid. This provided a definition of 'minder'. We did not ask if the caregiver was a registered minder. This would have been unreliable information, and it might have given offence.

13. By 'under-twos' we mean children who were under two years old at the time of the first interviews. Similarly with 'over-twos'.

14. It could be argued that in cases where, to us, the minder's care was obviously deficient, the mother would not, or should not, have left the child in the first place. But the interviewer was perhaps in a better position, during the course of a long interview, to assess the quality of care, and was able too to use systematic interview and observation techniques.

15. This is a minimum figure, representing those who made an approach to a nursery, local authority worker, or health service. Other mothers may not have tried for a nursery place because they knew the chances were remote. This is a possible explanation of the disparity between the inner and outer London figures. There are fewer nurseries in outer London; smaller proportions of children get places. Fewer mothers will know families using nurseries.

16. This answer is in striking contrast to an earlier one in which mothers were asked if they were happy for the child to go on attending the minder's. Eighty-six per cent of the mothers said yes to that. The huge difference in scores shows that the answer given depends on the question asked. Mothers are likely to defend their current arrangement for their child; they have a stake in hoping and assuming all is well. But if a good alternative is proposed, they can allow themselves to consider it. It may be that if offered a nursery place they would not accept it. But their expressed preference for nursery care parallels consumer preferences noted by Kamerman and Kahn (1981). It is also in tune with Bone's (1977, Table 3·5) finding that, among parents using different forms of care, those using minders are the least satisfied and a majority would prefer their child to go to playgroup, nursery school or day nursery. The sample day-nursery mothers too overwhelmingly (83

per cent) preferred day-nursery care to other care. Finally there is a striking similarity between the answers given in this study to those given to a similar question in the earlier two-year-old study. The research team had thought then that mothers' preferences for other care for their two-year-olds might be partly associated with their child's age; many children start at nursery school or playgroup at three. It was thought that mothers of under-twos might be happier with minding. The findings from the present study cast some doubt on this hypothesis.

17. See OPCS, 1980a, Table 4·28; and 3·52; Bone, 1977, Chapter 5; Bax, Moss and Plewis, unpublished report to DHSS, 1979.

18. This evidence about the length of past placements comes from data collected about the number of under-fives who had left during the twelve months before the interview. There were 108 of these children. The data was collected from those minders who had minded for at least a year, that is 85 per cent of the main sub-sample (52 of 66). The mean number of completed placements at these minders' was 1·5 (s.d.1·7). About a third of the minders had a stable group of children – none had left; but about a fifth had had through their hands three or more children.

19. We obtained from local authority day-care management staff in each of the four boroughs the number of families who were asked to remove their child from the day nursery in the last year. In three boroughs the number for the year was tiny: two, three and twelve, but in the fourth about six a month lost a place. In other words stringent reassessment of need for the place was carried out. In this borough it was considered that a child should be at home with his mother if possible, and his need for stability in his day-care placement was valued less highly. We do not know what policies are followed in other boroughs.

Chapter Five
Premises and Equipment

The mothers' experiences in finding and keeping a day-care place have shown some of the disadvantages of an unplanned day-care system. There were not enough places, especially in the inner boroughs, and those least familiar with the system got a poorer deal than the rest. Some children, all under two years old, had already moved on once or twice when we first saw them. A year later, most had moved from their minder. Very few people obtain a day-nursery place, and most mothers had to wait a long time for it. Their children were subjected to stop-gap arrangements, but in three of the four boroughs studied most could stay put once they got a place.

In this chapter we describe what mothers found at minders and nurseries – the housing and equipment for the job. Recommendations on standards are made by central government, but decisions on standards are devolved to the local authority. Standards may fall short of recommendations, and may vary between authorities. So some groups of people may fare better than others.

The mother who leaves her under-two in day care wants him to be cared for in safe, comfortable surroundings, where he has space and opportunity to play both indoors and outdoors. This is important for the child's daily experience, as well as the child-care practice and attitudes of the childminder. In Chapter 9 we describe the standards enforced or recommended for nursery schools, day nurseries and childminders in respect of premises and staff, and show how these vary. Education is the most rigorously controlled service and minding the least. The high standards which parents can see in operation in nursery school, and to a lesser extent in day nurseries, provide a yardstick by which they may judge less well regulated services such as playgroups and childminders. Parents want the best for their child, and one reason why many prefer other day care to minders may be that some minders do not provide safe, spacious premises, or a garden to play in. Both the Nursery and Childminders Regulation Act, 1948, and government circulars on day care recognize the importance of the physical characteristics of the day-care setting. The Act says local authorities may refuse to register nurseries and minders if they are satisfied that the premises are not fit, 'whether because of the condition thereof *or of the equipment thereof or for any reason connected with the situation, construction or size thereof* . . . to be used for the purpose'. The words we have italicized are supplied by the 1968 amendment, which strengthens the local authority's powers and brings equipment also within its direction.

Local authorities establish their own criteria for registering premises, and these vary. For example, some boroughs refuse to register minders who live above a certain floor, while others accept them. Standards may vary also between country and urban districts. However, central government has produced guidelines about 'fit' premises and equipment (in a Memorandum enclosed with the Ministry of Health Circular 37/68), and we used these as a basis for assessing whether the minders' housing and equipment were adequate for minding. We describe minders' housing in the light of these guidelines, and consider whether certain groups of children were in the care of minders with better premises and equipment, and whether the minders' housing compensated for the often poor housing of the children's own families. The main emphasis is on what conditions were like for minded children, because there is much more doubt and concern about minders' housing and equipment than there is about nurseries.

Two points must be made about this assessment. First we were in no position, as guests, to inspect the premises and this limited the scope and accuracy of the assessment. But we were careful to apply the same standards to all the minders and nurseries, so we do give some idea of the range of provision. Once we had made the assessment, we were able to to consider an important question – who got what? – and the answer to this showed that families facing other difficulties were also disadvantaged at minders' as regards housing and equipment. Secondly, we tried to stick to certain indicators – such as garden, safety equipment, prams – and to avoid emotive judgements or comments. We do not say much in this chapter about whether we would consider the premises and equipment at minders' and nurseries satisfactory if we were providing a service or using it for our own children. This is because these are very personal judgements and perhaps less reliable than judgements based as far as possible on DHSS criteria. The disadvantage is that this account of housing and equipment is not colourful, nor does it express appreciation of good conditions or horror at bad ones.

Minders' Housing

The childminders' housing varied widely. Some minders lived in council housing on new or old estates, in low-rise or high-rise blocks. A few lived in privately rented rooms in the basements of large houses and some were owner-occupiers in Victorian terraces or suburban semi-detached houses. Still others were housed in nineteenth-century philanthropic 'buildings' – blocks of inner-city flats, often in need of modernization. The bare facts about the 159 minders' housing are set out in Table 11. This shows wide disparities between minders' housing in inner and outer London. Most of the inner London minders lived in council housing, whereas in outer London over half owned their dwelling. Similarly, most of the inner London minders lived in flats or maisonettes, with no garden, while most of the outer London minders had a house, most lived on the ground floor and most had a garden. The characteristics listed (tenure, type, floor, garden) may affect the kind of care offered to the minded children. Ownership of the dwelling in general indicates greater prosperity, and the better-off minder will be better able to equip herself adequately for the job of minding. In one important respect outer London minders were better equipped than inner London minders – almost all had a phone (91 per cent compared to 66 per cent). This meant that minder and mother could get in touch with each other, and minders could contact the health and social services when they needed to for the children. Then if minders live above the ground floor (two-fifths of them did) they find it more difficult to take the children out, or to let them play outside, especially if there is no lift. Of the minders who lived above the ground floor, only 44 per cent had a lift. The relationship between the type of dwelling, height off ground and children's play out-of-doors was examined by Bone (1977, Chapter 5) who showed that higher proportions of children under five who lived in a house played outside than those living in flats. And children living above ground-floor level played out least. It seems that many minders live in housing conditions that are likely to restrict children's play.[1]

So not all the children, by a long way, spent their day in the sort of housing most people prefer for their children – a house and garden. This much is fairly obvious – city housing is as it is; and if, as a matter of policy, we opt for domestic day-care, then many city children will spend their days in flats, with little opportunity for outdoor activities. But apart from this broad contrast between flats and houses, what sort of picture do we have of the children's day-to-day environment at minders'?

The information set out in the rest of this chapter concerns the 66 minders

Table 11: Characteristics of housing of minders and mothers of minded children in inner and outer London

Housing	Mothers			Minders		
	all	I*	O*	all	I	O
Tenure:	%	%	%	%	%	%
own	46	12	57	44	3	56
council/housing association	28	30	26	42	84	30
other	26	58	17	14	13	15
Type:						
house	34	11	42	45	10	76
flat/maisonette	56	79	49	54	87	24
other	10	11	10	1	3	0
Floor:						
ground	43	35	51	61	30	87
first	33	28	38	16	24	10
other	25	37	12	23	46	3
Garden:						
own/shared	59	25	67	71	30	82
none	41	75	33	28	70	18
Number	64	32	32	159	75	84

*I = inner London boroughs; O = outer London boroughs.
Note: Data on tenure for the minders relates only to the main sub-sample of minders (N = 66).

(main sub-sample). Their housing and equipment, of course, affected all the children they cared for, but we have concentrated particularly on the focus children: the under-twos whose mothers we interviewed at home. Where comparisons are made with the children's homes, again these are the homes of the focus children.

What features of housing are important for children in day care? Provided the house or flat is warm and reasonably clean (and they almost all were), perhaps the main things are that children should have space to play and move about freely, and that they should be safe. The Memorandum certainly stresses space and safety. It sets out standards for the amount of clear space needed for children of different ages: 40 square feet for under-ones, 50 for one-year-olds, and 25 for over-twos. Where children are in full day care, in groups of up to seven children, the room where they spend most of their day, should conform to these standards, but, the Memorandum hastens to note, the standards should not be regarded as rigid. This is just as well considering the amount of space most people have in their living rooms, and the amount of furniture they have. For of course minded children tend to spend most of the day in the living room, amidst the minder's furniture and possessions. Very few minders will be able to provide a playroom (three of the 66 did). Where the minder has a large open-plan living area, in a new flat or house, the children may have plenty of space to play indoors. But in an older house or flat, rooms may be smaller. Furthermore, many minders kept a front room for their own family's use and confined the children (except in most cases for sleeping) to a smaller back room, next to the kitchen. This was typically a room crowded with furniture: dining table and chairs, easy chairs, sideboard, television set. For this study, we modified the Ministry criteria and attempted to assess merely whether the children had space to move about fairly freely and to make use of playthings. The assessment took into account the number of children cared for at any one time. Sixty-four per cent of the minders met this revised criterion. Here is an example:

> Large sitting room with sofa, easy chair, television. Space about 8 foot square in the middle. Two minded children (aged one and three years) had plenty of space for playing with bricks, pull-along toy, Galt baby trike. Also free run of the hallway.

And here is an example of a minder who had inadequate play-space:

> Large room with all the family's sitting- and dining-room furniture. Also baby's pram. Only space available for playing is the narrow 'corridors' between tables and chairs. Three minded children (aged two to four years) sat quietly playing with bits and pieces from a cardboard box. No room to put up constructions, or even lay out a puzzle undisturbed. Certainly no room to run about.

Apart from playing in the main room, it seems important that children should be able to move about – to play in the hall, for instance, and to make use of several rooms. In the words of the Memorandum: 'The children need to use the corridors and ancillary rooms'. This refers mainly no doubt to nurseries; but surely all children in day care should have access to more than one room, particularly where there is more than one child. Restriction to one room may impose uniformity of management on the children. For instance, they would probably all have to sleep at the same time. One room would also give inadequate scope for active play. Most children had the run of two or more rooms, but at 13 per cent of the minders' the children (where there was more than one) were confined to one room for eating, sleeping and playing.

The Memorandum also emphasizes the need for the home to be safe for the children. 'Heating appliances should be properly guarded, doors and gates to the street made properly secure, french windows and glass doors protected.' For the study, we noted whether fires and heaters in use at the time were properly guarded; and whether the play-space was otherwise safe.

Points we noted were: whether stair-gates were used where a toddler or baby had access to a landing; whether the children played in a passage with an open door giving unguarded access to the street; whether, if a child was mobile and had access to the kitchen, there was an unguarded cooker (guards which fit round the top of a cooker are available and at least one local authority insists on their use in playgroups). At 71 per cent of the minders' the play-space was rated as unsafe in one or more of these respects: 68 per cent of the minders had unguarded cookers to which the children had access; 12 per cent had inadequately guarded fires; four minders allowed children to play at the top of unguarded stairs, and one let the children play in the hallway with the front door open and unguarded access to the street.

We also took into account whether there was a garden, and whether it was safe and accessible. This again was in line with the Memorandum, which, though it does not specify a garden, strongly implies that there should be one, and says that it should be adequately fenced and easily accessible. For the purpose of considering minders' gardens, and the problems of supervision of several children, we thought that the garden should be accessible from the same floor as the living room so children could go in and out and still be seen, that it should be enclosed and that it should not have any grossly unsafe features (such as piles of rubbish or rusting equipment). Almost all the gardens met these criteria.

Overall assessment of minders' housing
So on each of these topics – space and safety indoors, and outdoors – some of the minders' housing was inadequate by D H S S standards and by ours. But not all the shortcomings were equally serious. For instance, children playing at the head of a steep flight of stone steps seemed in more danger than those near a short flight of carpeted stairs in a house; and while some children played in rather cramped surroundings, others were seriously overcrowded. So an overall assessment was made which allowed a minder's premises to be rated on a four-point scale, using the space and safety criteria already noted, and taking into account the seriousness of the shortcomings.

A small proportion, (9 per cent) all living in outer London, had safe housing with enough indoor space and safe garden or yard. For example:

> House and garden; safe heating; children kept out of kitchen while minder is cooking; no safety hazards. Children have plenty of space to play – indoors in glass-roofed extension and in sitting room; outdoors in safe, accessible garden.

> Minder lives in council flat – the converted ground floor of an end-of-terrace house, with its own garden. Children have the run of the flat. Enough space to play. Safe central heating. Minder has cooker guard (provided by the local authority).

A further 40 per cent had satisfactory premises except that the children did not have direct access to a garden, and/or there was no cooker guard. In many of these cases, the only disadvantage was that it was a flat above the ground floor with no garden. For example:

> Pleasant, tidy, council maisonette on fifth floor. Spacious indoor play-space, mainly because not much big furniture, and stairway and passageway wide. Children have the run of the maisonette, including bedrooms. Safe heating. Kitchen has door; minder says she mainly keeps the children out of it.

> Spacious semi-detached house and garden. Lots of safe play-space indoors and out. Central heating. Children have the run of the ground floor. Only snag – no cooker guard, and the children can wander in and out of the kitchen at all times.

So about half the minders were providing at least fair accommodation, given that it was domestic housing, in London. The rest of the minders were offering worse conditions. Forty-seven per cent had inadequate indoor space and/or safety hazards, in addition to lacking a garden and/or having an unsafe cooker. For example:

> Tiny living room. The front room is out of bounds for the minded children. The older ones can go upstairs, but Jilly is mostly in very small room with three-piece suite, dining table and chairs; this leaves a floor space which can't be more than one by two yards.

> Ground and basement maisonette. Children spend most of day in one basement room; sometimes allowed upstairs to watch TV. Also play in basement hallway. Basement room: rather dark and dingy; has double bed and one chair; cramped play-space. Children have free access to kitchen, which has unguarded cooker. Garden with large vegetable patch and small concreted area.

Finally, in a small proportion of cases (5 per cent), the premises were worse still: they were unsafe and/or seriously overcrowded. Four of these five minders lived in inner London. For example:

> Children spend the day in one room, about 12 by 14 feet. Six minded children present at the interview, and two holiday children (that is, school children on holiday). There was also a third school child cared for before and after school and when sick. The room had the normal domestic sitting-room furniture plus a dining table and chairs, three dogs, one cat, and a parrot.

> Maisonette with ground-floor sitting-room and own garden. Unsafe: no fireguard to fire; unguarded steep stairs down to basement rooms. Interview took place in tiny kitchen with all three minded children (aged 12, 13, and 17 months) on the floor. Unguarded cooker. Children had free access to the unguarded stairs.

Some minders then were unable to give the children a safe and spacious environment, and some seemed to us to be unaware of the dangers the children were exposed to. For instance, minders allowed children to run round their feet while they were handling hot pans, or said that telling a child not to touch a hot fire was a good enough precaution. Some of this no doubt can be put down to the view that what is good enough for one's own children is good enough for other people's. But while this view is understandable enough, it does not square with the principle that surely lies behind the standards laid down for day care – that if children are away from their parents then deliberate steps should be taken to ensure their safety and well-being. Nor will it do to suggest, as some people do, that day-care standards are middle-class standards and that it is objectionable in some vaguely moral sense to apply them to the whole population. Children of any class are susceptible to burns.

Equipment

To carry out their child-care work, minders need the tools of the trade. The list of things minders may need to cater for children 0 to 5 is long – child-sized furniture, crockery, cots, beds, pushchairs, toys, a washing machine, drying facilities, sterilizing equipment for bottles. But here we looked at only those things that all the minders needed to care for the focus child – playthings, a place for the child to sleep and some means of taking him out.[2]

Play materials

The Memorandum lists toys and improvised playthings, and mentions household equipment suitable for children's play. It says:

> Children have the same basic need to learn through play whatever their environment. It is a means of discovering and exploring the world around them, children combine elements of imagination, adventure, creation, co-ordination and manipulation in their play activities.

The emphases here are like those of writers on play – Garvey (1977) and Newson and Newson (1979). They emphasize the importance of toys as a means by which children can explore the world, and as 'pegs' on which to hang play. Exploration and play are seen as leading to greater understanding of the properties of things. And for children kept indoors most of the time, toys are especially important, because they have little chance to explore the natural world (cf. Uttley, 1976).

We asked the minders to show us the toys the study child played with, including toys for the pram or cot. We filled in a check-list afterwards, and noted the quality and quantity of the toys. The minders were also asked whether the child ever played with household objects, such as pans, spoons, colanders. Forty-one per cent of the focus children over the age of six months were allowed to do so. Of those who spent time in their cots and prams during the day, fewer than half (44 per cent) had a toy, whether a rattle, soft toys or swinging toy, during that time.

We assessed the adequacy of the toys available for the focus child, in the light of the child's age, the number, condition and variety of toys available, and the number of children who shared them. We also took into account whether the minder gave evidence of having considered the child's play. The assessment of toys was further discussed and sometimes re-scored at the weekly meeting of the research team. Of course, this was not a very precise piece of data-collection. We could not inspect the toys and had to rely on what was shown. But some of the minders had virtually no toys at all, or few for a particular age-group. We were able to divide the minders into those who had obviously inadequate toys and the rest. Here are some examples:
Adequate toys:

> A minder looking after only one child aged three months, who had a string of rattling beads hung across his pram, within reach of his hands, was assessed as adequately provided with toys for this age of child.

> Ginny, aged fifteen months, brought one toy from home. At the minder's she was allowed to play with kitchen things – tins and plastic containers,

and Mrs A said she loved playing the piano. She also had soft toys, book, building bricks, a tea-set, a handbag, a pushchair and a pull-along toy, all in good condition. She had no pram or cot toys, no drawing or painting materials and no riding or climbing things.

Inadequate toys:

> Gary was sixteen months old. His minder seemed not to realize that he needed or could have toys. He brought his own teddy from home. Otherwise he and two other minded children had only a toy pram and a few stuffed toys. The minder said he did not play with household objects. He attended the minder's for over ten hours a day.

> Minded children were aged 16 and 21 months. Very few toys: a few big teddy bears, a doll's pram. Minder said she got rid of most of the toys when her own child (aged three years) got older. The children had nothing to do but tumble about – they tumbled about her feet in the kitchen throughout the interview, while she cooked.

In all, 72 per cent of the minders provided adequate toys for the focus child, according to the assessment. Nearly half had at some time bought toys for minded children, but 56 per cent said they had never spent anything on toys. As with many aspects of minding, this is probably mainly because there is so little money in minding. When you are earning a wage well below what you could get anywhere else, you are not likely to give high priority to buying toys. Local authorities do not have much money for minding either, but some have responded to this problem by giving or lending toys to minders. In the study boroughs, two had given toys to many of their minders in the last six months (to 82 per cent in one borough and 30 per cent in the other). In addition, all four boroughs had a toy-lending service, but only a tiny proportion of the minders (4 per cent) had used it. Some found it difficult to get to a toy library; others may not have felt a need for toys, or been unwilling to take responsibility for keeping toys in good condition.

Push-chairs and prams, cots and beds
Minders need to be able to take the children out, and what sort of transport they need depends on the ages of the children. Some have a pram which accommodates the baby and a couple of toddlers. Others have double buggies. For many babies, the pram is also where they sleep during the day, and some mothers left their baby's pram at the minder's all day, for use as transport and bed. Most of the minders were managing at present as regards

transporting their group of children, although four said they had not anything suitable for taking all the children out. At best this meant few outings; at worst, it meant leaving children at home while they ran to the shops. Several minders commented that prams and buggies wear out and so were a recurring problem, which involved scouting round the area for cast-offs. Again, of course, minders' pay takes no account of this expense.

Minders also have to provide, or rely on the mother to bring, somewhere for the child to sleep. All the focus children had a sleep during the day, and while most of them slept in a cot or pram, a sizeable minority (two-fifths) slept elsewhere – on sofas, on adult beds (where they might be in danger of falling off), on the floor, or in their push-chairs.

Overall assessment of equipment
Next, we assessed the minder's equipment with reference to how it affected her care of the focus child and the child's day-to-day experiences. Fifty-five per cent of the minders were thought to be well equipped. They had adequate toys, a safe and comfortable place for the child to sleep and a suitable means of taking the children out.

In 39 per cent of cases the minder was inadequately equipped in one or more of these respects; and in a few cases (7 per cent) she was so ill-equipped as to cause serious concern for the well-being of the focus child. The main single reason why minders were rated as inadequately equipped was that they had poor toys for the focus child (28 per cent of minders). Others had poor sleeping accommodation and/or child transport (26 per cent) and two-thirds of these also had poor toys. There was no difference between inner and outer London minders on the equipment ratings. Here are examples of the ratings:
Good equipment:

> Mrs R. looks after five children in all, but Laura, eight months, is the only one who comes every day. There is a playroom well stocked with toys of all sorts, and Laura crawled round investigating them, chewing, rattling, during the interview. The minder has a cot in the bedroom for her sleep. There is a Snoopy toy in the cot for her. Mrs R. has a pram for taking the children out.

Less adequate equipment:

> Colin, aged 14 months, is minded with three other children, (aged 2, 3 and $3\frac{1}{2}$ years). The toys aren't very good or varied, not much the children can *do* with them – one pull-along toy, two rattles, and some animals.

Mrs L. has bought one cot, and the local authority has provided another. She has a pram for taking children out.

Mrs N. has rattles and soft toys for focus child (baby of 5 months). But both children (second minded child is 2 years) sleep on sofa, and Mrs N. also lacks transport – has only a single push-chair; has asked local authority for double buggy. Says she has difficulty getting out with the children.

Serious lack of equipment:

Julietta is 6 months old, and is one of four minded children with Mrs C. There are probably enough toys for her – rattles, soft toys, squeaky-toys – but nothing more demanding for the older children. Mrs C. is very ill-equipped. The children spend the waking day in her small kitchen/living room. She won't use a fireguard for the gas-fire and blocks their access to the cooker with a plastic bin. She has no play-pen or baby-chairs, so there is nowhere safe they can be left for a moment. During the interview, Julietta was left sitting in an armchair until she fell asleep. Then she was put in the bedroom to share an adult bed with a little girl of 16 months. Mrs C. has a push-chair provided by the local authority, but she has no pram or double buggy which she would need to take the children out together. In any case, she doesn't want either, because of the difficulty of getting it up and down stairs to her first-floor flat. When she goes out to the shops or to get a child from school, she sometimes leaves a child unattended.

The minded children are aged 18 months and $3\frac{1}{2}$ and $4\frac{1}{2}$ years. The minder provides virtually no toys – she says she can't afford them. The children have a box of toys, mostly provided by the council, but are not allowed to play with them, because it makes too much noise. There is a bike in the back yard. No cot for the toddler – she sleeps in a play-pen. No low chair for her to have meals – she eats on the floor or in the play-pen. Minder has a pram to take the children out in.

Who provides the equipment?

It is obvious that to be well equipped, minders must spend a good deal at the outset, and as they go on, depending on the ages of the children they care for. Toys get broken or lost. Cots and prams wear out. Since the minder has no income except what the parents pay, a good deal will depend on what she has in the house already, and on what she can afford. Fifty-seven per cent reported buying equipment at the outset, and a similar proportion had bought something later on.

However, there is another possible source of funds – the local authority. The local authority may help minders, under the provisions of Section 1 of the Children and Young Persons Act, 1963, as one of the measures designed to prevent the reception of children into care; or the local authority may have other funds from, for instance, Urban Aid, or from charitable foundations. In the four study boroughs, provision of equipment was very varied. We asked the 159 minders whether they had had any equipment loaned or given by the local authority when they first started to childmind, or since. One borough had lent or given items to more than half the minders we saw. In another borough, only one minder out of forty had received any help. In the four boroughs, 29 per cent of the 159 minders had received equipment at some time for their work. This might be a fireguard, or some toys, or a double buggy, or they were given a small money grant. This contribution, though valuable and perhaps crucial for the minder and the children, was only a small contribution to the initial and recurring costs of equipment that minders faced.

The costs of childminding are well known at local authority level, perhaps less well recognized higher up. The Memorandum says that childminding should offer care as good as that in a good home, and this perhaps assumes among other things that the good home is one that is already equipped for the care of children. This is not necessarily the case, even where the minder has young children of her own. The needs of a group are different from those of one or two children, and as children's ages change their needs change. Furthermore, of course, toys, prams, beds, bedding and crockery break and wear out.

Relationship between premises and equipment

We noted earlier that the very best premises were in outer London and the very worst mainly in inner London; the rest were fairly evenly distributed. There was no difference between inner and outer London minders on equipment. But there was a close relationship between premises and equipment. Table 12 shows this. We set the four ratings for premises against the three for equipment, and found that 33 per cent of the children spent their day in premises assessed as good or fair, and had the benefit of adequate equipment. On the other hand, 31 per cent of the children spent the day at minders' where both premises and equipment were less adequate and in some cases seriously unsatisfactory. The relative poverty of some minders may partly explain these groupings. The top group included some minders wealthy enough to own a house, and these would be able to afford the tools for the job. At the other end of the scale were the minders who lived in run-down dwellings, often cramped and unsafe; these were the minders least able to afford adequate equipment.

Table 12: Rating of minders' premises according to rating of minders' equipment

Equipment-ratings %	Premises – ratings %				
	Good	Fair	Less adequate	Unsatis-factory	Row total %
Good	4	29	21	0	55
Less adequate	4	10	22	2	39
Seriously lacking	0	0	3	4	7
Column total %	9	40	47	5	100

Number of minders = 66
Kendall's tau c = ·27; p < ·002

A complementary service?

So far it is clear that minded children may spend their day in a comfortable, safe, spacious, well-equipped home, or they may be in unsatisfactory conditions: cramped, unsafe, poorly equipped. Where a child lives in over-crowded conditions at home or has no garden, it is important that things should be better for him in his day-care setting. Day care, as the D H S S recognizes, should complement or supplement the care given at home: 'the sum total of home and group care should be such as to meet the all-round needs of the young child'. It seems unlikely that our haphazard day-care system is conducive to achieving this aim, and it was our impression that the system was not working well. We decided to compare the data on the focus children's housing at their own home and at the minder's home in order to throw some light on the question – were children who were disadvantaged at home compensated at the minder's?

Table 11 shows that twice as many mothers as minders lived in the least secure kinds of housing – the privately rented; and in inner London over half of them did so. This is housing that is likely to be cramped, and unlikely to have a garden. The table also shows that minders and mothers were likely to share disadvantages. In inner London, about the same proportion of both groups lived above the ground floor and lacked a garden. However, in outer London higher proportions of minders than mothers had their living room on the ground floor and had a garden. In general, children minded in inner London stand a greater chance of having poor housing both at home and at the minder's, than those in outer London. So how did the children fare in practice?

To take first of all play-space. Twenty-two per cent of the children lived in overcrowded conditions at home (1.5 or more persons per room). All but one of these children were at minders' where there was either inadequate indoor play-space, or no safe enclosed outdoor play-space. These children represented 20 per cent of the 64 children. Furthermore, compared with those who were not overcrowded at home, they were more likely to face one or both of these disadvantages at the minder's.[3]

A similar comparison may be made about gardens. The child's access to safe, enclosed outside space at the minder's was set against whether his family had a garden of their own. Again, those with a garden at home were more likely than those without to go to a minder with a garden.[4] Some of the children's families shared a garden with another family, and while this may not give as much freedom for play as an unshared garden it is better than none. What is striking here is that some children did not have access to a garden either at home or at the minder's: this was the case for 49 per cent of inner London children and 7 per cent of outer London children.

The relationship between the minders' and mothers' housing can also be considered more generally. For this purpose we grouped the mothers' housing into three categories, good, moderate and poor, using as criteria: amenities, overcrowding, height off the ground, and gardens.[5] On this basis, 50 per cent (25 of 64) of the households lived in good housing: in a house or flat, with all amenities, and not overcrowded. They all had a garden. Most had their living room on the ground floor. This group was weighted up in percentage terms, since most of them lived in the outer London boroughs. A second group, 28 per cent (24 of 64), lived in moderate housing. All but five of these lived in flats or maisonettes. All of them had sole use of all amenities, but two were overcrowded. Most of them lived above the ground floor or in the basement. All but two lacked a garden. The third group was smaller; 21 per cent of the households (15 of 64) lived in poor housing. All suffered from two or more of the following disadvantages: overcrowding; no garden; sharing or lacking an amenity; living above the ground floor or in the basement. This group also included all those who lived in rooms, not self-contained. We then set the mothers' housing against the minders'. For this purpose, we used the assessment of the minders' premises discussed earlier, and divided the minders into two groups, those providing good or fair conditions for the children (49 per cent) and the rest, whose accommodation was poorer, as well as cramped and/or unsafe. The result is set out in Table 13.

Table 13: Minders' housing compared to mothers' housing

Mothers' housing	Minders' housing good/fair	less adequate/ unsatisfactory	Row total %
Row %			
Good	59	41	50
			(N = 25)
Moderate	54	46	28
			(N = 24)
Poor	19	81	21
			(N = 15)
Column totals %	49	51	100
	(N = 32)	(N = 32)	(N = 64)
		Kendall's tau c = ·29; p < ·02	

The table shows that children whose housing at home was good or moderate got fairly equal proportions of good and poorer physical conditions at the minder's with a slight tendency for those living in the best housing to do best at the minder's too. But those children in poor housing at home were more likely than the rest to get poor physical conditions at the minder's. Eighty-one per cent of them did, compared with 41 per cent of those in good housing at home, and 46 per cent of those in moderate housing. As with play-space and gardens, there was a small group (17 per cent) who did badly in both settings. And there was another group who were compensated at the minder's for their moderate or poor housing at home – 19 per cent of the children. There were no significant differences between inner London and outer London.

So on the whole children were not being compensated at the minder's for the defects of their own home. This is not surprising. Mothers are likely to use minders who live nearby, and in some cases mother and minder will have similar housing. This point was made by Alan Little (1976) in respect of ethnic minority groups, some of whom live in run-down areas and so use minders living there too. There may also be less obvious mechanisms at work. Better-off minders are more likely than others to pick and choose among mothers, just as better-off mothers may pick and choose among minders. On both sides there is less urgency than for poorer women to make an arrangement, and more leisure to ensure that they get what suits them.

Mothers' place of birth and social class

We explained earlier that where mothers were born abroad, they were also brought up abroad (except in one case). Many had been in this country for less than ten years (37 per cent), including a smaller group (14 per cent) who had been here for less than five years. So our sample included many who were new to the country and its services. Table 14 shows what sort of premises and equipment the mothers got, according to their social class and where they were born.

First, housing at the minders'. Of mothers born in the British Isles, those in the professional classes did best, and those in the manual classes least well. Among mothers born abroad, there was little difference according to class. But among the professional classes (R G I and II), the mothers born here did significantly better than those born abroad.[6]

Secondly, equipment. For mothers born in the British Isles there is no class difference. But for mothers born abroad there is a difference which is highly statistically significant between non-manual and manual workers. The manual workers did strikingly less well than all other mothers. Ninety per cent were using minders who had equipment that was less adequate or seriously lacking.[7]

Looking at the figures more generally, we can say that more of the non-manual class mothers, whether born in the British Isles or abroad, got good premises and equipment for their child at the minder's. It is the manual workers who had most of the worst conditions.

Various possible factors may go some way to explain these findings. One is that the best educated mothers, those in the professional and managerial jobs, may be better able to choose a minder with high standards. There is a slight suggestion in the data that their buying power may be a factor too; these mothers paid slightly more per hour for the child than other mothers. A second possible factor is that being familiar with the services, and perhaps having the leisure to choose carefully, may account for these mothers' relative success. Another point is that some minders discriminate against ethnic minority and foreign-speaking mothers, and so for these mothers, of whatever class, the field of choice may be narrowed. The mothers who did

Table 14: Minders' housing and equipment ratings according to mothers' social class and place of birth

Mother's social class (RG)	Where mother born	Minder's housing - ratings %				
		good	fair	less adequate	unsatis-factory	N
I,II		15	57	28	0	17
III NM	British	12	41	46	0	10
III M, IV, V	Isles	0	36	56	8	6
I,II		0	39	61	0	8
III NM	Abroad	0	35	62	3	15
III M, IV, V		15	27	31	26	8

Mother's social class (RG)	Where mother born	Minder's equipment - ratings %			
		good	less adequate	seriously lacking	N
I,II III NM }	British	62	36	2	27
III M, IV and V	Isles	56	36	8	6
I,II III NM }	Abroad	68	32	0	23
III M, IV and V		10	52	39	8

Number of mothers = 64

Note: Students are included with mothers in R G I and II work.

worst were foreign-born mothers engaged in manual work. These are likely to be hard-pressed to find a minder quickly, may have to face racial discrimination, and may be less able to pay for the best. In addition, their unfamiliarity with the language in some cases and with available services, may restrict their ability to choose well.

The data on premises and equipment points up the disadvantages for the consumer of this private day-care system, where the local authority is not obliged to maintain high standards. Under the present policy the service children get at minders' is likely to depend on their parents' situation.

Day-nursery premises and equipment

There are obvious differences between the day nursery and the minder's home. The minder provides care for a few children in a domestic setting, the transaction is a private one and the local authority does not take responsibility for the standard of care provided. Day nurseries, on the other hand, are provided by the local authority for children in larger groups – usually fifty or sixty to a nursery; the children are ones deemed to be in need of day care; and the local authority takes responsibility for the standards: for premises, equipment and staffing. So standards at day nurseries are likely to be higher than at minders'.

First, the buildings used for the fifteen day nurseries. The Ministry of Health (now the DHSS) has provided guidelines for premises and equipment. Circular 5/65 (Appendix 1) recommends that buildings 'should preferably be single-storied, but where space on the site is limited, service rooms should be provided on an upper storey.' The appendix also says that rooms used by the children should preferably have 'direct access to ample outdoor play space'. In practice, eight of our nurseries were purpose-built, and were single-storied. Six of them were in large adapted houses, and here both ground- and first-floor rooms were used for the care of the children. One of the nurseries had been a residential nursery-cum-training college, and here too some of the children's rooms were on the first floor. So eight nurseries met the Ministry recommendation.

We studied 23 group rooms at the nurseries, those where there was at least one of our 44 focus children. All the nurseries had a garden, and they were all adequately fenced. But at one nursery staff considered the garden unsafe because neighbours threw rubbish into it, and so did not let the children use it. As far as access to a garden is concerned, 15 of the 23 rooms (65 per cent) had direct access, but in only 13 of them were children actually allowed to use the garden. However, at all the nurseries, except the one noted above, staff took the children outside in groups; and 63 per cent of the focus children had played outside 'yesterday', compared to 22 per cent of the minded children.

As with the minders, we made some judgements about the play-space. All but two of the 23 rooms were light and airy and all but two comfortably warm. In all the rooms the children had enough space to move about freely and use their playthings. In addition, at some of the nurseries, children spent some time with other groups, in their rooms, or their own group was divided up into smaller ones, and taken off to do painting, or for a story to another room. We saw no safety hazards in any of the nurseries. As far as space and safety are concerned, the nursery children were doing well, judged by the criteria used for the minders. On the other hand, the day-nursery children were more confined in at least one sense than the minded children: many more of them spent the day in just the one room – 65 per cent compared to only 13 per cent of the minded children.

Overall assessment of the nursery group rooms
Next we made an overall assessment of the nursery group rooms. On the criteria used for minders' housing, 65 per cent were 'good', and the rest 'fair'. Those rated 'fair' were those without access on the same level to a garden. None of the rooms was rated as 'less adequate' or 'unsatisfactory' – whereas 51 per cent of the minders' premises fell into these categories. This is not to say that, apart from the garden, the nursery rooms were all equally satisfactory for the children and staff. Comments from some of the staff made this clear. One matron, for example, thought the rooms were too large, and too few, so that too many children had to be cared for together. Another said the rooms were too small – not as regards the space available for the children, but because, when staff were absent, two groups could not double up together. Some of the nurses, too, when asked if there were any improvements they would like to see in the nursery, mentioned shortcomings in the premises. These were mainly to do with not being able to segregate small groups of children for special activities.

Equipment at the nurseries
This was also satisfactory according to the criteria used for assessing the minders' equipment. There were many and varied toys; adequate cots, mats and stretcher beds for sleep, and prams for outings; hygienic means of dealing with feeding bottles and nappies. Again, this does not mean that all the nurseries were equally well provided. In some cases, for instance, toys looked dilapidated and incomplete. A quarter of the nurses, asked if they would like to see improvements in the nursery, mentioned better equipment for the children, including toys. Compared with the minders, however, where more than half were assessed as being inadequately equipped, the nurseries were equipped to meet the needs of the children.

Standards at minders' and nurseries

This comparison between the premises and equipment of minders and nurseries points out the obvious: the nurseries offered children a much better deal. But the obvious does perhaps need pointing out. All the children in day care have the same needs, as the DHSS recognizes, but in practice only those families with acute problems can be reasonably sure of minimally acceptable standards for their children. For the researcher, as no doubt for the health visitor, social worker and mother, to go from many minders to day nurseries is to move into a different world. While some people may disparage nurseries as being bleak, starched or institutionalized, we tended to feel, as most of the mothers we talked to did, that safety, space and adequate equipment for the day's activities are important basics, things mothers should be able to assume when they leave their children in other people's hands.

The description given in this chapter of housing and equipment shows large contrasts between what local authorities accept at minders' and at nurseries, and between what they accept, as far as housing is concerned, in inner and outer London. The two contrasts illustrate different aspects of the same difficulty: where decisions about standards are devolved from central to local authorities, standards will vary. The reasons why standards are in practice higher at nurseries than at minders' are no doubt many. Local authorities are likely to be more concerned about standards within a service they provide themselves. Probably history too plays a part. The nursing profession has a long tradition of association with day nurseries and this may still be influential in the emphasis on large, light, airy rooms and on safe and hygienic washing and cooking facilities. The reasons why housing standards at minders' vary between inner and outer London boroughs must be largely to do with the housing available: for instance inner cities have more flats than outer areas. Also pressure on places is likely to be higher in inner city areas, so local authorities will drop their standards even lower to cope with demand. This was shown in the greater difficulties inner London mothers had in finding a satisfactory place for their child.

Factors of this sort may explain differences in standards, but they do not justify them. In other services, such as education, measures have been taken to ensure more even minimum standards, by imposing statutory requirements on local education authorities (this is discussed in Chapter 9). It is difficult not to conclude that standards for day care are allowed to vary so widely because day care for the general population has very low priority, for both central and local authorities.

Summary

As a setting for child care, the childminders' housing varied widely. The biggest differences were between types of housing in inner and outer London. Most of the minders in inner London lived in flats with no garden; most of those in outer London had a house and a garden. Children living in poor housing at home were more likely than the rest to attend minders with poor housing. If we take housing and equipment together, about a third of the minders provided a good setting for child care. That is, with regard to space, safety, comfort, hygiene and playthings, the children were well catered for by domestic standards, bearing in mind the fact that most inner London minders did not have a garden. There was also an intermediate group who did better as to premises than equipment, or vice versa. But 31 per cent did badly with regard to both. These findings suggest that local authorities did not make use of their discretionary power to refuse registration because of inadequate housing or equipment; and that they did not apply the guidance as to standards set out in the Ministry's Memorandum.

The nursery children who, unlike the minded children, were the responsibility of the local authority, were cared for in more spacious surroundings, with greater safety and more adequate equipment. The nursery children are, of course, thought to have special needs which place them in a priority category, and for them the nursery was able to 'complement and supplement' the home.

The tendency (statistically significant in some instances) was for the children of mothers born abroad and those whose mothers were manual workers to do worse at their minder's than the others. One possible factor here is the minder's prejudice against children of a different culture or language group. This may reduce the range of choice for some mothers. Also mothers use minders close to home, and some minders and mothers may share housing disadvantages or poverty. Some mothers may be better placed to choose well because they are well educated and can take their time to select a suitable minder; whereas others, who are unfamiliar with English and with the day-care services, as well as being hard-pressed to find a place for their children so that they can work, may choose less well.

While minding remains a private service, without effective regulation by the local authority, such inequalities are likely to persist.

Notes

1. Most families in England and Wales with a child under the age of two live in a house (89 per cent); for London the proportion is 59 per cent (OPCS, 1979a, Table 3.31) By the time the youngest child is ten to fifteen years old, 71 per cent of London families and 95 per cent of families in England and Wales live in a house. This preference for houses seems to be general, as data from another General Household Survey shows. Almost all those living in a house preferred this and two-thirds of those in other kinds of housing would prefer to live in a house (OPCS, 1980a, Table 4.28). We too assume in this study that families with young children are best served by housing close to ground level, with adjacent outside space.

2. For babies, minders may need equipment for washing and drying nappies and for cleaning bottles, but that depends on what the mother and minder have agreed between them. So though we asked about washing facilities and bottle-cleaning, we have not included the data in the assessment of equipment.

3. Eighty-nine per cent of the children who were overcrowded at home, were overcrowded at the minder's, compared to 49 per cent of those not overcrowded at home (tau = ·23; p < ·02), two-tailed test.

4. Eighty-two per cent of those children with a garden at home went to a minder with a garden, compared to 62 per cent of those with no garden at home (tau = ·19; p < ·05), two-tailed test.

5. A 3-point rating of the minded children's housing was devised, using the following scores:

	Score
Overcrowding (1.5 or more persons/room)	2
If on first floor or above, or basement	1
If lacks an amenity (bath, running hot water, indoor lavatory, kitchen) score 2 for each amenity lacked	8
If shares an amenity, score 1 for each amenity shared	4
If no garden (shared or unshared)	2
	17

Maximum actual score – 9

The scores were then grouped:

Group 1 – good housing scored	0 or 1
Group 2 – moderate " "	2 or 3
Group 3 – poor " "	4 or more

6. Tau = ·33; p < ·04, two-tailed test.

7. Tau = ·56; p < ·001, two-tailed test.

Chapter Six
The Child's Relationship with his Caregiver

Only one-third of the children were looked after by minders whose premises and equipment were up to official standards. Nevertheless, many people might object that these standards are not crucial for the child's well-being and that what the minder has to offer above all is loving, individualized care for the child – similar to that his mother gives him or to how the minder treats her own children. It is not difficult to set up this model of 'motherly' care in opposition to the 'institutional' care of the nursery. The first person to introduce the theme into the debate about childminding was Sonia Jackson (see page 44).

The attraction of this viewpoint, at a time of both public spending cuts and an increase in the number of mothers returning to work is obvious. The minder's service could be seen as inherently sound and needing only some small expenditure (for training, support and equipment) to render it totally acceptable.

The present study questions the assumption that the minder is a 'mother substitute' and that a policy for 'low-cost day-care' may be built on this foundation. But first a word about our own position on the caregiver as 'mother substitute' and about the criteria we used.

First we must emphasize that we do not hold that the relationship between the minder or nurse and the child should be equivalent to that he has with his mother. Such a relationship could produce emotional conflicts for all three parties involved, not to mention for the minder's own children. It is also possible that other ways of relating to the child have qualities to offer which are themselves of value. A study in the USA by Rubenstein and Howes (1979), for example, reported that caregivers in a day-care centre were more affectionate towards children, scolded them less and played with them more than did a group of mothers with their children at home. The present study investigates the notion of *proxy mothers* only because of the power this concept holds and because of the suggestion that 'motherly' care mitigates aspects of the minder's service which may be less satisfactory.

At this point a problem of definition arises. Within the context of social policy, the term 'proxy mother' may have more rhetorical than scientific value. Its use suggests a style of relationship different from that between children and nurses, or teachers, or playgroup leaders; a more personal, warmer relationship, in fact. However 'motherly' behaviour may differ between families and also across different cultures. Rather than attempt to define 'mothering' we took the behaviour of the mothers and children in the study as our criterion and measured the interaction of the minders, with the same children, against this.

We assessed the amount and kind of interaction between mothers and children and then asked questions which had a bearing on whether the minder was a mother-substitute. Did the child treat the minder as he treated his own mother? Did he behave in the same way in her house and in his own home? Was there as much interaction between them? Did his two principal caregivers react in the same way towards him? Did the way they talked about him suggest that they thought of him in the same way? Did the minder treat the minded child as she treated her own child?

Some answers and partial answers to these questions came from the 66 minders, the mothers and their children. There is also, for comparison, some information about the way nurses relate to children. The findings were drawn from both observation and interviews, and were derived from:
1. The adults' report of the child, his behaviour and any current problems.
2. The observer's subjective impression of the relationship between the adult and child and a check-list for the occurrence of certain behaviours.
3. An interaction count recorded during the first twenty minutes of the interview, in the case of children who were getting about by crawling or walking, and during a feed for the others.

An account of observation categories and reliability studies is given in Appendix D.

1. The adults' report of the child

As an introduction to the section of the interview on the child's behaviour we asked minders, nurses and mothers a general open question:
I wonder if you could tell me a bit more about him.
What sort of a child is he?

Would you say he was an easy child?

If no: What sort of things does he do/what is it about him that makes him difficult to look after?

If yes: Is there anything about him that's difficult?

The responses showed striking differences between the three groups of caregivers, differences in the extent to which the child was described in management terms. It seemed probable that this reflected the way the adults thought of the child.

Two broad kinds of response were identified according to whether the caregiver used an exclusively management definition or not. In the first, the management definitions (a) the caregiver praised the child, but only with respect to his being good or easy to manage, or presenting no problem about crying, eating, sleeping or playing alone. For example:

> Very good, no bother. *Easy?* Yes.
> She's very good on the whole. She lies down and sleeps without crying. A very lovable child. *Easy?* Yes.

(b) She praised the child, but added a reservation about a behaviour which made him less easy to manage: crying, being spoilt, whining, not liking to be alone, having a temper, clinging. For example:

> A good baby, not exactly placid, but going that way. *Easy?* Relatively easy, yes. *Difficult?* Only when he gets going with his screaming – sounds like a piglet, it goes through me.
> He's settled when his mother's not here. When she's here he cried a lot. *Easy?* Yes.

(c) She offered no praise for the child, but mentioned a current management problem. For example:

> He doesn't like me to leave the room; he cries. He's indulged a bit at home, I think. *Easy?* Definitely not – having to make sure he can see me all the time.
> Bad tempered, especially in the morning. If I hit him, he tries to hit me back. *Easy?* Sometimes he won't behave.

In the second kind of response, non-management definitions, (a) the child was praised, and attributes over and above being easy to manage were mentioned. For example:

> Very lovable, gorgeous child, very easy going. Quite a lot of go in him.

Very gentle, not spiteful or selfish. *Easy?* Yes, when he came he was very upset, but he settled down fine.

(b) In addition to (a), some reservation was made with regard to temperament or behaviour. For example:

Happy, noisy, mischievous, very active. *Easy?* Rather difficult because she's so demanding, but it's our fault (we play horse-back riding) – we don't let her get away with everything.

An extrovert. *Easy?* No, you've got to watch her all the time. She's always running with things – falling over – she runs into doors, falls over toys on the floor. Boisterous, she's very mobile, very light and active.

(c) The caregiver expressed worry about the child's development or behaviour; or the child was described as 'funny' or 'peculiar', or the description was largely in negative terms (what the child did *not* do), but without management problems. For example:

Bit slow with her stage of development. She's only just sitting up and she doesn't chatter a lot. *Easy?* Yes, she doesn't cry a lot. In fact we were worried to start with.

Placid, very quiet child – doesn't play with the others. Doesn't like to be interfered with. *Easy?* Yes.

Sixty-seven per cent of the minders, 29 per cent of the mothers and 36 per cent of the nurses described the children exclusively in terms of how easy or how difficult they were to manage. Minders were much more management-oriented than either mothers or nurses.

Perhaps for many minders the child was seen not primarily as an individual, presenting his own characteristics but as a component, together with the other children and her household chores, of the working day. Whether a child presented management problems or not may have been for many women what most readily came to mind when they were asked 'What sort of child is he?' The nurses were much less management-oriented than the minders. Looking after children may be more central to their work. Perhaps it was this together with their training (nurses in training write studies of individual children) that led them to differentiate between children other than by management problems, or the lack of them.

The mothers were the least management-oriented of all. There are, of course, other possible explanations for the differences than that they reflect differences in the relationships. Perhaps mothers found children less of a management problem than minders and therefore did not focus on this aspect of his personality. Again, perhaps the differences were to do with class differences between the three groups of caregivers. We will take both these possibilities in turn.

Behaviour and management problems

Did the children present fewer management problems for the mothers? In fact, the mothers reported less frequently than the minders that the child was 'easy'. This was true too of problems about the child's eating, sleeping and whether he was often miserable – although the differences between the two groups were not so great on these items as with the general question about whether he was 'easy'. In keeping with these differences, is the amount of irritability that the two groups of women admitted to. Most of the minders said that they rarely felt irritable with the child, while 22 per cent of the mothers said they were irritable at least once during the week and a further 14 per cent reported feeling irritable daily. For these items, although minders and mothers were responding about the same child, there was little or no correlation between their reports. So while minders focused more on management, they reported fewer problems. Data from the observations, to be described later, suggest that this, rather than differential reporting, is in fact the case – they had fewer problems.

Class and management definitions

Were the differences between the way minders and mothers described the child to do with social class differences? We showed earlier that more minders (judged by their past job) than mothers (judged by their present job) were in manual work. Differences between minders and mothers held good across social classes as they did when nurses were compared with minders who had previously worked in non-manual jobs. The differences were large and statistically significant.

2. Observer's impressions of the child's relationships with his mother and minder

Some of the items in the observation schedule, based on the Caldwell Inventory, make use of the observer's impressions (see Appendix D). Many of them are similar to those the casual observer might take away from a visit to a minder or mother.

On many of the items there seemed to be little to choose between the minders and the mothers. As far as the warmth of the caregiver's behaviour is concerned the child seemed to do almost as well at his minder's as he did at home. However, the mothers scored more highly on all but two items – the same proportion of mothers and minders slapped a child and the same proportion were warm towards him during a feed.

Still, 72 per cent of the minders kissed or caressed the child in the course of the interview and, although a much smaller percentage did so in the ten-minute feed observation (27 per cent, compared to 56 per cent of mothers) this provides further evidence of the impression of warmth in the relationship. It is perhaps from impressions such as these that the minder gains her reputation as a mother-figure. Two items which yield somewhat larger differences are those which show that the caregiver was helping the child to relate to objects and experience other than the personal relationship between them. Sixty per cent of mothers (compared to 23 per cent of minders) used a 'teaching style' during the course of a feed. They repeated names and qualities is such a way as seemed designed to attract the baby's attention. And 61 per cent of mothers (compared to 43 per cent of minders) did something to help the toddler to play during the interview. They got out toys, made suggestions or gave a helping hand with play that was under-way. However, these differences are not statistically significant.

3. Interaction observations

So far, this chapter has considered the minders and mothers: what they have reported and how they have appeared. The more systematic observations of interactions between caregivers and children present an opportunity to look at the child, to see how he – a more naive subject than either of his caregivers – related to them as well as observing how they interacted with him.[1]

Two types of interaction observations are considered: those of 'mobile' children during the first twenty minutes of the interview; and those of 'non-mobile' children during a feed. The data comes from matched observations; cases where a child was reported sick or off-colour in either or both situations have been discounted.[2] (Details of observation categories are given in Appendix D.)

Interview interactions

Twenty-five children over one year old were observed, first with their minder and then with their mother. On average, there were more interactions between the child and his mother than between the child and his minder. This was so whether the interactions were child-initiated, or adult-initiated. Before comparing the scores, however, it is necessary to take into account three variables which might have had an immediate effect on the number of interactions that took place or were scored during the observation. The first two concern the possible effect of the presence of other people (children or adults); the third concerns the observation category 'bodily contact' which limited the number of interactions which might be recorded by an observer.

The number of children present. Interaction between the study child and other children was not recorded, but the number of other children present was noted. In most cases there was one or more other children present at the minder's. This was so in only one instance at the child's home. We thought the presence of other children might have kept the study child occupied and diverted his attention from the minder, but the singly cared-for children actually initiated fewer interactions than children who were cared for in groups of three or more. As for the minders, while the four women who cared for one child scored high, there is little difference between the scores of those who cared for two children and those who cared for three or more. The presence of other children did not seem to suppress the number of inter-actions initiated, and certainly not in the case of child-interaction.

The presence of other adults during the observation. When another adult was present, it was noted whether he or she interacted with the child above a pre-defined minimum level. Such interactions took place during 16 per cent of minder observations and 52 per cent of mother observations, where the adult concerned was usually the child's father. These adults often seemed to see their task as diverting the child from the interviewee. In both situations interaction with another adult made for lower scores. The minders' scores were more affected – but the number of occasions where another adult interacted with the child at the minder was small (four altogether). These differences were not statistically significant.

Bodily contact with the caregiver. When the category 'bodily contact' was recorded, no other interactions initiated by the child and no 'touch' interactions initiated by the caregiver were noted. Episodes of 'bodily contact' took place in twenty of the observations with mothers and fifteen of those with minders. In these cases the scores must be treated as minimum scores.

The child's interaction with another adult and episodes of 'bodily contact' with the caregiver should be taken into account partly because they may help to explain some of the variability in the scores and also because of the extent to which they affect the comparison between mothers and minders. The means of total scores and subscores are set out in Table 15.

Table 15: Mean number of interactions during the observation

	CHILD-INITIATED INTERACTIONS							
	Touch		Object		Bodily contact		Total	
	mean	*s.d.*	*mean*	*s.d.*	*mean*	*s.d.*	*mean*	*s.d.*
To minder	0·9	1·3	1·7	2·6	1·2	1·4	3·8	3·9
To mother	1·8	1·8	1·8	2·3	2·8	2·8	6·4	4·7
*T value	T = 68 p < ·01		non sig		T = 71·5 p < ·02		T = 83·5 p < ·05	

N = 25

	CAREGIVER-INITIATED INTERACTIONS									
	Touch		Object		Speak		Admonish		Total	
	mean	*s.d.*	*mean*	*s.d.*	*mean*	*s.d.*	*mean*	*s.d.*	*mean*	*s.d.*
Minder	1·28	1·8	0·44	0·7	3·8	4·3	0·72	·84	6·2	5·2
Mother	1·68	2·2	1·6	4·5	5·9	4·7	1·72	2·6	10·9	9·3
*T value	non sig		non sig		non sig		T = 85·5p < ·05		T = 93·5p < ·05	

N = 25

	TOTAL INTERACTIONS	
	mean	*s.d.*
Minder observation	10·0	8·2
Mother observation	17·3	12·1
*T value	T = 74 p < ·02	

*Wilcoxon's signed rank matched pairs two-tailed tests.

In every category there was more interaction when the child was at home than when he was at his minder's; he initiated more interaction with his mother and she with him. The greatest differences are to be found on the part of the child. He touched his mother, whether a simple touch with the hand or a more prolonged episode of physical contact, twice as much as he did his minder (4·6 times in twenty minutes as against 2·1). As far as giving objects was concerned, there was little difference in the two situations. The difference between the amount mothers, compared to minders, presented the child with something, is due to the high score of one mother, reflected in the high standard deviation. The mothers tended to speak to the child more (5·9 episodes against 3·8), and they 'admonished' him more than twice as often. This is in keeping with the fact that they, more than the minders, reported difficulties in managing the child. All in all there were 73 per cent more interactions between mother and child than between minder and child. It seems that, as with the differences between the way the two groups talked about the child, the mothers were more involved with the children and they found them more of a handful.

Underlying the mean scores, however, there is a great deal of variability, as the standard deviations indicate. There was rather less at the mothers' than at the minders'; the average total scores were 10·0 with a standard deviation of 8·2 at the minders' and 17·3 with a standard deviation of 12·1 at the mothers'. A partial explanation may be found in the variables which affected the observation or its scoring, referred to earlier. What of variables to do with caregivers and children? Is it possible to account for the fact that while six of the children did not initiate interaction with their minder at all, and two minders similarly ignored the child, there were six children who initiated eight or more interactions with her and four minders who initiated ten or more interactions with the child?

The following variables were *not* related to the scores: the social class of the minder or mother; the age of the child; the length of the current placement; the age of the child when his mother first returned to work; the number of placements the child had experienced. Three variables *did* tend to relate to the child's score at the minder's: the minder's attitudes towards the child (whether she gave a management definition of him); the length of time she had been in the job; and the child's sex.

The minders' scores were hardly affected by these variables, but the children's scores tended to be, with the greatest (and only statistically significant) difference occurring in the score categorized according to the minder's attitude towards the child. Where the minder had given a non-management score, the child approached her nearly three times as often as for the rest.[3]

An examination of the data has thrown no further light on the variability of the scores. Some may be accounted for by the variables just discussed, some by the observation method and some by individual differences – extreme scores may play a large part in variability in a small sample.

That children interacted more with minders who spoke about them as individuals, than with those who talked about them only in management terms, suggests that to classify minders in this way has some validity and that the sort of definition used reflected an underlying attitude towards the child. A question which might be asked is whether the attitude is brought about by the amount the child interacts, or if the child interacts according to the minder's attitude. Again an explanation may be found somewhere between the two. The more personal the relationship, the more the child is responded to as an individual with his own qualities and needs. This in turn makes it more rewarding for him to interact with his caregiver and as he does so the more he reveals about himself for her. Evidence from the present study suggests that this is generally the case with mothers; they had a high inter-action rate and they defined the child in personal terms. Nurses also generally talked of the child as an individual. Unlike most of the minders, the reasons they gave for taking up their work were mostly to do with interest in or love of children. It may be that developing a relationship with another person's child is not so intrinsically rewarding for many minders. Perhaps there are benefits for her in a child who does not make personal demands, who is kept at arm's length, so to speak. As we shall see (Chapter 7) some minders had many children whose comings and goings they supervised during the day. To relate to each one personally, and do the household jobs, might have imposed too large a burden. In any case, for many minders the way they managed the children seemed to pay off. They mentioned fewer behaviour problems than the mother, they 'admonished' the children less, and they tended to have less difficulty in managing a feed (page 122). Some minders were aware of this and remarked how much better behaved the children were for them than for their mother. So far, it does not seem that most minders are a 'substitute mother' for the young child, to the extent that they were like the children's own mothers.

Interaction during feeds

The 'non-mobile' children were observed during a ten-minute feed. The results presented here refer for the most part to matched observations, matching referring not only to the same child being fed in each situation but also to the type of feed: whether bottle- or spoon-fed. (Some babies were fed in both ways.) In order to compare feeds of differing lengths, a quotient was obtained by dividing the number of each behaviour observed by the number of minutes in the feed, or type of feed. There were three feeds where the care-giver changed so frequently and quickly between spoon and bottle that timing was impossible. These have not been analysed, nor have feeds where the child was reported sick or off-colour in either situation. There are six matched bottle-feeds, which come from eleven feeds with mothers and fourteen with minders, and eleven matched spoon-feeds from fourteen mother and nineteen minder feeds.

The results show a tendency (statistically significant for the baby category) for more vocalizations per minute, whether by adult or baby, when the mother was feeding the child than when the minder was feeding him.[4] The only exception to this is that the minders 'exhorted' rather more – encouraged the baby to feed – during the bottle feed. The rates of baby's babble and the adult's utterances and 'exhorts' are set out in Table 16. As well as the matched observations, the results of all the observations are set out for comparison.

Table 16: Minders', mothers' and babies' vocalizations per minute during a feed

Feed	Caregiver		Matched observations Adult Utter	Adult Exhort	Baby Babble	All observations Adult Utter	Adult Exhort	Baby Babble
Spoon	mother	mean	5·75	0·44	2·5*	5·8	0·72	2·5
		s.d.	(2·99)	(0·57)	(1·7) N = 11	(2·6)	(1·2)	(1·8) N = 14
	minder	mean	4·1	0·39	0·83*	3·3	0·4	0·8
		s.d.	(2·6)	(0·26)	(0·72) N = 11	(2·3)	(0·5)	(0·7) N = 19
Bottle	mother	mean	4·5	0·06	1·4	3·0	0·09	1·3
		s.d.	(3·8)	(0·09)	(2·4) N = 6	(3·2)	(0·18)	(1·8) N = 11
	minder	mean	1·89	0·1	0·13	2·19	0·18	0·22
		s.d.	(1·39)	(0·12)	(0·2) N = 6	(1·4)	(0·27)	(0·36) N = 14

* Difference between two rates of babble during the matched spoon-feed statistically significant, p < ·05, T = 7·5 Wilcoxon matched pairs two-tailed test.

The rates of vocalization in the matched pairs are very similar to the rates in the whole set of observations. An exception is with mothers' utterances during a bottle-feed and minders' during a spoon-feed, for both of which the matched scores are rather higher than is typical for the whole set of observations. The most striking differences between the feeds given by a mother and a minder was in the number of times the baby babbled in the course of the feed. He babbled 25 times on average during a ten-minute spoon-feed given by his mother but only one-third as much when his minder fed him. The bottle-feeds show an even greater difference although this is not statistically significant. As well as the babies babbling more with the mothers, the mothers talked more to the babies. What is more, there was a positive correlation between the mothers' talk and the babies' babble. This was not so with the minders and babies. The correlations are set out in Table 17.

Table 17: Correlation between caregivers' utterances and babies' babbles

	Correlation between utterance and babble	
	spoon-feed	*bottle-feed*
Mother	+ 0·53	+ 0·72
Minder	– 0·06	– 0·1
	N = 11	N = 6

It seems as though there is a relationship between the amount mothers and babies 'talk', but that with the minders there is no connection between them. Again, as with the interaction scores of mobile children, there is some variability in the score. The small numbers concerned have unfortunately made it impossible to arrive at any explanations for this.

Nursery feeds. Five spoon-feeds in the nursery met the criterion described for mother and minder feeds; the child was not off-colour or sick.[5] The number of subjects is very small; nevertheless this slight piece of evidence suggests that the nurses' feeds resembled the minders' more than they did the mothers'. The nurses scored 2·2 utterances per minute (s.d. 2·0) and the babies scored 0·8 babbles per minute (s.d. = 0·6).

Other feed observation items. On many of the observation items there are only small differences between the mothers' behaviour and the minders'. We have already noted (page 115) that as many minders as mothers gave an impression of warmth towards the baby but that the mothers used a teaching style more and kissed their babies more. As for difficulties during the feed, there was a tendency for the mothers to have more problems than the minders.

Comments and Summary

Data from caregivers' reports, from our observation of their behaviour and attitudes and from timed systematic observations were used to consider whether the child interacted with the minder in the way he did with his own mother. Some comments on the limitations of the methods should perhaps be made here. The investigation was limited in scope by the situation of mothers and minders – for instance, we could not ask to spend all day, or parts of several days with these busy women, and so get a fuller picture. However, the methods used do permit comparison with our earlier study and with the Oxford Study (whose findings will be considered at the end of the next chapter). Secondly, while mothers and minders may behave differently with the child, *this is not in itself a criticism of the minders' care*. It does, however, question any ready assumption that the minder is a *substitute* or *proxy mother* for the child and that this is her main strength. A third point is that the differences in style between minders and mothers may relate in part to differences in their age and length of motherhood. The woman in her thirties who has reared two children may behave differently with a baby from the women in her twenties caring for a baby for the first time. The size of the sample did not permit analysis of this point. It is a topic which could be investigated further; it suggests that the quality of being motherly is too imprecise and varied to be of use in evaluating day care, however attractive it may be for policy-makers.

What emerges from this study of relationships is that the minders were, for the most part, unlike the children's own mothers. This is not to say that they were harsh or cold towards the children. They were, however, more concerned with management than the mothers were, and the child presented them with fewer behaviour problems. More of them found the child 'easy'. They scolded the child less and checked undesirable behaviour less frequently. The observers' impression was that this was not because the minder ignored or accepted behaviour which the mother would have reprimanded; it was rather that the child was often less active at the minder's. A certain passivity may have made him easier. Certainly he behaved differently in the two situations. There were no, or only very small, correlations between how he was reported at home and at the minder's as far as potential problem behaviours were concerned. Neither was there any correlation between the amount a child interacted with his mother and with his minder. Most of them interacted much more with their mothers. They were especially more likely to touch their mothers than their minders and to get close to them physically. In the less personal interaction of presenting objects, there was very little difference in the number of interactions between the two groups. At the minder's, however, presenting objects formed a greater percentage of all interactions. There was a group of children, almost a quarter, and mostly boys, who seemed to relate little to the minder and initiated no interaction during the observation period. None of the children behaved like this with his mother. There were some minders with whom the children interacted more than with others. These were women who placed less emphasis on management and described the child more as an individual – in fact they tended to be less typical of minders and more like mothers (or nurses) in this respect.

Notes

1. Evidence about inter-observer reliability is given in Appendix D.
2. There was no need here to weight the data with regard to the age of the child, since only over-ones were included in the interview observation, and only under-ones in the feed observation. And a comparison of inner and outer London observations showed no statistically significant differences in the amount of interaction between caregivers and children. So these observational data have been analysed without weighting (see Appendix B for detail on the weighting).
3. 5·8 (s.d. = 4·2) compared with 2·0 (s.d. = 2·5) [F = 5·38; p < ·03]
4. The categories 'cry', 'extended cry', 'sing' and 'laugh' have not been analysed because they occurred rarely. See Appendix D for categories.
5. There were two cases where the baby was bottle-fed, but these have been discounted.

Chapter Seven
The Child's Day

Social contacts

> From the child's point of view a good minder can provide him with informal care in familiar surroundings that is the nearest substitute to his own home . . . for many children under three and those with special problems this is much more in tune with their limited capacity for social contacts than the communal experience of a day nursery. (DHSS/DES, 1978)

This passage from the Joint Letter suggests that the child at the 'good' minder's will have relatively few social contacts and that this is particularly appropriate for the youngest children. While the underlying assumption may be debatable, the value which the Departments place on limited social contact is used as one criterion against which to measure the child's daily experience.

First, how long did the children spend at minders' and nurseries each day? It seems that most minded children are there for a good stretch of the working day. Three-quarters of the 361 under-fives at the 159 minders were there for 30 or more hours a week, and this was true for the youngest children – the under-twos – as well as for the over-twos. In our study we focused particularly on children in full-time care (defined as 30 hours or more a week) and in practice the 66 focus children were with their minder for, on average, $42\frac{1}{2}$ hours a week. Children who go to a day nursery are less likely to have a mother in full-time work. They may be there to give their mothers a break, for instance. So though some attend the day nursery for hours to cover a working day, on average their day may be shorter. The 44 day-nursery under-twos were there on average for $38\frac{1}{2}$ hours a week. So children spend long hours at minders' and nurseries, far longer than playgroup and nursery-school children. What happens to them while they are there is perhaps all the more important.

Whom do they spend the day with? Does the minded child spend the day with one or two other children in a family-like setting? Does the nursery child, as the Joint Letter suggests, have many more social contacts? The Memoranda enclosed with Ministry Circulars 36/68 and 37/68 suggest as a firm guide that a minder should care for not more than three under-fives including her own. In practice of the 159 minders a third were caring for three under-fives. But there was a wide range in the number – from one to seven children. If we look just at minders who minded at least one full-time under-two (since we are interested in what happens to these children), then 19 per cent of the minders had just one minded child, 26 per cent had two, 33 per cent had three, and 23 per cent had four or more.

The Memoranda state that the number and age of the minder's own children, and schoolchildren cared for before and after school, should be taken into account when the local authority determines how many under-fives a minder may take. When we took these children into account, we found that the under-twos were quite likely to be part of a large group of children. The number of school-age children at the 66 minders' is set out in Table 18. It can be seen that 73 per cent of the minders had one or more schoolchildren of their own and that 66 per cent of the minders regularly took in over-fives. Some of these came only in term-time before and after school; some came in the holidays too – probably for the working day; and some came only in the holidays or when they were ill. If we include the children who were regularly present (not those cared for only in the holidays or when sick) and the minder's own five-to-eleven-year-olds, then the minders cared for a number far in excess of the Memorandum's guidance, on average 4·7 children each, ranging from one to twelve. The ratios are shown in Table 19, with the nursery figures set out for comparison.

Each minder cared for slightly fewer under-fives overall than the nurses, who cared for 3·6 children each, on average. The table shows the range of contacts possible between a full-time minded child and other children under the age of twelve regularly present at the minder's. Each of them had on average nearly four other children to mix with. The situation at the nursery was different: nursery children's social contacts depended, not just on the size of the group they were in, but on various other factors (we will come back to this).

Most minded children also saw various adults during the day – the parents of other minded children, or the minder's husband or relatives. We too met other adults at minders' when interviewing, in about a quarter of the cases. Then a few of the children (17 per cent) also went to a playgroup or a drop-in centre with their minder. So many of the under-twos at minders' did have several social contacts there, both with children and adults. Perhaps more important for their daily experience are the implications of the high child–adult ratio for the care the minders gave the children. The minders' day with the children and the many jobs she did for them, is described below.

So the minded children had opportunities for more social contacts than might be supposed from the statement quoted at the beginning of this chapter, and the nursery children enjoyed a favourable caregiver–child ratio, compared with the minded children (Table 19). But a straightforward comparison between the two settings is impossible, because it is not a matter of comparing institutional care with domestic care, but of taking into account the very varied patterns of organization to be found in the institutions. In the fifteen day nurseries in the study, 23 groups (each with its own room or rooms) were included for detailed study, and each of these had at least one focus child. The groups were organized according to the age of the children, but with some variety between nurseries. The different forms of organization are shown in Table 20.

Twelve of the groups contained babies only, or toddlers only, and a further six had children who were mainly in their first two years. Only five of the groups had toddlers mixed with older children. In none of the nurseries were babies in family groups. These different age-bases of the groups made for differences in the daily timetables: examples of these will be given later. They also made for differences in staffing ratios, with the family groups having proportionately fewer staff than the baby groups. Appendix I to Circular 5/65 suggests that one nurse to five children is a 'reasonable standard' and that it may have to be increased if there is a high proportion of young children. (The Appendix also says that student nurses may be counted in the ratios, with three students equivalent to two nurses.) There was a very wide range in the staff–child ratio on the day of the interview – from one group where staff outnumbered children, to another where one nurse cared for six children (see Table 21).

There was also a wide range in the number of children in each group. Thirty per cent of the groups had six or fewer children, and 39 per cent had ten or more. Similarly there were differences in the number of staff (nurses and students) to each group. Half had one or two staff, the rest three or four.

These differences have been given in detail show how much variety there was in the grouping of children according to age, in their numbers in each group, in the number of staff in each group, and in the staff–child ratio. We

128 Childminding and Day Nurseries

Table 18: Percentage of minders who cared for school-age children (5- to 16-year-olds, main sub-sample of minders)

	Percentage of minders who cared for					
	1	2	3	4	children total	
Before/after school	6	8	3	0	17	
Before/after school and in holidays	12	5	7	3	27	66
Holidays and when sick	12	8	3	0	23	
Own school-age children	32	30	9	3	74	

Number of minders = 66

Table 19: Ratio of caregiver to children regularly present at minders' and day nurseries

	Adult–child ratio			
	at minders (main sub-sample)		at nurseries*	
Children	mean	s.d.	mean	s.d.
Under 5 years	1:3·0	1·2	1:3·6	1·0
5–11 years	1:1·8	1·4	–	–
0–11 years	1:4·7	2·1	–	–

Number of minders = 66
Number of nursery groups = 23

* The ratio does not include any student nurses present. There were 18 students working part-time in the 23 groups.

noted earlier that there was a higher staff–child ratio at minders' than in nursery groups. It is also interesting that for seven of the 23 nursery groups, the average number of children on the register was slightly lower than the average number of children (including schoolchildren) at minders' (4·6.s.d. = 1·5 at nurseries; 4·7, s.d. = 2·1 at minders'). The difference in the range

Table 20: Organization of nursery groups containing focus children (under-twos), according to the age of the children in the group

Type of group	Age-range of the children	Number of groups
Baby	Under 15 months	5
Toddler	12–24 months	7
Babies and toddlers	up to 27 months	6
Family groups	16 months – 3 years	2
	12 months – 4 years	3
	Number of groups = 23	

Table 21: Nurse to child ratio in the nursery groups 'today' (excluding students)

	One nurse to						
	0·5–0·9	*1–1·9*	*2–2·9*	*3–3·9*	*4–4·9*	*5–5·9*	*6 children*
Number of groups	1	1	6	10	3	1	1
					Number of nursery groups = 23		

of numbers of children present is also less marked than might be expected. At minders' the range was from one to twelve children who attended regularly, while in the nursery groups the range was from two to thirteen children on the register.

It is clearly difficult to generalize about day-nursery groups, and in some cases the sizes of nursery and minder groups are not all that different.

As with children at minders', day-nursery children were likely to see other adults as well as the nurses – mainly mothers and domestic staff. Some mothers spent part of their day at the nursery, either to settle their child in or because they needed support during the day. This had happened 'last week' in seven of the 23 groups. And of course mothers came and went all day to bring and collect their children. In addition, other adults, mostly domestic staff, often spent time playing with the children. This had happened in about a third of the groups 'last week'.

A further complication is added by the re-grouping of children during the day. Thirty-nine per cent of the groups joined together at the beginning or end of the day. At these times there were few children present, and few staff too, because of the shift system whereby half the staff started and ended work an hour before the rest. So the joining together of groups did not affect all the children. During the main part of the day, when most of the children were present, there was also some joining of groups: for their sleep after lunch and for indoor play. This allowed nurses to take a lunch break, or provided the children with space for more boisterous play.

All in all, it seems that in general the nursery children had more social contacts than the minded children did, but the distinctions between minding and nurseries are not clear-cut. While many minded children saw a lot of people, some nursery children saw few.

How the children spent the day

This is a difficult subject. To do it justice, it would be desirable to spend a long time at each minder's and in each nursery, observing daily activities. However, this was not feasible.[1] In any case it is difficult to make comparisons between the two settings, for, as we have explained, numbers of staff at nurseries, and numbers of children in both settings varied widely. Here we draw on what the 66 minders and 44 nursery nurses told us about their day with the children.

Both nursery staff and minders tended to organize their day within a timetable. For minders this included being at home when parents came with their children and again when they collected them. Minders had many routine jobs to do for the children: cooking, housework, laundry, shopping. Most of the minders said they coped well with all this; only 12 per cent had any problems. The high child–adult ratio had implications for the number and type of jobs minders did for the children. They took children back and forth to playgroups and nursery schools, and older children to and from school. Or they had to be at home when the schoolchildren came, before school, after school, and in some cases at midday too. The fact that some children were not present all the time reduced the work in some ways but increased it in others. When the schoolchildren or any part-time under-fives were not about, then the minder had greater opportunity to interact with the full-time minded child. On the other hand, the coming and going of children during the day imposed a routine on her. She had to be at home to receive children, and also when their parents came to collect them. In many cases she had to keep a strict timetable in order to take children to school or playgroup and collect them afterwards. This was so for 66 per cent of the minders. Minders also had to make extra meals and snacks for the older children, especially in the school holidays. This list of jobs takes no account of caring for the children more generally – talking and playing with them, and supervising them. This picture of the minder's busy day caring for several children of varying ages may be interpreted as providing a desirable setting for the youngest children. Perhaps they enjoy seeing several people and going on trips to the primary school; perhaps one of the strengths of minding for young children lies in this variety of experience. It is clear that a minded child is quite likely not to have the undivided attention of the minder, and that the facts run contrary to what seems to be assumed by promoters of minding. For many children, being minded is not like being at home with their mother and perhaps a brother or sister: it means being part of a highly structured day with an adult who has many calls on her attention. Some minders had many children and many commitments. Taking into account the numbers of children under twelve cared for part-time and full-time, the numbers present at any one time, the minder's housing, the number of trips to schools and pre-schools, the hours worked as a minder and (for 11 per cent) the hours worked in a part-time job, we agreed that a group of minders stood out from the rest: they had too much to do.[2] This group was 29 per cent of the main sub-sample. On average, this over-burdened group was looking after 6·7 children (s.d. = 2·1) compared with the rest, who had 3·9 children (s.d. = 1·6). There is evidence that these minders offered poorer care than others. On the assessment concerned with child care (see below) the overburdened minders did much less well than the rest. Twice as many of them were rated as offering 'less satisfactory' or 'poor' care. It would seem then that what is proposed as one of the strengths of the minder – that she offers flexible care, and can go on meeting children's needs once they start school (see, for instance, DHSS/DES, 1978), may impoverish the service she gives to the pre-school children, because she may have too many responsibilities.

In the nursery groups, the different age-bases of the groups, the differences in the size of the groups and staff–child ratios, all made for different routines from one group to the next. In the baby groups, for example, the feeding schedules, mixing feeds, sterilizing bottles, changing and bathing the babies, dealing with their nappies, provided a framework for the day. In groups containing fewer of these youngest children, physical care of the children imposed a less rigid routine. Most nurses had some jobs to do during the week – dusting, washing, tidying up – but our impression was that these jobs were much less onerous, responsible and time-consuming than those of the minders. The nurses were after all backed up by cleaning, catering and laundry services. In some respects the day-nursery children kept to a stricter timetable than the minded children. In all the nurseries, a mid-morning drink, dinner and tea appeared from a central kitchen at set times. Only 16 per cent of the children, compared with 60 per cent of the minded children, rested when they felt like it, rather than at a routine rest-time.

Routine toilet-training was also more frequent at the nursery. Seventy-two per cent of the nursery children, compared with 45 per cent of minded children were being, or had been, trained.[3] Whether toilet-training is to be welcomed as one means by which children grow towards independence, or deplored because it subjects children to the wishes of adults, is debatable. One reason why the nurseries trained the children was to prepare them for moving into a group of older children. Toilet-training was seen as one of the tasks of the toddler nurses. This was a need which the minders did not have, and they may not have thought it appropriate. Nor perhaps did they all have time for frequent routine potting, during the day. There is a similar contrast in the matter of self-feeding. Only 39 per cent of the minders allowed the child to feed himself at all, and this included children who were allowed to hold a spoon during a feed. In the nurseries, the policy seemed to be to encourage the child to feed himself as soon as possible, no matter how messy the result, and 74 per cent of the children did so. The minders did not seem to value the child's independence in this so highly; and of course it is quicker and more efficient for an adult to feed a child than to let him try to feed himself.

Another difference between the two groups was in playing out of doors. Sixty-three per cent of the nursery children had played in the garden 'yesterday', including those playing on a rug (the babies not yet walking). Only 22 per cent of the minded children had played outside. It will be remembered that many minders did not have a garden, especially those in inner London. However, most of the minded children did leave the house 'yesterday' – 70 per cent compared to 12 per cent of the nursery children. Forty-seven per cent had accompanied the minder to and from school with older children, and nearly half of these had made two or three such trips. Other expeditions with minders were to the shops (frequently mentioned) and to the local park (36 per cent of the children had been there in the last week).

There are various possible reasons why the nursery children went out little. Staff may see this as an unimportant experience for the children, especially as there was usually a garden at the nursery. There was also less need for the staff to go out themselves. Finally, even if nurses did value outings, as means by which the children might learn about the world, nevertheless the nursery routine, especially for the youngest children, did not provide enough unoccupied time.

As for playing with the children, about the same proportion of minders and nurses (82 per cent and 78 per cent respectively) said that they had played with the child on the previous day. (It should be remembered, however, that in most of the groups other nurses – apart from our interviewee – were present who could have played with the child). We included in this category minders and nurses who made references to short bouts of unstructured play – for instance: 'We had a game when I changed him', as well as those who described more sustained purposeful activities together, such as playing with a form board. What is disturbing is that 18 per cent of minders did not report even minimal play with the child, during a day which lasted on average eight and a half hours.

So there were differences in the children's daily routines and activities which spring from differences between the settings. The nursery routines, whether outdoor play, set rest-times, or self-feeding, arose to some extent from constraints within the institution, the facilities available, and also from the knowledge and values of the staff about child care. The minder was also influenced by the constraints of her premises, her timetable, the needs of the other children and her attitude towards child care. This study does not evaluate the different experience of the child in the two settings. On the face of it, if a source of contact with the local community is valued, then the minded children did better than the nursery children; if outdoor play is valued, the opposite is true. But we did not explore what happened during the outdoor play, or during the outings. We do not know if, during outings, the caregiver brought things, people and events to the child's attention, if she talked to him about them, and if she labelled things which caught his interest. Nor do we know about the nature of his outdoor play – to what extent and how it involved other children and adults, how much talk there was, and how much unhampered running about and exercise. Without such information it is not possible to describe adequately the child's experience – let alone compare how he fared in the two settings – beyond saying that there were differences.

One suggestion may be made here about routines. It is often assumed that the nursery is inevitably routinized in its child-care attitudes and practices and the minder is praised in contrast for her flexible informal care of children. What seemed clear from what the caregivers said about their day was that while both minders and nurses were operating under constraints, these controlled the minders more inexorably than they did the nurses. Minders were bound by their many commitments, and might, for instance, be just unable to find more time to play with the children. They had no resources to juggle with. But the nurseries could almost certainly re-think and re-plan their policies and practices on aspects of child care if they chose to. We return to this topic in the last two chapters.

Quality of care

The assessment of quality of care
The Memorandum enclosed with Circular 37/68 says that

> Child minding should provide as good a standard of care as would be expected in a good home and it is the minder's first duty to care for the children, even if she has to carry out domestic duties. She should have opportunities to talk and listen to the children and encourage them to form a warm relationship with her.

One of the purposes of this study was to evaluate the minder's child-care practice.

Our assessment was made according to what the minder reported and what was observed in the course of the interview and/or feed observations. (There was no attempt to carry out the same assessment in the day nurseries.[4]) The main criteria adopted for making the assessment were first, that the minder's practice should not present a possible source of physical harm to the children and secondly, that there was evidence that she understood, in the words of the Joint Letter (DHSS/DES, 1978) that children needed more than to be 'merely minded'; they needed 'intellectual and social stimulation'. We noted whether the minder kept an eye on the children's safety and well-being; whether she initiated interaction with them and responded to demands for attention, talk, affection and play. And we noted what she said about the importance of playing and talking with the child. The assessment was then made on a three-point scale:
1. *Good.* The minder gave no evidence of poor practice, and some evidence of good practice. For example:

> Minder seemed capable, caring about the children, and friendly towards them. She kept a good eye on their activities and took action where necessary: picked up a child who was nodding off and put him to sleep on the sofa; admonished three-year-old when he poached on another's play territory. Minder said she believed in talking to the children, and reported spending a lot of the day with them, being available to help and chat. She was very amenable to the children's approaches – they brought her objects, sometimes needed and got help, were hoisted up on her knee,

and she replied to their questions helpfully. Plenty of toys, all over the floor, and the children active and busy.

Child C. aged 17 months, is the only minded child. Warm, loving relationship; plenty of interaction and play during interview. Mrs N. was able to describe the child in a lively way – her love of dance, rhythm. Says what C. likes most is following her around and helping her with the housework, but in the afternoon they settle down and play together.

2. *Less satisfactory.* The minder presented some evidence of poor practice but not such as to cause immediate serious concern for the children's wellbeing and/or safety. For example:

Jimmy, aged 14 months, spent two separate half hours on the pot during the interview (Mrs L. strong on training). Juney (focus child, aged 7 months) was constantly ignored; so was Jimmy, who made many overtures to the interviewer – as did the other children. When Juney wants to sleep she does so on the floor and stays there until she wakes up. Other children sleep on the sofa. The children were highly disciplined, tidy up toys very quickly and efficiently. No Lego allowed on the floor. Mrs L. maintains a cool, supervisory role. Speaks to them as adults. Says she smacks the children if naughty. The interviewer got the impression that her punitive, distant manner results in the children being regimented. When she left the room the children 'erupted' a bit, got noisy, squabbled.

Other minders rated 'less satisfactory' included those where the subject child spent the whole interview unprotestingly confined to a pram or low chair, awake but with few or no toys and little or no interaction with the minder or with anyone else.

3. *Poor.* The situation caused serious concern for the children's well-being and/or safety. This category included minders who left the children unattended while they left the house; and those who gave the child little social stimulation, judged by their behaviour during the interview and their report of daily activities. One minder reported that the three children spent most of the day alone upstairs in cots and a play-pen, coming down only for meals and to see television in the afternoon. Here are others:

Minder very busy with own family responsibilities – a full day with husband about some of the day and two children: one at primary school, the other at nursery school. The minded children (13 months and 2 years) played about her feet in the kitchen while she cooked. Occasionally she intervened if they showed signs of hurting one another. No suggestions for play. Provided almost no toys – 'I got rid of most of them when my children got older'. Just a pram and odd dolls. Said she didn't have time to play with the children.

Minder left front door ajar – easy access to street. She didn't monitor child's whereabouts and activities when we were talking and the child was out of the room. She took long phone call in another room and left fretting child with me; he didn't know who I was; she didn't ask me to look after them. Minder has evening job and leaves children whose mothers arrive late with her own ten-year-old; leaves the minded children strapped into their prams/push-chairs, also leaves child sleeping alone in the house.

The minders were rated as follows: 51 per cent, good; 31 per cent, less satisfactory; 18 per cent, poor. There was no significant difference between inner and outer London minders, but most of those who left children unattended lived in inner London (5 of 7).

We then considered which children went to minders with less good childcare practice. As with the minders' premises and equipment, it was children whose mothers were born in the British Isles who tended to come off best. The differences between the two groups arise mainly from the fact that foreign-born manual workers' children got the less good minders. Ninety-four per cent of mothers in manual work who were born abroad used minders rated as less satisfactory or poor, compared with 61 per cent of mothers in manual work who were born in the British Isles.[5] Apart from this, there was little or no relationship between mothers' social class and the assessment of the minder, whether or not the mother was born abroad. The finding that manual workers born abroad do less well, is open to the sort of interpretation given earlier with regard to the minders' premises and equipment. On child-care practice, there is evidence that parents do become aware that all is not well, and this in spite of language or cultural differences. There was a high positive correlation ($\cdot$68) between whether or not a child stayed with a minder, and how her child-care had been assessed (see Chapter 4).

Overall assessment – housing, equipment, and child care
To make an overall assessment, we devised a three-point rating, based on the individual ratings already described. The child-care and equipment assessments had been made on a three-point scale, and the housing assessment on a four-point scale. To combine the three assessments, the first two points on

the housing scale – 'good' and 'fair' – were put together. The overall assessment of 65 minders was made as follows:

1. The minder obtained the top rating on all three assessments. Her housing was rated as 'good' or 'fair', she was assessed as 'well equipped' and as 'good' on child-care practice – 26·5 per cent.
2. The minder obtained the middle rating on one or more of the three assessments: her housing or equipment fell into the 'less adequate' category, or her child-care practice was rated 'less satisfactory' – 54 per cent.
3. The minder obtained the lowest rating on one or more of the three assessments: she had 'unsatisfactory' housing, and/or a serious lack of equipment, and/or 'poor' child-care practice – 20 per cent.

Judged on our criteria just over a quarter of the minders were offering a reasonable service. The rest were much less satisfactory and the care they gave was worrying in respect of the children's safety, well-being, happiness and/or development. The 20 per cent rated (3) gave very serious cause for concern. We would have wished to remove a child immediately from these minders.

Which children attended which minders?

As with housing and equipment, we decided to see whether some families got better minders than others, using the overall assessment. The assessment was set against the mother's social class and country of birth. As before, those in the higher social classes and those born in this country did better than the rest for their children. Twice as many of the children with mothers in manual work as those with mothers in professional and managerial work (RGI and II) were the minders whose overall service was rated lowest (Table 22), and three times as many of those children with mothers born abroad, compared to children of mothers born here (Table 23).

If an analysis is made controlling in turn for social class and the mother's place of birth, there is a tendency for both of these to correlate, within the different groups of mothers, with the overall assessment of the minder's service. Although these correlations are not statistically significant, items from the analyses are telling. Thus, 47 per cent of mothers in Classes I and II, born in the British Isles, used minders who obtained the highest rating. Only 6 per cent of mothers born abroad and engaged in manual work did so.

Table 22: Overall assessment of minder's service according to mother's social class

	Overall assessment			Row total %
	1	2	3	
Mother's social class (RG)				
I,II	41	43	16	38
III NM	19	65	16	39
III M,IV,V	16	51	34	23
Column total %	26	54	20	100

Number of minders = 64

Kendall's tau c = ·21; p < ·02 two-tailed test

Table 23: Overall assessment of minder's service according to mother's country of birth

	Overall assessment			Row total %
	1	2	3	
Mother born:				
British Isles	36	54	9	52
Abroad	16	53	31	48
Column total %	26	54	20	100

Number of minders = 64

Kendall's tau c = ·31; p < ·007 two-tailed test

Children of mothers born abroad

So there is reason to think that the child of a mother born abroad, especially if she is in manual work, will get a poorer service at the minder's. The study suggests a reason for this. As noted earlier, minders who were overburdened with children and tasks (29 per cent of the main sample) offered poorer child care than the rest. What is disturbing is that almost twice as many of the children of mothers born abroad, compared to children of mothers born here, were at these overburdened minders: 38 per cent compared to 21 per cent.

There is evidence on this point too from the interviews with the 93 minders (the ones with whom we did a short interview). We found 22 per cent of them were 'over-minding' – caring for four or more under-fives including their own. In fact the mean number of under-twelves cared for by this group was 6·4. The 93 minders were asked the country of origin of all the children currently attending. This information may be rough in some cases, but probably distinguishes between children of parents born in the British Isles, and those of foreign-born and ethnic minority parents. The information was used to determine what proportion of children from each broad group were with minders who 'over-minded'. Twenty-four per cent of children from the British Isles were with those who 'over-minded', compared with 45 per cent of children from elsewhere (see Table 24). Children from Africa and those of West Indian origin scored highest, at 56 per cent and 46 per cent respectively.

Table 24: Number and proportion of children from national groups/ethnic minorities who are with minders who 'over-mind' (secondary sub-sample)

National/ ethnic group	(1) Number of children at minders who 'over-mind'	(2) Number of all children at minders	(1) as % of (2)
British Isles	14	59	24
West Indian	13	28	46
African	14	25	56
Asian	17	41	42
European	9	23	39
Other	2	6	33
All non-British Isles	55	123	45
Totals	69	182	38

Secondary sub-sample of minders N = 93

It was noted earlier that ethnic minority and foreign-born parents are poorly placed to get good child care in the private market, compared to parents born here and white parents. They are likely to be discriminated against, to have past placements (see Chapter 4) and, as we show later (Chapter 9), to get on relatively badly with the minder. The study provides some reasons why they may be dissatisfied, and why they may remove their children from minders: poor physical conditions and poor child-care practices by the minder, and because their children are likely to suffer from being minded in large groups.

Summary

By and large, minded children had fewer social contacts than nursery children, but the demarcation between the two settings was not absolutely clear. Nursery children had more favourable adult–child ratios than minded children, and the ratio of minders to under-fives was only fractionally lower than the ratio of nurses to under-fives. If all the children under the age of twelve cared for daily are taken into account, each minder looked after, on average, 30 per cent more children than the nurses did.

The organization and staffing of the nursery groups was very varied, but in spite of the differences between groups, there were distinct differences between the nursery child's daily experience and the minded child's. Nursery children played out of doors more, and minded children more frequently went on outings. Nurseries placed more emphasis than minders did on the child becoming toilet-trained, and learning to feed himself; and more nursery children than minded children had to take their rest at a routine time.

As for the minders' child-care practices, half of them gave no evidence of poor practice, but the other half did, and in nearly a fifth of cases there was serious cause for concern. Mothers born abroad, especially if they were engaged in manual work, were more likely to get poor minders for their children.

When the assessments of premises, equipment and child care were put together, we found that just over a quarter of the minders were offering a good service; but nearly a fifth were offering poor care in one or more respect. Again, children of mothers born abroad and children whose mothers were in the lower occupational groups received a poorer service.

Discussion

In this and the previous chapter we have set out our findings on the minder's attitudes to child care, her relationship with the child and the child's daily experience at the minder's. Data on housing, equipment and child care was drawn together to provide an overall assessment of how the children fared.

It may be useful to consider the findings of the Oxford Study (1980), which used methods somewhat similar to ours, and came up with comparable findings.[6] The Oxford research team found that their 66 minders had good housing – all but one had a house and garden, though inside and outside space was cramped in some cases. There were few children per minder, and over two-thirds of the focus children were singly minded.

Oxfordshire was a county with few working mothers, with minders described as coming from 'close knit, deeply rooted, semi-rural and probably middlingly prosperous families', and with virtually no newcomers to the county or ethnic minority women among either mothers or minders. There was also greater stability among the Oxfordshire children, given that they were children in each of the first five years of life, and therefore had had more opportunity for changing placements than children in either of our London studies. Parents seemed more satisfied with the minder than our mothers did. But still the research team found serious deficiencies in the daily experience of a substantial minority of the children.

In particular, there were about sixteen children (24 per cent) who seemed to lose out on most counts. All these children had cramped play-space or restrictions on messy play (usually both) and had not been taken out much or at all in the last week; all but two had a very poor selection of toys, and twelve of them had only a small yard to play in or no garden at all. Furthermore, thirteen had neither played actively with the minder 'yesterday', nor had a close relationship with her husband, and eight had no other under-fives to play with. The authors note that 'some children may be taken out too much, perhaps experiencing rather tiring, frustrating days with little time for play'.

The Oxford Study also examined the relationship between the minder and child, and his interaction rate with her and with his mother. On interaction, using measures similar to ours (Mayall and Petrie, 1977), they found that the child approached his mother more than he did his minder, but they accounted for this by the greater number of other children present at the minder's. When the number of children in both situations was taken into account, there was still more interaction with his mother, but not at a statistically significant level. A possible explanation of the difference between this and the findings we describe in Chapter 6 is in the differences in the samples. The London children, for whom an unobtrusive count of interactions was made during the interview, were all in full-time day care and aged between one and two years. Some of the Oxford children were part-time and some full-time, and they were aged from one year to just over five. Some of the older children especially (and a third of them were over four) may well have played with each other rather than approach their minder (some of the children had formed close friendships). Nevertheless, they noted that at the minders' 71 per cent of the children 'were characteristically rather detached and inactive. They did nothing very much or were occupied in solitary play.' Twenty-six per cent of the children were described as behaving like this at home. From this and other evidence the authors conclude that while minders are well disposed 'they fail to get close to the children and often do not give them much warmth or physical attention'.

In spite of some differences between the London and Oxford samples, a common conclusion was reached: that for a substantial minority of minded children their day-care experience is inadequate, and the minder is not generally a mother-substitute for the child. This is not unexpected in the light of much earlier research and writing about minding, although it conflicts with recent aspirations.

It is a black and discouraging picture. Improvement in the childminding service is long overdue. But to describe and deplore poor conditions does not amount to blaming minders. It is important to stress this. Most of what was poor at minders arises from their conditions of work, which in turn depend on social policy towards day care.

Many minders, especially those in inner London, lived in housing unsuitable for child care. Housing with cramped conditions, no garden and unsafe play-space may be more common in London than in some areas, but is almost certainly to be found in many cities and industrial areas. Only the Oxford Study (1980), which took place in a relatively favoured area, has so far found no serious cause for concern about minders' housing. The registration of minders in poor housing must be related to the scarcity of other kinds of day-care places and to social policy which places low priority on this.

Minders are often asked to take children back and forth to playgroups and nursery schools; indeed the DHSS/DES Letter (1978) specifically recommends that older pre-school minded children should be taken there to gain educational experience. These frequent trips *may* be enjoyable and stimulating for the children, or they may not. They do impose routines and burdens on the minder. Again, this recommendation is a low-cost measure. An alternative would be to offer three-year-olds all-day places at nursery schools and playgroups (see further discussion in Chapter 11).

Minders work a long day to accommodate the needs of working mothers. Presumably they take on minding because it suits them, but these are hours imposed by a casual low-cost approach to day care, which assumes that the length of the caregiver's day and any effects of this on the child are unimportant. Minders are likely, during a day lasting about ten hours (our minders worked on average a 47-hour week), to try to get some of their domestic jobs done, as well as having to do many routine chores for the minded children. This will mean less time to give to talking and playing with the children. Such a long working week must also be tiring, and many minders may have insufficient energy to cater fully for the children's needs.

Minders are encouraged by day-care policy (or the lack of it) to take over-fives. There is virtually no provision for school-age children after school and in the holidays, so mothers turn to minders as the only form of help. Minders are poorly paid because the pay comes from the mother's earnings, and minders set the rate low enough to make it worthwhile for mothers to go out to work. (Our minders were paid an average (gross of expenses) of £9.24 per child per week (or 22p an hour). The Oxford Study (1980) reported similarly.) Under these circumstances, an extra few pounds for school-age children is likely to be welcome. In some cases a child who has been with a minder in his pre-school years continues to come to her after school and in the holidays. For these children, this may be a good option. And minders told us that the older children helped to look after the younger ones. But in general this arrangement does not seem to be in the best interests of the under-fives at minders'.

Caring for school-age children is a national problem. Simpson (1980) has estimated (for 1978) that 525 000 children aged five to fifteen including 250 000 children aged five to ten, are regularly left alone after school, and a further 150 000 schoolchildren are left during the school holidays. And he points to official neglect of the problem. Though some local authorities provide schemes for school-age children, most of these are during the holidays and then may not cover all holidays, or they are evening schemes, which do not cover the crucial hour or two after school.

There is a further point about minders' low pay. Few well qualified or well-to-do women (in good housing, well equipped) will take on minding, for such long hours, for such a low return. Either they will go out to work and earn better money, or they will not work at all. A sample of minders is likely to contain a good proportion who are poorly qualified, poorly off, poorly housed, who work a long day with many jobs, and who care for many children, both under- and over-fives. These characteristics are not conducive to good child care. Some minders will not be able to equip themselves well for the job. Some will just not have the time or energy to respond sensitively and carefully to each child's needs. Some will not see the need to. Some will be housed in conditions that are unsuitable for child care.

There are also less tangible problems at minders, related to the fact that minding is a low status job. Local authorities seem fairly unconcerned at the point of registration about standards for premises and personal fitness, or so it seems to many minders we have met. Later, if help is given, it is likely to be low-cost help – a few toys, some second-hand equipment, or a meeting once a week in a hall with poor facilities. When a minder is in trouble, with a parent defaulting on pay, or criticizing her, the local authority is unlikely to offer much help. Minders have little incentive to go out of their way to provide high standards of child care, however much they are exhorted to do so.

In Chapter 9, we discuss how minders and parents get on together, and in Chapter 10, we look at childminding as a job. The point to stress here is that under prevailing circumstances we are lucky that some minders offer good care, and it is not surprising that many do not.

Notes

1. We did not think we could ask to be present at various times in the day at the minders', without the risk of losing many of our sample.
2. The overburdened minders were identified as follows. Two-thirds of them cared regularly for six or more under-twelves and in addition they had one or more of the following 'burdens':

    A 50-hour or more week

    A part-time job

    Two or more regular trips to pre-school or primary school

    Unsuitable housing for the numbers of children, either because it was cramped, or because the minder could not oversee the children unless everyone stayed together (for example, because kitchen and playroom were on different floors).

    Or they gave evidence of physical or mental strain.

    The remaining third had four or five under-twelves regularly present and two or more of the above 'burdens'.

    On the child-care assessment (discussed on page 000) 80 per cent of the overburdened minders, compared to 39 per cent of the rest, were rated as offering 'less satisfactory' or 'poor care' (tau = ·34; p < ·001) two tailed test.
3. It will be remembered that higher proportions of minded children than day-nursery children were under a year old. The difference is rectified by the weighting procedure, restoring to the sample of minded children their true representation in the population (see Appendix B).
4. We did not attempt an assessment of quality of care in the day nursery. First, the interview took place in different circumstances – other nurses often took over the care of the group while we interviewed our subject nurse and so her practice was not observable in a setting comparable to that of the minder. Secondly, the nurse was more likely, because of her training, to know what is currently regarded as good practice and less likely to admit in an interview to the sort of grossly inadequate practice which minders in our earlier study reported. So the two sets of caregivers might be giving information that could not be compared.
5. Tau = ·66; p < ·01 two-tailed test.
6. The Oxford study of childminding is summarized in Chapter 3.

Chapter Eight
Health Services for Children in Day Care

Young children make heavy use of the health services. In their first year especially they are likely to be taken to the child health clinic frequently for weighing, check-ups, advice and immunizations. Any congenital disorders or defects may be diagnosed and treated. Parents are likely to play safe with young children and take them to the doctor whenever they suspect something is wrong, whereas for older children or for themselves they may wait and see (Locker, 1981). It is generally recognized, too, that one of the health visitor's main responsibilities is to the young family. But where children are in day care, it may be difficult for parents to meet all their health needs; and they may slip through the net of surveillance by health service staff. Parents may be unable to take their child regularly to the clinic if the hours are unsuitable. And if the child is ill, problems may arise about who should care for him, and who is available to do it. Health visitors may not have enough contact with parents and day-care staff to advise both sets of caregivers and check on the child's overall health and welfare.

Before the reorganization of social service and health departments in 1971, the local health authority was responsible for children in day care. Its role was stressed in the Ministry of Health Memorandum to Circular 37/68 (para. 18). Although responsibility has passed to the social service departments, overseeing the health and welfare of children in day care is still seen as a responsibility of the health authorities. The Department of Health and Social Security in its recent letter recommends the maintenance of close links between health staff and day-care services (DHSS/DES, 1978, para. 20); there should be 'regular health surveillance' of all children in day care and 'health visitors need to co-ordinate the care given to the child at home and in day-care'. For more specific recommendations, Circular 37/68 contains the most recent guidance to local authorities. It points out (para. 19) that children remain the responsibility of their parents while in day care, and the minder should obtain parental consent before seeking medical attention for the child, except in emergencies. Where the parents do not ensure regular medical surveillance, the minder is to be urged to complement their care by taking the child to the doctor or child health clinic.

It seems desirable for the health services to oversee the health of children in day care. We describe how the minded and day-nursery children fared, and then consider whether the health service itself is adequately structured to serve the needs of the children and their parents. The data on the minded children refers to the main sub-sample only (64 focus children).

The minded children

We asked both mothers and minders whether they had been visited at home in the last six months by a health visitor. Only 29 per cent of the mothers had been visited, and 35 per cent of the minders. In all, 55 per cent of the focus children had been seen in one setting or the other. Of course the health visitor may have come in some cases to see the minder's own children, or other children than the focus child. We did not ask about this, since information is likely to be unreliable.

A second kind of health surveillance is carried out at child health clinics. Almost all the children (87 per cent) had been taken there at least once in the last six-months. Most of the children (71 per cent) had gone with their mother,[1] and some of these also went with the minder. A few (15 per cent) had gone only with the minder, mainly for weighing, immunizations, or advice on a specific topic, rather than for a check-up. The five children who had not been to the clinic at all had also not been seen either at home or at the minder's by the health visitor. This small group of children were all aged over one year. After this age check-ups are recommended at six-monthly intervals, so it is possible they had been taken just over six months before the interview, and were being routinely seen at the clinic.

Seeing to a young child's health needs is time-consuming. Some mothers had taken their child to the clinic many times in the last six months. Fourteen per cent went seven or more times and the average number of visits was 2·5. Children also saw the doctor either at his surgery or at home; again a small group (9 per cent) saw the doctor seven or more times and the average number of visits was three over the last twelve months.[2]

In addition to clinic and GP visits, some children had been to hospital during the last twelve months. A small number – seven (14 per cent) – had been in-patients, and in some cases had attended out-patient departments too. And a further twelve children (13 per cent) had attended out-patient or casualty departments.

Children also have to be looked after when they are ill. Some children get frequent minor illnesses, especially colds – a quarter of the children were having colds at the rate of one a month (over the last three months). Looking after an ill child can be a problem for the working mother. Since they started work again after the child's birth, 49 per cent had taken some time off work because their child was ill, in most cases for less than a week. Where the child had been ill during his present placement – too ill to go to the minder – we asked who had cared for him. In all but two cases, the mothers had done so: they had taken leave, paid or unpaid, or had used part of their holiday entitlement.

It might seem from this account that these children had more illnesses and used the health services more than most, and it is worth considering data from another study on this point. The Thomas Coram Research Unit's medical research team studied child health in two small areas in inner London.[3] Data was collected on almost all the under-fives over a four-year period. The sample contained children from all social classes, and a wide range of nationalities and ethnic groups. About 17 per cent of the mothers worked where the child was under two, including about 10 per cent working full-time. The comparison data is set out in Table 25. The TCRU data was collected in a slightly different form, but the comparison with the present study shows that the use of health services by our minded children was *not* higher than that of a general population of under-twos in areas of inner London. However, for some kinds of illness the minded children were doing less well than the TCRU children. Twice as many of them were having colds once a month. And twice as many had had two or more attacks of bronchitis (confirmed by a doctor or health visitor) during the last year (13 per cent of 56 children). Perhaps, as it is often said, children in group care are prone to these illnesses. But it is worth repeating that a high proportion of the children lived in poor housing (see Chapter 5).

The day-nursery children

It is difficult to make a clear comparison between the minded and the day-nursery children for several reasons. Most of the nursery children had frequent contacts with doctors – both GPs and hospital doctors. At least eleven of the 40 children had a day-nursery place partly because of their health or danger to it – they had a serious or congenital condition, or were under threat of violence at home, or had been harmed at home. So some of

Table 25: Proportion of children who have used medical services (minding and nursery samples) with comparison data from TCRU survey

% of children	Type of medical service			
	in-patient once or more	*out-patient/ casualty once or more*	*GP 7 times or more*	*N*
TCRU (1974-79):				
By the age of 6 months	9	28	4	337
By the age of 12 months	15	45	12	266
Between 12 and 24 months	15	43	10	275
This study (1977-78):				
Minding sample, over the last 12 months	14	20	9	64
Nursery sample, over the last 12 months	36	62	47	39

Source: Bax, Hart and Jenkins, unpublished data. See also their report to DHSS (1980).

their health needs usually met by health visitors and clinics may have been met by doctors. Table 25 shows that the day-nursery children went to the doctor or to a hospital far more than the minded children. Some of them spent time in hospital and in addition were seen at out-patient or casualty departments, and went many times to see their doctor.

To give an idea of how much the children used the health services over the last twelve months, we devised a criterion for low use: no in-patient stay, no visits to out-patient or casualty departments, and fewer than seven contacts with the GP. This criterion is arbitrary, but it gives a rough measure of frequency of use and the amount of illness, as well as the time and worry involved for the mother. Sixty-five per cent of the minded children had been well and trouble-free by this criterion, compared with only 19 per cent of the day-nursery children.

As far as the preventive health services go, day-nursery mothers are offered a rather different service for their children compared with other mothers. Health visitors may visit the nursery and see several children and discuss them with staff, although the mother may not necessarily be there too. The local health authority usually provides at the nursery the equivalent of the service offered at child health clinics – monitoring the children's health and development by a visiting doctor. So how well were these services covering day-nursery children?

First, what part were health visitors playing? We did not ask if the focus children had been seen by a health visitor at the nursery, since this would have been difficult to establish reliably. Rather more of the children had been seen at home in the last six months, compared with the minded children (43 per cent against 29 per cent). This still seems low coverage for a population at some risk, but it may be explained, if not justified, by the high use of the other medical services by the families.

As to attendance at a child health clinic, the picture is complex. Only 45 per cent of the children had been taken there in the last six months. Many mothers said there was no need because he was seen at the nursery by a doctor (65 per cent or 26 of 40 mothers). But mothers did not always know when this had last happened; and only four of the mothers said they were ever present at a consultation at the nursery. No doubt there are problems here: mothers may be at work, or they may not turn up on time. One nursery matron said she discouraged mothers from coming because they made trouble. But it would seem desirable for the mother to be present at a consultation about her child.

All fifteen nurseries were visited by doctors, according to local authority staff. In practice we found wide variations in how often they visited. In the four sample boroughs, local authority day-care management staff said, variously, that a doctor visited, once a week (one), once every two weeks (two), every four to six weeks (one). Nine of the fifteen matrons confirmed the management staff's view of the frequency of visits. But five of the rest said visits were much less frequent in practice, and one that no doctor visited at all (Table 26). There were few other visitors to see the children, although six of the nurseries had a regular visit from a speech therapist. Health visitors and social workers tended to come irregularly.

Table 26: Visits to day nurseries by health and social service staff, according to matron

	Frequency of visits						
	1/wk	*1–2wks*	*1–3wks*	*1/mth*	*1/year*	*irregularly*	*none*
Visitor:							
Doctor	2	4	1	6	–	1	1
Health visitor	1	1	–	–	–	8	5
Social worker	–	–	–	–	–	10	5
Speech therapist	4	2	–	–	1	2	6

Number of nurseries = 15

A complementary service?

The health visitor

Data on both minded and day-nursery children show that the health visitor service was not adequately covering these children. This confirms and amplifies data from earlier research. In our first study (Mayall and Petrie, 1977, Chapter 8), health visitors had visited 41 per cent (16 of 39) of minders in the last six months. In 29 cases we were able to establish from the minder and mother of the focus child (all were aged between two and three years) whether he had been taken by either of them to the child welfare clinic in the last twelve months. Eight children (28 per cent) had not been taken, and six of these had not been seen at the minder's either. The Oxford Study (1980, Chapter 6) came up with similar findings. Forty-three per cent of the mothers said they had never been visited by a health visitor, and only 27 per cent (17) had been visited in the last six months. Ten of the 27 children had never been seen at the minder's.

The health visitor's array of tasks is formidable as shown by Hicks (1976, para. 498), who quotes the long list given in the 1969 Mayston Committee's Report. Hicks analysed Health and Personal Social Services Statistics (1973) to show a drop in the numbers of under-ones and under-fives seen by health visitors, over the period 1965 to 1971, with an increase in the number of people over the age of 65 seen over the same period. This trend is discussed in the Court Report on the child health services (1976, 4.21). The Report notes (17.28) that numbers of health visitors were 50 per cent below what was recommended by the Jameson Committee Report on health visiting (1956) and restated by the DHSS in its Circular 13/72. The Court Report recommends that children should be seen by a health visitor twelve times during their first year, four times during their second year, and twice a year thereafter until they are five. It also proposes the establishment of Child Health Visitors (17.25,26) to concentrate on overseeing the health of under-fives and their families.

Court's proposals are supported by Bax and Thompson (forthcoming) who stress that the most important function of the health visitor is to oversee maternal and child health. They note that the Court proposal for child health visitors has been rejected by the Health Visitors' Association and is likely to be rejected by the DHSS. The Association argues in favour of generic health visitors to survey the health needs of all the family, from babyhood to old age. But Bax and Thompson point out that, especially in urban areas, the problems of mothers with young children are complex and should be given high priority. Furthermore, at least in urban areas, small nuclear families are likely to predominate over extended ones, and a specialist service for young families is therefore particularly appropriate in cities.

The need for more health visitors to oversee the needs of under-fives at home is clearly recognized. Given the increasing load on health visitors, it would seem desirable either to increase their number, or to appoint specialist workers to oversee the needs of families with under-fives.

It could be argued that to stress the health visitors' role with regard to children in day care is outdated. Now that children come under social services departments, they could be supervised from there by childminding workers. But it is important for the child's health and development to be overseen, and for his caregivers (his mother and others) to have the opportunity to seek advice and help. The health visitor seems the appropriate person to do this, rather than a childminding worker. Furthermore, it is important for the child to be seen in both settings – at home and in day care – preferably by the same person, to achieve consistent and complementary care. Social services departments do not have a responsibility to visit parents of under-fives. A possible way forward would be to develop a day-care service where social services staff were responsible for keeping up contacts with both parents and day-care staff. This is the formula adopted in Denmark, for instance (see Chapter 11 for further discussion).

Taking the child to the medical services

The data on attendance at the child health clinic indicate that most of the minded children had been taken in the last six months. However, 13 per cent had not – all of them aged over one year – and another 15 per cent went only with the minder. These findings are rather better than those in our earlier study, where 28 per cent of the two-year-olds had not been taken at all during the last twelve months. This is to be expected, since clinic attendance drops off in the third year. The Court Report quotes attendance figures for 1971 to 1973 which show a dramatic fall in the proportions of over-twos attending the clinic (see Table 27).

We noted earlier that some minders saw to some of the children's health needs themselves. Thirty-one per cent had taken the child to the clinic in the last six months, and a few (11 per cent) took him to the doctor, either on their own initiative, or when asked by the mother. Minders expressed virtually no dissatisfaction about this: if they were asked to do it or did it on their own initiative, it was willingly done. So it would seem that some minders are offering a complementary service, as recommended by the DHSS (see

Table 27: Proportion of children attending child health clinics according to age (England and Wales), 1971–73

	Under 1yr	1-1·11yrs	2-4yrs	all under-5s
	Child's age			
1971	80·0	71·4	28·3	46·3
1972	79·4	72·4	27·5	46·5
1973	80·0	73·0	28·0	46·6

Source: Court (1976), Chapter 4, Table 1.

above). Whether this is desirable is another question. Minders have a busy day (see Chapter 7). For either social services staff or mothers to suggest that they should help in this way may lead to problems. Social services staff probably leave it to the minder to consider what help she will offer the mother on this. But that means another area where mothers and minders may be in doubt about what responsibilities the minder has taken, or should take (see Chapter 9 for fuller discussion of this topic). From the children's point of view, waiting about in a clinic is not necessarily enjoyable; and they may prefer to go with their mother to see the doctor and nurse. And is it desirable for children to be seen without their mother? The mothers have their children's medical and social history and are responsible for their care; and so it is the mothers who can best help the doctor in diagnosis and treatment, and who most need to be informed and advised. This is difficult if they have to be contacted at one remove.

With families where the child is at day nursery, it is especially desirable for mothers to be present at meetings with doctors and other health professionals. These families are likely to be among those having most difficulties with their children. The children may have developmental or behavioural problems; some of the mothers will be very young, or inexperienced, or under great stress. Most of them probably both need and want help with rearing their children. Consultation at the nursery, with nursery staff, doctor and mother all present would seem the best way of helping these mothers. In the sample nurseries this sort of help was sometimes given where the child was handicapped. For instance, at one nursery a physiotherapist came from the local hospital to teach the nursery nurses and the mother how to give remedial help to a physically handicapped child.

Working mothers and their children's health

The data on the children's use of health services and the mother's part in this, raise a more general question. Should recognition be given to the need for a working mother to see to her child's health and welfare requirements? We have described the number of times the mother took the child to the clinic and the doctor; the incidence of treatment at hospitals; and the extent to which mothers had to take time off work to care for a sick child. None of this is exceptional; these are the normal responsibilities of mothers. But they add up to a lot of time which the working mother has to take out of work, as unpaid or holiday leave, or, for the lucky ones, as paid leave. Those who get paid leave to care for their child are likely to be those in higher status jobs where employers value their services highly. The study data tend in this direction, but the numbers are too small for analysis. The Court Report (1976, 9.33) recommends that child health clinics run evening sessions to meet the needs of working mothers. This might solve some mothers' problems, and might allow fathers to participate too, but it does not seem in the best interests of the child or parents that they should set off to the clinic at the end of a long day. Nor would this proposal help mothers to see to their children's other health needs. There is a growing European movement to introduce employment measures to take account of children's health needs and parents' need for time to see to them (Hughes et al, 1980, Chapter 3). Sweden has gone furthest to implement such measures: either parent is entitled to twelve days' paid leave a year to see to the child's health needs, or to introduce him to a day-care placement (Swedish Ministry of Health and Social Affairs, 1977). Parents are also entitled to 60 days a year paid leave to look after their child if he is ill (Federation of Social Insurance Offices, Sweden 1980).

The Swedish example points up a problem that has not yet been faced in this country: if measures are introduced to help mothers combine work and child care, this may decrease their attractiveness as employees. For this reason, and also in the name of equal opportunities for men and women (as parents and as employees), Swedish legislation has emphasized both parents' roles in child-rearing responsibilities and commitments. So far we have concentrated on the needs of mothers, since in practice it is mainly they who combine work and child care. In the final chapter we will broaden the discussion to include fathers.

We are leaving proposals about childminding and nurseries to the final chapters, where the service as a whole is considered. However, the health service coverage of children in day care is a rather separate topic, and we will add a final note here. We have shown how far the services covered the sample children, and indicated that our findings confirm those of other studies. We would argue that the parents, not day-care staff, are the appropriate people to see to the child's health needs, and that since young children make heavy use of the health services, the needs of parents, including working parents, to see to them should be an important consideration when planning services.

Notes

1. Where the mother took her child to a G P clinic offering the same kind of service as the child health clinic, we counted this in as clinic attendance.
2. Where a mother reported more than six contacts with the clinic or doctor, we gave it a score of seven, because her memory was likely to be less accurate for larger numbers. So the averages are a minimum estimate of the rate of visits to clinics and doctors.
3. Bax, Hart and Jenkins, 1980.

Chapter Nine
Accountability

We have discussed the needs of mothers and young children in the light of what is offered at minders' and day nurseries, and whether the standards set by the DHSS are met in practice. A question which lies behind consideration of needs and standards is how far is the service accountable? Does it respond to the needs and wishes of the people who use it? Is it in any sense answerable to them? And is it in any way answerable up the line to the public body – the local authority – which monitors or provides it? Can the consumer hope for redress, if the service is poor, either by appealing to the people who offer it – the minder or the nursery staff – or up the line to those responsible for registering the service or for providing it?

Accountability is a complex word, comprising several separate but related concepts (Kogan, 1979; Sinha, 1979). First, responsibility, accepted for a defined task; secondly, the rendering of an account of the task discharged; leading to the third – the judgement of performance against agreed criteria; and the fourth, sanctions – penalties or rewards that can alter the performance. A relatively simple situation which involves all four aspects of accountability is when a house-owner makes a private agreement with a builder to do work on his house. The builder and owner agree on the job; the builder agrees to do it; he renders an account giving a breakdown of costs; the owner assesses the work; he pays, or withholds payment until he is satisfied.

In this example the task performer is accountable to his employer. In public services, such as the social, health and education services, where the employer is a local authority, the situation is complicated by the existence of the consumer. The consumer does not pay the bill directly, but does use the service. In all these fields, two kinds of concern have been voiced. First, that the employee (the social worker, nurse, teacher) should render a better account to his employer: this involves problems of task definition, assessment and sanctions. Secondly, that in some sense the service-givers should render an account to the consumer, not only in cases of complaint, but as a normal part of operating the service. So the consumer has two main demands. In case of complaint, mechanisms for redress should be available, and the service should be answerable to him. He should be able to expect efficient use of resources and reasonable standards of performance by currently accepted criteria. A hard-line reply to these demands for power to affect the performance of an assumed responsibility is that the consumer can always vote out of office the council or political party he judges to be a poor performer of tasks. But this long-term and imprecise form of power is widely accepted as inadequate. Increasingly people believe they have the right to be involved in the running of their social services (Blackstone, 1979). The growth of consumer groups, community health councils, parent–teacher associations shows something of public unrest. At government level, recognition of the consumer's desire for a voice is seen in the establishment of an ombudsman for administrative affairs, and of royal commissions, such as Skeffington (1969) on public participation in planning, and Taylor (1977) on parental roles in education. However, in most service fields the consumer can only hope that the service-giver will carry out the task with a sense of responsibility for the consumer's interests. The account is rendered to the employer, ultimately the Secretary of State, who may invoke sanctions. In medicine there have been extreme cases where, for instance, a patient's health has been permanently damaged by a mistake in treatment. The area health authority has been held responsible and has paid damages to the patient. In less extreme cases, for instance, where the patient thinks a nurse is not discharging her responsibility properly, the assessment of the task, its performance and possible sanctions for non-performance, have to be considered in relation to the complex structure of roles and duties in the hospital. This is not within the knowledge or competence of the individual patient, though his interests can be advanced through the area health authority.

The central issue in these two health service examples – task definition and the assessment of performance – remains a difficult problem. It is even more difficult in the social services and education. The care of the under-fives illustrates some of the problems.

Nursery education

Nursery education is the most carefully defined and controlled kind of pre-school care. It comes under the broad umbrella of the Education Act, 1944. Nursery schools and classes, like primary and secondary schools, are required by law to provide for pupils 'opportunities for education offering such variety of instruction and training as may be desirable in view of their different ages, abilities and aptitudes' (Education Act, 1944, Chapter 31, section 8(1)). Standards for premises and teacher qualifications are controlled by statutory instruments; local authorities must conform. Teachers must be qualified as teachers; criteria for qualifications are specified. An exception is that in nursery schools and classes people with other child-care training, such as nursery nurses, may be appointed as assistant teachers, subject to approval by the Secretary of State.[1] What is to be defined as education is up for decision, but the balance of power seems to be in the hands of the Department of Education. For instance, parents who wish to provide education at home must conform to the Department's standards; and training courses for teachers must be approved by the Secretary of State. What goes on in the classroom will be dictated largely by the teaching profession's current views on education. While this dual control from above may be frustrating for parents if they wish to change practice or attitudes, or if they wish to complain, it does provide a ladder (however rickety) of accountability from the classroom teacher to the Secretary of State. It also offers some guarantee of minimum standards.

The long-established power of the teaching profession over the aims and methods of education is now being challenged by parents. Debate centres on ways in which dialogue between the profession and parents could be improved.[2] Perhaps there are two main aims here: to work towards clearer and more explicit goal definition; and to provide structures which recognize teachers' responsibility towards parents and the need for schools to respond to parents' wishes, that is, to be more accountable to parents.

Most debate on accountability in education has related to the secondary-school level. This is presumably because conflicts between the needs and wishes of children, parents, industry, the universities and society at large have been greatest here, and because the passports school-leavers are thought to need for adult life depend on testing procedures widely thought to be inadequate, inaccurate and misleading. Debates about primary schooling died down after the removal of the eleven-plus test. However, there is now concern about the curriculum, especially among ethnic minority parents, some of whom have set up classes to remedy what they see as the deficiencies of primary schools. The implicit ideologies of primary schools have been attacked too by teachers, who have sought to alter the relationship of teacher and pupil and the approach to learning (see, for

example, an account of the William Tyndale affair in David, 1978).
At nursery-school level, it has been argued that the most appropriate role
for parents at present is to help their children achieve within the education
system, rather than influence its content (Blackstone, 1979). But for parents
an important concern at present is the curriculum itself: what are the
purposes of nursery education and what are the best means of achieving
these? For many years it has been widely assumed that a main function of the
nursery school is to promote language development. Yet Tizard's recent
work (1980) on adult–child conversations suggests that nursery-school
teachers are less successful than mothers, both middle-class and working-
class, at encouraging children to converse. Ethnic minority parents are starting to challenge the free-play approach and to ask for more structured,
formal teaching. Some parents whose main language is not English are
asking for English teaching to be given high priority for their nursery-age
children. It seems possible that pressure will grow, via research and parents'
groups, for nursery teachers to redefine their aims and methods, to make
them more explicit to parents, and to consider including parents in the
decision-making process about the curriculum.

Day nurseries

In pre-school education, then, there are statutory requirements on premises
and staff training, and some control by the DES over teacher training.
Standards of provision are thus controlled both by legislation and by the
teaching profession. Control by the law and by the DHSS over private
nurseries and minders is less firm.[3] The Nurseries and Childminders Act,
1948, gives local authorities the power to impose standards. Recommendations on these were set out in Circular 5/65, and revised and expanded in the
Memorandum enclosed with Circular 37/68. For day-nursery staffing, it is
recommended that the matron should be a qualified nurse or nursery nurse;
more recently a social work qualification in addition has been recommended
(LASSL (78)1, para. 19). Other staff should be nursery nurses or in
training as such. The training of nursery nurses is run by the National
Nursery Examinations Board (NNEB), an independent organization whose
courses are not formally subject to approval by the DHSS, although it acts
in an advisory capacity. In practice, it is probably the case that most day-
nursery children are in the hands of a trained nursery nurse (see Chapter 1).

As to accommodation and equipment, a recommended model for a fifty-
place nursery is described in Appendix II to Circular 5/65. The curriculum
for nurseries and minders is, as for education, left vague: 'The sum total of

home and group care should be such as to meet the all-round needs of the young child. To achieve this there should be a good standard of co-operation between the parents and those responsible for the care of their children during the day' (Memorandum with Circular 37/68, para. 14). This suggests a service complementary to the home. More recently it has been recommended that local authorities should aim at 'improving the education content of the various forms of day care' (DHSS/DES, 1978, para. 15). Standards for day-nursery premises and staffing are in the hands of the local authority. The programme of activities (the curriculum) at the nursery, as at the nursery school, depends on the staff, and will be affected by their training. But though defining and carrying through a coherent curriculum is difficult in any child-care or education setting, the nursery nurse is perhaps less well placed to do this than the teacher. Training for nursery education takes place within a framework of concepts of education covering the nursery years to higher education, which perhaps offer a relatively coherent ideology. Nursery nurse training is part of no such professional structure of thought. The definitions of what care at a day nursery should be may be less clearly defined, and there may be more variation in practice between staff and between nurseries.

From the parent's point of view, the day-nursery service offers less assurance than the nursery school of minimum standards for accommodation, staffing and curriculum. Responsibility for choosing what standards to impose rests with the local authority rather than with the Secretary of State. In cases of complaint parents may be able to go no higher than the local authority. For instance, if a child has been poorly cared for by untrained staff, parents cannot bring pressure to bear on the local authority from the Secretary of State. On the other hand, it might be thought parents will have more say over what goes on than they do in nursery school. Part of the day nursery's traditional function is to help parents, and to help them care for their children. One might suppose therefore that the nurses would see communication with parents as important, and allow parents scope for affecting the care of the child at the nursery. In contrast, while nursery schools have traditionally paid lip-service to the importance of parental interest and co-operation, in practice they have focused on the child alone.[4] An important factor is that both nursery schools and day nurseries are in scarce supply. Parents may be inhibited by gratitude or fear from challenging what is offered, unless they are heavily provoked or exceptionally strong-minded. We shall see later what the day-nursery mothers' experiences and views were.

Childminders

Standards for private nurseries and childminders are covered in the same broad list of recommendations as for day nurseries (Memorandum enclosed with Circular 37/68). Little is known about private nurseries, although it seems likely that local authorities vary widely in the regulations they enforce.

On accommodation and equipment at minders' the Memorandum notes that standards may be adapted to take account of the domestic environment. In practice, local authorities probably enforce some fire and safety regulations at the time of registration, but otherwise register most applicants, if they consider them personally fit. This is because the person is likely to start childminding, whether registered or not. Standards of accommodation at minders' therefore depend on local housing standards. In the Oxford study, all but one of the 66 minders had a house and garden; by contrast London minders are more likely to live in flats without gardens (see Chapter 5). Standards of housing also relate to the social class of the minder: in London they are likely to belong to manual workers' households; in Oxfordshire the class mix was greater.

It may seem superficial to emphasize standards for accommodation and equipment but it is necessary to show how far private day care lags behind state provision and the differences in the responsibility taken for these standards by the local authority. In discussions on accountability in education, accommodation and equipment have not been seen as important issues, because it could be assumed they were more or less adequate. Discussion has focused on the curriculum and staff responsibility, on authority structures and on the responsiveness of the curriculum to parents' wishes. But more recently the clock has been set back and such things as inadequate provision of textbooks have become important issues. Whatever the issue, however, if parents wish to argue that standards, say for space, safety or equipment, are not up to DES specifications, the local education authority is answerable to them, and the ultimate appeal is to a ruling on the implications of the law. But in private day care the urgent problems for the parent remain at a basic level. Are the premises safe and suitable for child care? Will the child have access to enough and suitable toys? Is other equipment suitable for the task? If the parent thinks the service is inadequate, there is no appeal beyond the minder. The local authority has fulfilled its role in enforcing local regulations at the time of registration. Study data described earlier (Chapter 5) indicated that many minders' housing and equipment were not adequate.

As to staffing, there is a crucial difference between the recommendations made for minders, and those for nursery staff (Memorandum with Circular 37/68, Section 6). There is a firm recommendation that day-nursery staff be trained or in training; while 'it is desirable that some opportunity for training should be offered to all who care for children in private groups'; and for childminders 'it might be appropriate to organise short courses'. As already noted, most authorities probably comply with these standards for day-nursery staff. Very few minders are trained, even by the short course. Yet much depends on the minder's understanding of the needs of children. The list of recommendations on the care, health and feeding of the children makes it clear that a minder: will need to be skilled in child care and education, and aware of the importance of establishing and maintaining a good working relationship with parents; must be willing and able to spend most of her time with the children; must be able to provide play-space indoors and, preferably, outdoors, or to lead frequent expeditions to parks and playgrounds; must provide equipment and toys for the differing needs of the children, according to their age (paras 14, 15, 16, 17); must be willing to see to a child's health needs where the parent does not (paras 19, 20); must be willing and able to discuss the child's health with local authority staff (para. 21); must have a good knowledge of diet and be able if necessary to improve, with the parent's co-operation, on his home diet (paras 23–26). All this suggests well-to-do women, with spacious indoor and outdoor play-space, trained in child care, willing to devote themselves most of the day to child care, and with few distracting responsibilities. Some characteristics of minders in this study have been described earlier – their previous work experience, and the child's relationship with his caregivers and his daily experience.

As things stand, the control of child-care standards, and of health and safety standards at minders' are in the hands of people who have in general no training, and no backing from a profession, and only their own experience as mothers to build on. They are also busy and in some cases over-burdened women. It must be noted too that the recommendations include many exhortations to local authority staff to help minders in their work. The possibilities for improving minding through such recommendations will be discussed in the last chapter.

There is a further problem about standards at minders'. There is so little opportunity for anyone to help the minder to do a good job, and to be responsive to interested people's views and wishes. Minders offer the service that is least open to the public. Plenty of people – other staff, current and prospective parents, doctors, health visitors, local authority staff – may spend lengthy periods in nurseries. Apart from the occasional health visitor and minding worker, only the two or three current parents go regularly and frequently into a minder's home, and it is difficult for anyone to sit about and observe the activities there. So the form of care with the lowest standards for training and almost certainly the least well enforced standards, is also that which is least subject to the checks of observation by people interested in standards of child care.

Parents of minded children are using a private service. There is no line of accountability stretching upwards. The minder is not in any way accountable to the local authority (who registers her) for the service offered to the children. The local authority's statutory duty stops at the point of registration, when it assesses the minder and her premises for fitness (see Chapter 2, for the local authority's legal responsibility).

If parents are dissatisfied with the care given, what redress have they? A pointer to the minder's legal relationship with the local authority was given in the report of an incident in which a child was scalded to death at a minder's (*The Guardian*, 8 November 1978). The local authority was exonerated from any responsibility, since it had carried out its duty in registering the minder. The mother had previously complained to the local authority about the care given by the minder, and had asked the local authority to help in finding another minder, but the responsibility for leaving the child with the minder was found to be the mother's. It is clear, then, that parents must seek redress directly from the minder. Probably the best they can hope for is that the minder is insured against accident to the minded children.

What kind of responsibility for the child does the minder take? This depends partly on the contract made between parent and minder. For instance, it would be possible in theory for them to agree for two hours a day to be spent on nursery education, or to more precisely defined activities, such as singing games or painting. Failure to do this by the minder could then lead to the parent withholding payment or removing the child. In practice, however, this sort of thing is highly unlikely. Parents and minders are more likely to agree on hours, payment and the provision of goods for the child. Where supply is scarce, parents are likely to keep their demands to a minimum. Established tradition says that minding is offered on a take-it-or-leave-it basis.

It might be argued that parents arranging for care by a minder are in much the same situation as people buying shoes or choosing a private school, and that they can similarly exercise their responsibility to choose a service they consider adequate and appropriate for their children. There are objections to both analogies. Shoes can be returned, usually without permanent damage to the buyer; child care is not returnable and may do lasting damage. Also the goods and services are not on display as in a shop or school; they cannot be vetted in advance of take-up. Parents cannot spend long enough at the minder's home to weigh up the quality of the service on offer. They have little choice of other minders, or of other kinds of care. A more general objection is that assessment of a child-care service demands skills and experience which young parents may not necessarily have. Because of this, standards, as in medicine and education, need to be controlled and assessed by experts, as well as by consumers.

How the contract works out in practice depends partly on the relationship between minder and parent and on their view of what sort of care the minder is to give the child. An important difference between minders and mothers is that minders tend to be older women, more experienced as mothers, and more used to having children about the place. Parents' relationship with the minder is likely to be at least partly influenced by their recognition of the minder's experience and the long hours of service she is giving for very little return. With little other choice they are likely to fall in with what the minder offers, rather than discuss what they would like for their child.

The arrangement between minder and parent has some characteristics which together make up a contract different from that made in other child-care settings. It tends to be an individualized arrangement, based on the needs and demands of parent and minder. Money enters into it, more than into most forms of day-care, and may be a source of dissatisfaction on either side. The service is often offered on the basis of superior knowledge and experience, but without the backing of a profession or training. It has to be accepted on trust by parents, for they can make only the most superficial assessment of its quality. It may be seen by some minders as a reciprocal service: offered on its own terms as part of the give and take of community life; it may even be seen by some as a favour, a gift, in which the payment is a mere token.

Summary

In summary, there are wide disparities between minimum standards of care offered at minders' and those in other forms of pre-school provision. And while there may be general difficulties for parents in affecting the standards of care their under-fives get, these difficulties are particularly acute for parents of minded children. It seems likely that parents' tolerance of minding has more to do with the scarcity of other forms of care than with their satisfaction. The rest of this chapter is concerned with what data from the study tell us about accountability at minders' and day nurseries.

Mothers and minders*

As shown earlier, mothers using minders in the four boroughs were offered widely varying standards of care in terms of availability, stability, accommodation, equipment and the caregiver's practice and attitudes. While some minders offered good care, on every topic considered there was a substantial group who did not. Minding is not, on the evidence described, a reliable service. Mothers cannot be sure that the child will be accepted and kept on; that he will be safe; given opportunities to play, reasonable amounts of attention and opportunities for interaction. He may even be left unattended in the house. In these respects the local authority is failing to intervene in the private market to ensure minimally acceptable standards. Given the present policy on day care, it would be difficult for them to do so (see Chapter 2). Yet the DHSS and successive governments have accepted responsibility for ensuring reasonable standards in the private sector. Recent statements to this effect have been made – by the then Secretary of State for Health and Social Services (Jenkin, 1979) and the Under-Secretary of State (Young, 1980).[5] We would argue that it is not possible for the private market to provide an acceptable day-care service at prices which mothers can pay. This point is discussed in the last chapter.

The arrangement made by mother and minder is private, but in the four boroughs contract forms were used by some minders. These forms set out a list of agreements and are meant to be signed by both minder and parent. They tend to cover such aspects as weekly rates of pay (by the hour or week); pay if the child is away on holiday; pay if the child is ill, or if the minder cannot take the child, for instance, because of illness or family crises; length of notice for ending the arrangement. In addition the form may specify who is to provide food, nappies and other equipment. The minder may agree to take the child to the child health clinic, or to a playgroup – who is to pay for that may be specified too. These contract forms have been devised to reduce conflicts and uncertainties about pay and responsibilities. They are becoming common among local authorities, but vary in detail. We asked our 66 minders if they had rules or conditions that they told a mother about when she came to make the arrangement. The question was left open-ended, with

---

* Since the data discussed here were collected from mothers (not from mothers and fathers) it is appropriate to talk mainly about mothers, not parents.

no prompts, in order to see what the minder perceived as important. Few of the minders (15 per cent) mentioned a contract form, and these mostly referred to its stipulations on hours and pay. For the rest the most commonly mentioned topics were pay (35 per cent), hours (38 per cent), and equipment for the child which the mother was to bring – bottles of milk, nappies, change of clothing (31 per cent). A few (19 per cent) said they asked about the child's likes and dislikes, his progress ('milestones') and routines. Others (11 per cent) referred to their own routines, and to what they were willing to offer. Six minders (9 per cent) said they had no rules or conditions.

In general minders seemed to find this topic uninteresting. They replied briefly and sketchily. Some said you had to come to agreements on specific matters as you went along; this seemed to be done especially in the case of holidays. The Oxford team reported similarly. Three-fifths of their minders did not recall mentioning anything in the way of rules or conditions to the mother (Oxford Study, 1980, Chapter 4).

From the mother's angle the contractual arrangements look equally imprecise. Asked about what rules or conditions the minder had mentioned at the outset, mothers could remember little beyond hours and pay. Most (86 per cent) said they were satisfied at the time with the arrangement; a few were dissatisfied with the amount of payment, and the request to pay for absence and holidays.

If arrangements are made informally, without much attention to detail, or to a binding contract, how well do they work out in practice? The minders were asked whether there had ever been mothers who had not kept to the rules and conditions specified. Half of them said they had had some kind of problem in the past, mainly to do with hours and payment. Some had asked mothers to remove the child because they did not stick to the agreed hours, or did not pay. Minders were also asked a series of questions about how the contractual arrangements with the focus child's mother were working out, in respect of weekly pay, pay when the child was absent, pay when the mother was late and holiday pay. Half were currently dissatisfied with one or more of these, and three-fifths of this group had also at some time had difficulties with other mothers. So it seems that many minders felt dissatisfied with the day-to-day working of the arrangements; many told bitter stories of disputes and unpaid debts. Whether minders or mothers were in the right in these disputes there is no means of knowing. The point is that the informality of the arrangements seemed often to lead to misunderstanding, abuse and conflict. At the worst, the children were pawns in the game.

How well were the mother and minder getting on together on the child's behalf? How far were the minders responsive to the mothers' wishes, and are there factors that work against this responsiveness?

The first thing to consider here is whether the mother and minder were regularly talking with each other about the child. This is important if the child is to receive consistent care, in which the two women complement each other's caregiving. It also serves as an indication of how far the mother is able to make her wishes clear, and how far mother and minder are able to reach agreement on how the child is to be cared for. We asked mothers about four topics – the child's sleeping, eating, toilet-training, and his health and progress.[6] Had she talked during the last month with the minder about each of these? Most said they had and were confident they knew how the child was doing (see Table 28). A small group (16 per cent) were not up to date on two or more of the topics. A striking inconsistency was shown in the information from minders and mothers about toilet-training: 27 per cent of the children were being trained in one setting and not in the other, and in four cases the other caregiver was in ignorance of this.

We chose these four topics because caregivers would need to know the other's practice in order to take over confidently from the other in looking after the child. But they are only a minimum, and the criterion used – over the past four weeks – is generous. In an interview designed to intrude as little as possible on these busy women's time, it was not practicable to establish finer detail about each caregiver's knowledge of the child's hours away from her. But discussions between minder and mother are seen in a rather different light if answers on 'yesterday' are considered. These showed that communication varied from detailed friendly discussion, to handing over the child at the door with minimal exchange of information (see Table 29). Sixty-four per cent of minders said they had had a chat yesterday about the child with his mother or father. This is somewhat higher than the Oxford finding on a similar question in which only 46 per cent of minders and mothers had talked yesterday about the child (Oxford Study, 1980, Chapter 4). But the Oxford focus children were of all ages up to five years, and probably the need for daily information may seem less pressing to both caregivers as the child gets older. In our earlier two-year-old study, 58 per cent of minders and mothers had talked about the child in the last week.

It would seem then that, judged on these fairly generous criteria, a majority of mothers discussed their child reasonably frequently with minders. However, two other kinds of information suggest that in some cases relationships are not happy and constructive. The minders' willingness to cooperate with parents, and their practice with regard to current parents, was assessed in the light of various kinds of information collected during the interview: their accounts of their contact with parents; evidence

Table 28: Proportion of mothers who have up-to-date (last four weeks) information on child-related topic

	Sleep	Eating	Toilet-training	General health and progress	No information on two or more topics
Minding sample N of Mothers = 55	80	90	83	71	16
Day-nursery sample N of mothers = 33	70	52	76	61	38

Table 29: Proportion of caregivers who chatted 'yesterday' with mother, with comparison data from Oxford Study

	Child-related talk	General talk	No talk	Talk with other nurse	Did not see minder	Total (%)
Minder-mother/father N = 63	64	11	24	n/a	0	100
Nurse-mother N = 42	55	33	7	5	n/a	100
Oxford Study: minder-mother (N = 63)	46	27	11	n/a	16	100

of their willingness to co-operate reasonably with parents; any expression of hostility or disapproval towards parents, including racial discrimination. On the basis of this information we thought most minders (80 per cent) were co-operating well with mothers. Here are two examples of the interviewer's notes:

> Minder spoke warmly about her current mothers. Good level of co-operation with focus child's mother, yesterday and over the last month.

Minder mentioned specific topics: 'I tell her if anything's happened during the day – if she's said a new word, how her walking's coming on, her health'. Concerned to help mother to do the best for the child – some co-operative efforts by mother and minder to see to child's health problems.

Daily chat with parents about sleep, eating; minder and mother have discussed toilet-training in last month and agreed on common tactics. Minder has responsible attitude to parents; non-judgmental, co-operates with them for the child's good. No derogatory remarks about parents.

But in a fifth of cases, we were worried by what the minder indicated about her relationship with parents. For example:

Minder disapproves of child's mother because she works full-time. Disparages her child-care practice. Minder and mother do talk to each other about the child; but minder ignores mother's wishes on aspects of child care. Doesn't use nappy cream as requested. Feeds child solids from a bottle, instead of spoon-feeding; says child won't spoon-feed (but she does at home, interviewer noted).

Minder gave evidence of racism. Her currently minded children are all Arabs. But she says she won't take blacks, especially Moroccans: they have nits, and the parents don't pay.

Poor level of discussion with parents – no day-to-day chat about the child. Poor co-operation over last month. Evidence of conflict over washing nappies and keeping child clean. Mother dissatisfied that she is given dirty nappies to take home and that child is often dirty too. But minder said she wasn't willing to alter her practices on this; the mother must take it or leave it.

Although minders and mothers were not asked their opinion of each other's child-care practices, some made comments during the interview. Minders said that the mother had not co-operated with them on some aspect of child care; mothers said that they had made a request (a reasonable one in the research team's view) on a child-care matter, and the minder would not co-operate. Examples of minders' comments are:

His mother keeps asking me to keep him for the night. It's not right for her to ask me to do that. And it's not good for the child to be away from his mum for so long.

His mother feeds him out of tins. She won't take it from me that he's better off with mashed, real food. But she listened to the health visitor.

She keeps him up too late at night – it's so that she gets a bit of time with him. Then he's tired next day. I have talked to her about it.

And examples of mothers' comments:

She lets him unplug the TV at the main switch. She told me she lets her boy do it and she has to treat them the same.

She keeps him strapped in his pram, and she keeps him there sleeping too long. Then when I get him home he won't sleep at night. He needs to run about during the day. But she says that's how she arranges things.

I worry that she doesn't talk to him much. I can't get her to see that he needs a lot of attention.

In all, 21 per cent of minder/mother pairs told us about difficulties in agreeing on how the child should be cared for. Not surprisingly, some of the minders in this group were also among those we assessed as having a poor relationship with parents. In all, 26 per cent of minders belonged to one or both groups.

The data referred to here depend on answers and comments given by minders and mothers during an hour-long interview. Such interviews could not give anywhere near a complete picture of relationships, but they did reveal a good deal about attitudes. Probably in some cases we heard about only some of many conflicts and misunderstandings that may have threatened the continuance of the placement. On the other hand, some mothers indicated that they were pleased with the minder except for one or two aspects – for instance, that she gave the child too many sweets, or left him to sleep for too long. In such cases we did not feel that the placement was likely to break down because of the mother's dissatisfaction. But many placements with minders do end because mothers are dissatisfied, as most studies have shown (including this one – see Chapter 4). Mothers often refer to poor standards of child care: that the child is not kept clean, that he is left to sleep all day, is not taken out, or is not given enough attention. With the youngest children especially, problems arise when the two halves of the child's day do not complement one another. For instance, when a child who has slept too long during the day will not settle down to sleep at night; or when a child's digestion is upset by unsuitable feeding at the minder's; or when a child is being toilet-trained in one setting but not in the other.

It is worth speculating whether there are aspects of the arrangement between minder and mother that are conducive to disagreement, misunderstanding and disapproval, and may lead in some cases to ending the placement. Possibly, too, there are some factors that inhibit minders from responding to parents' wishes.

We suggested earlier that the contract made at the outset is often ill-defined, and that identification of what must be decided, and clarification of responsibilities, are perhaps left too vague. More generally, it seems possible that there is an area of unresolved difficulty in the expectations of each side to the arrangement. The mother may initially think that she is handing over her child to the care of someone who will do her best, within reason, to care for the child as the mother would herself, and who will offer individual care based on what the mother wants. This may seem at first glance a reasonable expectation, since the child is to be cared for by one person, a mother, in her own home. (A contrasting situation is where a child goes to a nursery; there may be tacit understanding on both sides that while there he conforms, within reason, to the procedures and norms of the nursery.) But the minder may not see it like that. She may consider that she is running a small group with its own procedures, routines and norms. This is especially likely if she has been minding for some time and has established ways of coping with her own domestic jobs and with the minded children, and particularly so if she has many children to care for. Data on these points have been discussed earlier (Chapter 7). It can be argued that it is unreasonable to expect a minder to respond more sensitively and carefully to mothers' wishes than caregivers at nurseries, nursery schools and playgroups.

Contrasting characteristics of minders and mothers may also make agreement and good relationships difficult. Minders tend to be older than mothers and to have larger, longer-established families (see Chapter 1). Minders are also mothers, but they have typically opted for life at home with their young children, while the mothers of minded children have chosen to work. We did not ask for minders' attitudes to working mothers, but other studies provide information. In our earlier study (unpublished data) we found that 31 per cent of minders were firmly against mothers of young children going out to work, and a further 17 per cent had reservations: they thought mothers should not work unless they had to. Similarly, the Oxford Study (1980, Chapters 3 and 5) found that a quarter of the minders were 'very opposed' to mothers going out to work, 45 per cent in all were generally against, and the rest gave only qualified approval. Under these circumstances some minders may feel that they know more about child-rearing than the mothers do, and that they are in an important sense more committed to child-rearing, because they have opted for it full-time. Some mothers' and minders' comments showed they were well aware of the contrasts between them. Some mothers accepted the minder as a granny-figure, advising them about child care; but others resented it if the minder insisted on making the decisions and imposing her own child-care practices on the child. The fact that minders are concurrently fulfilling roles as mothers and child-care staff gives them an edge over the working mother, in terms of conventional views about motherhood. In this respect they are similar to the playgroup leader with her own under-five, who may also claim moral superiority over mothers who choose to leave their children rather than participate in the playgroup's activities. No doubt, too, child-care workers in many settings disapprove of working mothers, but many of these mothers will be working only part-time. The mother of a minded child will, typically, be a full-time worker, and so presents a stark contrast to the minder caring for children all day at home.

Some minders and mothers may have extra difficulties. Mothers born and brought up abroad accounted for three-quarters of those who did not discuss the child much (Table 28). Some pairs of minders and mothers spoke a different language and could not communicate well, or in some cases not at all directly.[6] So some foreign-born mothers (nearly a fifth of all the mothers), whether because of language difficulties or for other reasons, were not discussing their child much with the minder. Minders are likely to be used by foreign-born and ethnic minority mothers (see Chapter 2); and minders are poorly placed to solve problems of communication and mutual understanding. Nursery and playgroup staff may be tackling these problems by a variety of methods: staff–parent meetings; toy libraries; use of specialist staff; enlistment of other mothers with particular skills; encouragement to mothers to spend time at the nursery in order to familarize themselves with activities and to get to know staff. These attempts may be piecemeal and only partially successful, but they are a start. Minders can call on no outside resources to help them with mothers.

Finally, while the minders came mainly from manual workers' households, the mothers were mainly in non-manual jobs (see Appendix F). Minding has traditionally been offered and used mainly by working-class women, but there is an increasing trend for middle-class mothers to go out to work, and presumably fewer of them can now afford in-home care. Some of the differences in child-care practices and some of the difficulties in communication may have resulted from class differences between minders and mothers. The study does not provide enough contrasting cases to study this. But some implications of the fact that minding is offered mainly by working-class women will be considered in the next chapter.

We have discussed the extent to which minders are responsive to parent's wishes, in the light of data on the contract and day-to-day communication between mother and minder. This raises other questions. What does the minder take responsibility for? How far should a mother expect the minder to follow her wishes? How far is it up to the minder to devise routines and activities for the day? These problems are particularly difficult when considering babies and toddlers. Mothers need their children to be consistently looked after, and it is important for them to maintain a major say in how they are cared for. More difficult is the question of what for older children one would call the curriculum – the programme of daily activities aimed at forwarding the child's skills and development. As minded children get older, this problem becomes more obvious, since comparisons can be made with the programme at nursery schools and playgroups. Indeed, the DHSS/DES Joint Letter (1978) suggests that care for these children at minders' should be supplemented by attendance at schools and playgroups. But probably mothers of younger children recognize the problem too. Many expressed a preference for group care and some moved their children on to nursery or playgroup (Chapter 4). For while mothers who use group care for their child may be reasonably sure that staff have some training or experience in child care and will aim to help the child develop as well as to care for him, mothers using minders have no such assurance. Few of the minders (14 per cent) had any previous child-care training or work experience, and while some of them probably offered a stimulating and varied environment for the child, some probably did not. The 'curriculum' in domestic day-care is in general ill-defined, as Kamerman and Kahn (1981) report. It may be that one reason why some mothers find minding unsatisfactory, or at least risky, is that no one is clear exactly what it is the minder undertakes, or should undertake, to do. In some cases mothers may have expectations of the arrangement which are not shared by the minder. Some mothers, for instance, were unhappy because the child was not being encouraged to speak by the minder; and we heard of one (extreme) case where a mother removed a three-year-old because the minder refused to teach him to read.

Mothers and nursery nurses

The day-nursery mothers and nurses were asked the same set of questions about the four child-care topics (see page 166).[7] The mothers were less well informed than the minded children's mothers about their child's day at the nursery (see Table 28). And 38 per cent of them were not up to date on two or three of the four topics, compared with only 16 per cent of the minded children's mothers. Again, there was evidence of inconsistent management of toilet-training – for 40 per cent of the children there had been no discussion over the last month between the two caregivers, even though the child was being toilet-trained either at home and at the nursery, or in just one setting. The pattern of chat 'yesterday' between mother and nurse was different from that between mother and minder (see Table 29). More of the mothers talked to someone at the nursery, but many talked about topics other than the child. It would be unwise to stress these contrasts. It is possible that the two sorts of staff and the two sets of mothers report differently. But it is worth suggesting some factors that may allow day-nursery mothers to remain in ignorance about their child's day, even though they feel able to sit and chat with staff.

First, day-nursery mothers may find it relatively easy to go into the child's room and sit and chat with a nurse who is on duty anyway at the end of the day, in a nursery which is open to parents. By contrast, a mother going to pick up her child from a minder has to go into her home, and may find her already involved in the activities and commitments of her own household. But it may be easier for the day-nursery mother to talk about herself, her day, even her troubles, than to talk about her child. She may feel relief that he is cared for during the day, and may assume or hope all is well, being unwilling to upset the hard-won arrangement. Furthermore she, and possibly the staff, may assume that how the child is cared for at the nursery is for staff to determine. Certainly some mothers commented that they did not like to ask about the child's day, because it was not their business. And the nurseries did have established routines and procedures (see Chapter 7). It is likely that a major problem in the relationships between mothers and nursery staff is that mothers feel inferior. They are the recipients of a preventive, welfare service, which implicitly denigrates their competence as mothers, and which has been granted to them often only after a long waiting period. These feelings may be accentuated by the expertise and competence of staff. A personal impression that may be shared by some mothers is that nurseries are usually clean, spacious, well equipped – they are designed for child care; and as you go in, you feel you are entering a rather large, well organized establishment (a bit like a school or hospital) whose goals and methods you are incompetent to challenge.

Secondly, there are some features of nursery organization and practice that may make good communication between mother and staff difficult. To start with, the child was in most cases (84 per cent) the responsibility not of one nurse, but of the nurses in charge of the child's group. So the mother in some cases found it difficult to get precise answers to her questions about the child, and may have been deterred from asking further questions. Then all the sample nurseries operated a shift system for staff, so that on some days a nurse started and ended work early and on others started and ended late. In practice, taking into account the times when mothers brought and picked up their child, this meant that for only 18 per cent of the mothers were all the child's nurses on duty at both ends of the day; and for 41 per cent of them, the staff were not all on duty at either end of the day. This is likely to mean, as some mothers said, that it was difficult to contact the person who knew exactly how long the child had slept, what he had eaten, whether he had played outside, and so on.

Finally, some mothers felt that the nursery was unwelcoming or inconsiderate to parents, or they were unhappy about some aspect of child-care practice at the nursery (11 of 35 mothers). As with mothers of minded children, this is anecdotal information; it may be a minimum score. But some mothers' feeling that they were excluded from participation in the care of their child at the nursery may have led them to talk little to staff about the child.[8]

Summary

We have discussed how far minding and day nurseries were responsive to the mothers' need to ensure consistent care for their children, and their wish to be well informed about how the children spent the day. A problem with minding may be that there is little consensus about what minders take responsibility for. Yet at the day nursery, where routines and programmes are perhaps better defined, a mother may feel powerless to affect what happens to her child.

Mothers using both forms of care are poorly placed to make the service more accountable to them. The mother of a minded child is using a private service; she is the employer to whom the account is rendered. Yet she is in a weak position to stipulate what she wants, because she has so little other choice. Minding is therefore a private transaction in which the employer's sanctions cannot be applied. Furthermore central and local government have not been willing to enforce reasonable standards to protect children and their parents. At the day nursery, reasonable standards are in practice enforced for both premises and staff. But the mother, as client of a welfare service, may find it unresponsive to her needs and wishes for herself and her child.

Notes

1. The Education Act, 1944, Section 10, lays a duty on the Secretary of State for Education to make regulations prescribing standards for premises. The most recent version of these is given in Statutory Instrument 1972 no. 2051. The list covers, for nursery schools and classes: the site, outdoor playing space, accommodation for adults and children, storage space, kitchen facilities.

   Staff training is covered under Schools Regulations, 1959 (Statutory Instrument 1959 no. 364, section 16). Only qualified teachers may be employed as teachers in maintained schools; details of acceptable qualifications are given. An exception is made in the case of nursery school and class staff: persons not qualified as teachers, but who have completed a course of instruction in the care of young children (NNEB or equivalent) may be appointed to the assistant staff (Administrative Memorandum 21/73). Teaching qualifications include successful completion of various courses, which must be approved by the Secretary of State (Statutory Instrument 1975 no. 1054), and qualifications defined, in various categories, by experience in teaching. (Taylor and Saunders, 1976.)

2. See Lello, 1979; Becher and Maclure, 1979, Elliott et al., 1981.

3. The regulation of private nurseries and minders by law is described in Chapter 2.

4. Clift, Cleave and Griffin (1980 Chapter 2) quote from Hadow (1933) and Plowden (1967), both of which refer to parental roles in children's education, but with the emphasis on parents co-operating with school aims, rather than on schools taking parents' views and wishes into consideration. The gap between lip-service to parents and staff opinions is indicated by the results of a study (Chapter 5) which included an open-ended question on nursery-school staff's perceptions of their aims; this produced no direct mention of parent-participation or co-operation with parents.

5. An excerpt from Jenkin's speech is given in Chapter 11, Note 2.

6. For these questions, 55 pairs of mothers and minders gave answers. Nine pairs have been omitted: one mother had little time to spare for the interview; in eight cases the mother spoke insufficient English for these questions (but one of these spoke the same language as her minder). So seven pairs of mothers and minders were not able to communicate well with each other.

7. Thirty-three pairs of mothers and nurses replied on these questions. Two mothers spoke poor English; five were unable to answer fully because of their psychiatric state. According to the nurses, three of these seven, including the two with language difference, did not talk much to them about the child.

8. Examples of day-nursery mothers' specific dissatisfactions with the day nursery: they fall into two groups:

   (a) *Child care and communication*

   You never know how he's being looked after. You just have to hope. I go up to his room each morning, but you can't stay long or matron's after you.

   Staff don't keep a good enough eye on him. He keeps having accidents. They say, sorry, but he's cut his eye.

   They don't tell me things. There was whooping cough in the nursery, so she caught it. Also German measles. They didn't tell me. I would rather have kept her away.

   I wanted him to be only breast-fed (child, four months old) but they harassed me.

   (b) *Problems with staff or with the terms of the contract*

I don't like Matron. She told me to stay the first two days, to settle him. Then on the second day she told me I was stopping the nurses doing their work.

The nurses won't let me stay and watch him play (child has just moved up from baby to group room).

At first they only gave me a place for two days a week, so I couldn't get a job.

They said she had to be picked up by 5.45, and I couldn't always get there on time (working mother).

Part Three
Discussion: Towards a Day-care Service

Chapter Ten
Minding and Nurseries: An Assessment

If all the findings of our study are considered together, what kind of picture do we get of childminding? And how do day nurseries compare?

How good a service is childminding for children and their mothers?

Probably many readers will know of mothers who speak glowingly of their minder: she's a second mother to him; he loves going there; I wouldn't move him. They may know of other mothers who tell of poor conditions: arrangements abruptly ended, perpetual anxiety about their child's well-being, disquiet and guilt at having settled for relatively poor care. Our findings show that minding is a chancy business, with some mothers standing more chance than others of getting the better end of the market. On every topic we looked at, some minders were offering a good service, and some a deplorable one. In the first place, minding is unstable and children who are minded are likely to have to move from one minder to another. This is partly because there are just not enough day-care places available, and mothers settle at first for what in the end they cannot tolerate; partly because there is a rapid turnover of minders; and partly because arrangements are made in a hurry and there is little time to settle children in or for mothers and minders to work out mutually satisfactory arrangements. The service offered is chancy too, in terms of housing, equipment and child care. Only about a third of the minders provided a good setting as regards space, safety, comfort, hygiene and playthings; and half gave cause for concern about child-care practice. Altogether a quarter of the minders were offering a good service and nearly a fifth a very poor service in one or more respect.

Perhaps the most disturbing finding of all was that mothers in manual work and mothers from abroad got a poorer deal than others. The pattern was consistent: mothers in manual work and mothers born abroad were using the minders who offered the poorer premises, equipment and child care. In addition, mothers from abroad, or belonging to ethnic minority groups, faced discrimination against them at about a third of the minders. It is not surprising then that these mothers were also more likely than others to use minders who were overburdened with chores, and in charge of many children (six, on average). If anything, this picture under-represents the problems encountered by ethnic minority mothers. In planning the study, we chose boroughs with a high rate of mothers working and with a high proportion of ethnic minority families. In practice, only a quarter of the mothers interviewed came from the main groups who have repeatedly been found to face discrimination and poor services – those from the West Indies and Asia. The rest of the foreign-born mothers came from Europe and a variety of other countries. So it may be that the findings, though shocking, are less so than they would have been had we chosen to study, say, mothers of West Indian origin. Furthermore, of course, the study was about registered minders. Unregistered minders, where standards are even more a matter of chance, are almost certainly much used by ethnic minorities.

It has long been clear that people from ethnic minority groups have particular difficulties in getting satisfactory services in this country. The problems they meet in housing and employment are well documented. There is increasing concern about how inaccessible and unresponsive the health services are.[1] And as far as services for young children are concerned, there is mounting evidence of disadvantage and parental dissatisfaction. Perhaps the central problem is to do with differences in cultural patterns and (for some groups) in language. Parents who speak little or no English, who have different views on child-rearing, different diets and dress, and different expectations of services, have difficulties in finding day-care services that are understanding, considerate and responsive.[2] Some of these parents do not use the services either because they know little about what is available or because they see the services as inappropriate to their needs or hostile or unresponsive. Yet many of the children are in need of day-care places, if by 'need' we mean that their parents are at work, that they live in poor housing, that they have poor opportunities at home for play or for learning English.

Providing services for a multicultural society where some groups are heavily disadvantaged means taking special care to plan for these groups, to offer flexible services, responsive to people's wishes and circumstances. This in turn means that staff must be educated, perceptive and willing. Childminding as at present organized and staffed is very unlikely to offer an adequate service to ethnic minority children and their parents.

The wide range in the quality of service offered by minders is well known to those who work in social service departments. It may be less well recognized by influential people who, if they use minders at all will use good ones, and may be impatient of claims that varying standards exist, or that they are unacceptable, or that some mothers consistently get a bad deal. It seems to us that a service which is so chancy and where a substantial proportion of caregivers offer sub-standard care is plainly unaccceptable. Mothers and children should not be exposed to the risks inherent in privately organized childminding, either through the luck of the draw, or because they belong to certain occupational or ethnic minority groups or are new to the country. Behind the recital of figures given in the chapter on availability and stability, and behind the discussion of DHSS criteria for day care lie the anxieties and frustrations of mothers – about their child's welfare and about their own work. Underlying all are the assumptions of social policy – that using day care is a private decision by mothers, and that society allows it but does not facilitate it, and furthermore encourages the existence of poor quality care. These assumptions are inappropriate in a society where a quarter of under-fives have a working mother at any given point, and where half have a mother who works at some point in the child's first five years.[3]

Apologists for childminding tend to point to recent improvements – the injection of local authority money and staff; the formation of local minder groups and of the National Childminding Association which work towards improvements (see Chapter 11). Such improvement schemes are testimony to the serious and kind-hearted wishes of minders to offer a better service and reflect local authority concern for the welfare of young children. They probably improve the daily experiences of many children. But it is the general level of standards that needs improvement. All mothers should be able to assume that all minders offer acceptable day care by the standards of the day. Mothers should not have to struggle with an unplanned system until they find something they can, however unwillingly, accept. In other words, piecemeal improvement schemes will not provide a stable, satisfactory day-care service. This point of view may be thought inflexible, even unsympathetic. It is certainly out of tune with today's fashion for make-do-and-mend. But child-care standards are too important to be left to chance and individual effort.

Childminding is an unreliable service. There is no guarantee of a place when and where a mother wants it, or that the minder's premises, equipment and child care will reach acceptable minimum standards, or that the place will go on being available for as long as the mother needs it. The detail of what the minder offers (food, outings, play, visits to the clinic, washing of clothes) and the fee are matters for individual negotiation between mother and minder, and the agreement made can be altered at a moments's notice.

One reason why childminding is unreliable is that it is a private arrangement, subject to few requirements that might produce a service of more even and acceptable quality. A minder can offer what she feels like offering, and withdraw it too when she feels like it. Compare the Danish minder, employed by the local authority: she signs a contract which specifies her conditions and work and what services she is to provide (see Chapter 11). The unwillingness of local authorities in this country to impose conditions or constraints on private minders no doubt results from fear of jeopardizing such a sensitive system. Many minders might give up minding if the service they were to give were determined externally. But the main reason why childminding is unreliable is that it is provided on the cheap. It has been promoted explicitly as a low-cost solution to the demand for day care, and the effect of keeping costs down is to decrease the quality and reliability of what is offered. This can be seen most clearly in the contrast between DHSS standards for housing, safety and equipment, and what we found. Local authorities are faced with impossible alternatives: to register all or most women who apply, in order to keep an eye on them and perhaps improve them; or register only those who meet the standards. Given the high demand for places they are likely to opt for the first alternative. But they have few resources for improving standards after registration. Such grants, loans and gifts as they make are a drop in the ocean.

In reality, of course, costs are not kept down. They are borne by minders and mothers. To visit these women makes one vividly aware how heavy is the burden they carry, compared with the contribution made by society. Minders work long hours at an insecure, poorly paid job, whose conditions of work would be totally unacceptable for any unionized group. Minders who give a good service do so by digging into their own pockets – to pay for prams, toys, crockery, and so on, and for replacements and repairs to their own belongings, furniture, carpets, wallpaper and paintwork. The mothers also work a long day, both at work and looking after their children, and they carry the financial costs of childminding too. It is a measure of the weakness of women in our society that they accept the present position and seem unable to change it.

Is childminding a neighbourly service?

Minding is seen by some as a service offered by good neighbours to mothers in need. Minders offer child care as a neighbour will offer to do shopping for someone housebound, or give a person without a car a lift to hospital. These are services given not so much for immediate or tangible return, but more in response to a feeling of obligation in a community to help a person in need. On this view, the money that changes hands between minder and mother may be less a fee than a token of thanks, as well as a contribution to the costs of caring for the child. This seems to lie behind Brian Jackson's (1976) reference to minding as a working-class community response to adversity. It is perhaps implicit in the call by Lady Plowden and others at the Sunningdale Conference on low-cost day provision for the under-fives (1976), for the use of community resources to provide day care. The authors of the Oxford Study (1980) formed the opinion that 'many minders liked to feel that in a sense they were doing the mother a kindness', that they were helping out mothers who had a difficult time and could afford to pay little. However, they also note that once minders joined discussion groups (for instance, in connection with the 1977 BBC television series for childminders) pay became a major discussion issue.

So, are minders motivated by the reciprocal obligations of one member of society towards others, are they helping out mothers less fortunate than themselves, or carrying out a neighbourly service?

It is clear to anyone who knows minders that on the whole they are kindly, concerned women who accept responsibility for the child during the day and will put in extra work to cover emergencies. Minders will keep a child after hours, take him to the doctor if he falls ill, temporarily take on an extra child for a desperate mother. These are the good deeds of a neighbour, who recognizes and meets the needs of a child or mother and offers a service irrespective of reward. They contain an element of sacrifice, of time, effort or money. In these respects some minders offer a service that goes beyond what parents could in general ask or expect of a nursery school, for instance. They are being good neighbours.

But many minders also weigh up the gains and losses of minding against those of doing other work or no work, much as anyone does. Certainly women with children or other home commitments generally settle for what will suit the family and themselves best, all things considered. An important factor here is money. The money paid per child to a minder offers little gain, net of expenses, compared to a good job. On the other hand, where a minder has a pre-school child of her own (36 per cent of our minders) or a child under sixteen (78 per cent), this amount can be traded against her wish to be at home for her children, and perhaps too against the costs, financial and emotional, of using day care herself. In addition, minders may take on more than three under-fives (26 per cent of our minders), or school-age children (66 per cent). At this point, minding begins to look like a good option for a mother, if she likes the company of little children, by contrast with the costs (in time, money and strain) of travelling to work, and the costs (in tiredness, boredom, conflict) of working outside the home.

The earning power of minders is also relevant. Most of our minders (73 per cent) had worked in shops, as secretaries or as other office workers, or in manual work. The mean gross wage for women in manual jobs at the time (1978) was £48; and for shop and office workers (classed as III non-manual), between £38 and £52; secretaries and shorthand-typists led the class III non-manual field with a gross average rate of £57 a week (Department of Employment, 1978). These rates may be compared with an average of £9 per minded child, or £27 (before expenses) for three under-fives. In many cases the minders could add on a few extra pounds for school-age children.

Viewed as a job, childminding has serious disadvantages. Minders are exploited, insecurely employed, under-paid, over-worked. In addition, they lack adult companionship, may feel isolated and are mainly confined to the house and immediate neighbourhood. But minding also offers advantages, especially when compared with the kinds of jobs most of the minders had done. The minder organizes her own time, she takes orders from no one, and she is not harassed by the demands of an employer, or by a strict, imposed timetable. Minders, then, offer child care at a rate somewhat below what they could earn elsewhere, but minding offers them benefits that they may prefer, at least for a time.

Data discussed in Chapters 6 and 7 support this argument. Minders take up minding because it fits in with their domestic commitments, and they continue to mind for as long as it does so. In this respect they behave like other workers. Our findings suggest that, while they work as minders, many women arrange their work-load, their day, their relationships with the child and his mother, to suit themselves. This is shown in their attitudes to the child, expressed in a description of him (see Chapter 6), and in some of their child-care practices, for instance, on settling-in (see Chapter 4). Possibly some minders adopt strategies like keeping the child at an emotional distance to make daily life with him easier (see Chapter 6). Then most of the minders were willing to offer day care only to some children, those acceptable in their house (see Chapter 4). And, as suggested in Chapter 9, the setting and enforcing of the contractual arrangement seems to come from the minder's side. It is she, if anyone, who gets the mother to pay for holidays, and who asks the mother to bring certain items of equipment or food. She may also ask for the child to be removed if the arrangement no longer suits her.

If this accurately describes the terms on which many minders offer day care, the service is unlikely to be responsive to the needs and wishes of parents, except on the most superficial level. It will be offered and sustained on a take-it-or-leave-it basis. Mothers who would like to see a cooker-guard or better toys cannot act with other parents to improve things, either by pressurizing the service or by fund-raising (as a group of mothers of playgroup or nursery-school children could). Mothers who want to see more attention paid to their children can make no appeal either to or against the minder; and may indeed have poor information about how the children spend the day.

Finally, of course, there is no reason why minders should be expected to offer more good deeds to neighbours or to strangers than the rest of us do. The mistake is in supposing that they are different from most citizens; that they are offering a child-centred, neighbourly service to the community for little or no return. It is possible too that some of the reluctance to face problems posed by working women and their young children stems from the assumption that the community is providing and providing well.

Community care – women as caregivers

Women are traditionally cast in the role of caregivers of the young, the old and the infirm, and the tradition is still powerful. The idea that men are the economic providers and women the housewives and mothers has been supported and promoted by psychologists, doctors (especially in baby books), sociologists, and professionals in law, education and social work (Rapoport, Rapoport and Strelitz, 1977, Chapter 2). This stereotype has allowed policy-makers to assume that women are, on the whole, potentially available as free or cheap labour.[4] It is also assumed that their role is generally nurturant, individualized in approach and child-centred. The Rapoports' thesis is that this model of men's and women's roles as well as of the conjugal nuclear family has been increasingly challenged in the 1970s, and the issue now is how to acknowledge in policy and practice the diversity in attitudes and behaviour, without chaos and confusion.

Many commentators have noted that the care of the dependent (young and old), and of the frail, ill or handicapped, rests on the family's shoulders. For family, as Wilson (1977) says, read women. She points to the function of the social work profession in supporting the premises on which the welfare state was constructed: that women would care for men and for the dependent. Moroney (1976) argues against those who claim that the family is losing these caring functions, and demonstrates its continuing importance in the care of the old and the mentally handicapped child. We have referred earlier (Chapter 4) to the assumptions of policy-makers that women will care for the handicapped. Land (1978) analyses recent social policies on income maintenance and community care to show how women have been encouraged to stay at home to care for the family. Both Labour and Conservative parties have recently reaffirmed their desire to strengthen the family so that women may care for its dependents. A Conservative Secretary of State for the Social Services has argued (Jenkin, 1979) that to provide child-care places at public expense for the generality of working mothers would be to encourage parents to believe that 'they can do what they like and it is the duty of the State to look after the children'.[5] Labour party policy differs only in that it gives greater emphasis to the need to introduce measures to enable women, if they so wish, to combine paid work with household duties (Coote and Hewitt, 1980). Coote and Hewitt also point to the contrast between the TUC's paper endorsement of equal opportunity and its unwillingness to promote it. One major stumbling-block is men's desire to retain their status as family wage-earners; another is the powerlessness of women in trade unions. All in all, the attitudes of policy-makers look traditional, coherent and unchanging. Against these powerful forces are arrayed: the fact that more women, especially mothers, do now take on paid work, and the efforts of relatively powerless groups, mainly of women, to persuade more powerful groups to recognize the implications of women's changing behaviour and attitudes.

The promotion of minding as a major form of day care rests on the assumption that though the behaviour of some women may be changing, there remains a pool of women who are available to offer child care and who do not seek or need proper recompense. An important ingredient of this view is that normal women are motherly; that those who are mothers will readily generalize their mothering to other children; and that their reason for taking on the care of other people's children is that they wish to mother them. (We have discussed the findings on this topic earlier (Chapter 6).) The relationship between ideas about women as caregivers and childminding is worth considering in some detail.

The links between the child in care and the child in day care were shown in Chapter 2. The 1871 bill to introduce controls over foster mothers sought to cover day-care mothers too. Seventy-five years later some factors that led to the reform of provision for children in care under the 1948 Children Act were probably instrumental in leading to legislation for children at minders and in private nurseries in the same year. Indeed, as in 1871, there was some thought of legislating for both categories under the same act. As Parker (1966, Chapter 2) says, evidence was brought that institutions for children in care had disadvantages and deficiencies; and there was a new emphasis on the importance of the child's relationship with his principal caregiver. But two further points were important: there were not enough places in institutions, and the obvious alternative of fostering was cheap. So in the 1948 Act fostering was specifically promoted by a statutory requirement that children be boarded out wherever possible. By 1963, half the children in care were fostered, whereas from 1900 to 1939 the proportion was never higher than a fifth.

So there is a close parallel with childminding, where legislation to control standards was introduced at a time when the need for day-care places was unmet by nurseries; and the alternative of minding was a cheap form of care offered by women at home. The 1940s revulsion against institutions for children in care was not immediately matched by distaste for day nurseries. Presumably this was because, as the Curtis Report made clear, the defects of some of the old poor-law residential institutions were gross. Day nurseries, on the other hand, were run by local authorities, and had perhaps acquired a good reputation during the War. When revulsion did come in the late 1960s, it was based not on knowledge or on studies of day nurseries, but on a swing in favour of individualized care by mothers, as well as on the cheapness of minding.

Since the 1940s, fostering has changed in character. Before that children were often fostered on a semi-permanent basis. They would become an extra child of the family, often taking its name, and were in fact semi-adopted. The legislation in 1948 insisted on the principle of restoration to the parents wherever possible. Foster parents were asked to take on an altogether more difficult role, in which they recognized the natural parents' rights, and kept the child at some distance, with the ever-looming threat that he might be restored to his parents (Parker, 1966, Chapter 6). The similarity of this new role to that of the minder is evident. Both share the care and responsibility for the child with the natural mother, and are asked to carry out many of the functions of the mother. The minder may well cope with the inherent problems by keeping her distance from the child, by avoiding commitment (and some rewards). She will of course take less responsibility for the child than foster parents, and may seek to minimize contact with the mother in order to avoid discussing the difficulties of a situation in which two 'mothers' share the child's care. (see also Oxford Study, 1980, Chapter 9).

Policy, then, has relied on the use of women with no special skills to carry out these kinds of child-care work, and it has become increasingly clear, first for foster parents, and more recently for minders, that to do the work well is difficult and requires a high level of skill. How has the problem been resolved? In fostering, recognition of the importance of the job has led to some changes. Nowadays foster parents are drawn from all social classes. Knowledge of the problems they may face has led to reasonable payment in the case of 'difficult' children, though fostering is still not in general a well-paid job. A central strategy to improve both services has been the use of professionals to help caregivers acquire child-care skills. The caregivers are then viewed as clients, rather than equals.

Childminding workers do various jobs: they interview applicants; they may arrange provision of toys or safety equipment; they may offer day-to-day practical advice to minders, and in a few areas to parents. But their main function is to improve the minder's child-care practices. This may be done by visiting her, encouraging her to attend group discussions at drop-in centres, or a more formal training course, and encouraging her to take the children to a playgroup. This method of improving a service is essentially make-do-and-mend. Instead of staffing the service with people chosen for their suitability in terms of personality, experience and training, they are recruited irrespective of suitability, and all then rests on their voluntary self-improvement.[6]

This strategy is unlikely to succeed. It was suggested earlier that many women do childminding because it is convenient and compatible with their domestic commitments. Furthermore, they have no reason to suppose they are deficient as caregivers – not only are they successful mothers, but they may compare themselves favourably with the working mothers they deal with. For these reasons they may resist attempts to improve their practice. Moreover, many work as minders for a short time only and efforts to improve them may be wasted. And those who most need improvement may be those most likely to resist change. The question of whether training minders offers hope for improving the service will be discussed further in Chapter 11.

Why have attempts to improve minding followed these lines? It may be that minding, which is regulated under social service rather than education departments, is seen as a branch of welfare for poor working women rather than as a day-care service for the population in general. Because the system is run mainly by unqualified working-class women, it has been tempting to see them as clients needing help. Perhaps this is why it has become common practice to appoint local authority staff to help minders, instead of, for instance, making annual grants to each minder for equipment, telephone expenses, or help with the housework. In the London boroughs studied, the ratio of minding workers to minders was on average one to 55. At current rates of pay (in 1978) for such workers (say £10 000 a year, including overheads) each minder could be given an annual grant of about £180 instead. This is a crude calculation, but it illustrates an alternative strategy for improvement. It is a strategy that would rest on the premise that the minder was a trusted competent colleague, rather than a client. It is worth noting in this connection that until recently it has been possible to rely on the idea that most families who used minders were themselves working class. Thus minding was provided (like fostering) both by and for people who could be seen as different from, and in various ways inferior to, those who managed the system. This is certainly no longer true of the children's families. The idea that minding is a welfare service for the deprived can no longer be sustained in the face of the increase in the numbers of working women of all classes who use minders.

The use of low-paid or unpaid women as child-care workers in a society where the behaviour and expectations of women are changing presents other problems: women may no longer be available for the work, and it is undesirable to use them.

The first point concerns *the nature of the job and the willingness of people to do it*. The data on the availability (Chapter 4) indicated a shortage of minding places; some local authorities even operate a priority system. Many minders stay for only a short time in the job. Return visits showed that a quarter had stopped minding since the first contact a year earlier, and 74 per cent of those had minded for less than five years. The Oxford Study (1980, Table 3·6) found that 92 per cent of ex-minders had minded for under five years, including 54 per cent who had minded for less than two years. It may be too that as the difficulties of the job are recognized more, fewer women will wish to do it. Then, as suggested above, local authorities and policy-makers may find that if they attempt to recruit a more suitable work-force, the number of applicants decreases. Those who are suited to minding are also suited to better jobs elsewhere. If they recognize the difficulties of minding, they may be unwilling to consider it except at a high price. The possibility of a local authority campaign to recruit women with experience or training in child care is considered in Chapter 11. At least it would help in future policy-making to know whether they were willing to childmind, and if not what would induce them to.

In the related field of fostering, the old view that foster parents should be given only token payment (to discourage unsuitable applicants, and to emphasize emotional commitment rather than the financial transaction) may be giving way to a recognition that people should have a reasonable financial return for the expense and hard work of bringing up a child. This has not yet been reflected in the general rates of pay,[7] but some recruitment projects offering higher rates are in operation, and these indicate that foster parents with skills to care for handicapped children or difficult teenagers can be found.[8]

But fostering probably offers greater rewards than minding, in terms of long-term emotional commitment to the child. In schemes where minders are more rigorously selected, and paid (usually at about the rate for untrained nursery assistants), there have been difficulties in recruitment. This was so in Lambeth (Willmott and Challis, 1977) and in Hackney (Hackney Sharing Care Scheme, 1980); it is also a problem in other countries – in Denmark, France and Sweden. (Schemes of this kind are discussed further in Chapter 11.)

The second point is that *it is undesirable to encourage the provision of child care by poorly paid women within a private system.* This is because women's status in society will be further down-graded, and because the service will be poor and standards of child care will suffer.

If women are encouraged to work in poorly paid jobs, this reinforces acceptance of their low status as workers and adds to their difficulties in getting their pay and conditions of work raised to equal men's. The ambivalence towards minding is shown in the fact that minding was not until 1980 classed as a job by the Registrar General, though minders were taxed if their income reached appropriate levels (OPCS 1980c). It has been classed as homeworking and its conditions of work deplored by the TUC (1978b). The TUC has also urged that minders be trained and paid on the same scales as other child-care workers (TUC, 1978a), but since 1978 no further progress has been made.

We have tried to show that the unreliable and in some cases downright poor service offered by minders results in part from the motivation and circumstances of those who are willing to childmind. Day-care services provided with few resources will be poor. This is true of playgroups too. They will flourish mainly in areas where women have financial security; elsewhere the survival and quality of the playgroup will be affected by women's need to go out to work.

One particular feature of the service needs discussion here. It is commonly assumed that though there is a shortage of minding places, nevertheless minding is on offer to all comers. But this is not so. Minders may and do pick and choose. In particular they may opt against babies, handicapped children and children from ethnic minorities. Under the present system they cannot be required to take a child. Is it desirable that they should be? If minders were salaried employees of the local authority, would it be reasonable to ask, as part of the terms of their contract, that they take any child sent to them by the local authority? Some people argue that it would be unreasonable, because looking after a child in your own home is a very personal, intimate affair and the child's well-being depends largely on the one caregiver being happy with the child. That sort of reasoning seems to inform the Race Relations Act's exemption of events within private homes (see page 68). But childminding is now promoted as the major form of day care, especially for under-threes, and it follows that it should be seen as a day-care service, not as a quirky system subject to the caregiver's private and in some cases racist preferences. One would not expect the personal preferences of staff to influence admissions to playgroups, nursery schools and day nurseries. This is not to suggest, of course, unreasonable demands by the local authority for a minder to take, say, a baby, where her circumstances would make that difficult. The local authority worker and the minder would obviously want to consider together what would be best, given her housing, her family and the children already with her. But a major advantage of turning minders into salaried employees with contractual obligations could be to reduce discrimination against parents and give them more equal access to the service.

To encourage the provision of child care by poorly paid women at home also encourages the belief that it does not much matter what sort of care children get. Some people argue that what some minders provide is much the same kind of care as some children get at home. After all many children do not have fireguards and gardens. But the government department responsible for day care has set standards high, on paper, and there seems no reason why some kinds of day care should be exempted. Furthermore, if the state is offering recommendations it surely must, as it does, propose what is acceptable according to current knowledge of children's needs. It is also an important principle accepted by the DHSS that day care should complement what children get at home and compensate for any disadvantage they may suffer there.

In practice, however, things are different. The status of child care as a job in Britain is low, and this accords with the low priority given to providing services for children. There is reluctance to help parents care for their children whatever the child's age. Services tend to be provided grudgingly and at a lower standard than education services. There is an almost complete absence of services for school-age children after school and in the holidays. Standards for staffing at minders' are set low. Even at day nurseries, which cater for children deemed to be in need of care, staff may start to train at sixteen, with in the main no higher qualification than O levels, and their training lasts for only two years. By contrast, teachers in nursery education start to train after A levels, for three years. Policy in Britain towards the care of children pays lip-service to the importance of ensuring children's wellbeing and welfare, but in practice everyone concerned – staff, local authority workers, perhaps even mothers – is encouraged to agree that poor or variable standards are acceptable.

Day nurseries

This chapter has been mostly about childminding because it was the main focus of the study. Minders and day nurseries provide for differently defined groups of children. Childminding offers a service to the general population, although in practice it may be selective. Day nurseries are provided for only a very few children, about one in a hundred. These children come from families with many problems.

We studied day nurseries mainly in order to compare them with minders, and this determined the sort of data collected. We studied premises and equipment, staff qualifications and mobility, the child's day and some aspects of the nurses' relationship with the child. But a detailed study of the children's daily experience remains to be done. Is it possible to say anything about the relative merits of the two services? Or to put it another way – given a choice, which would one choose for one's own child?

An obvious point is that the physical circumstances in which children spent the day at nurseries were far better and more consistently good, than those at minders'. Children had safe space to play indoors and outdoors, with adequate equipment. It may be a superficial comment, but it is important nevertheless: the nursery premises had been planned, or the existing housing converted, with children in mind, and to meet DHSS criteria. The environment complemented the children's home environment as the minder's did not in many cases. This is an important advantage of the nursery, at least for urban children. It will be recalled that many of the study children, whether they went to minders or nurseries, had poor play-space at home: 41 per cent of minded children and 67 per cent of nursery children had no garden; 22 per cent and 13 per cent respectively lived in overcrowded conditions.

What about the amount of attention children were likely to get from their caregivers? Nurses and minders were each looking after about three under-fives, on average; but many minders also cared for over-fives, and if they are included then minders each cared for nearly five children, on average. Furthermore, minders tend to have many tasks and commitments which may reduce the time they can give the children, whereas nurses are there mainly to care for the children, though they too have some other jobs to do. It is safe to say that the opportunities for interaction were at least as great for nurses as for minded children. As to the quality of the attention, some indication is given in the way minders and nurses talked about the children. Many more minders than nurses (67 per cent compared to 36 per cent) discussed the focus child exclusively in terms of how easy or difficult he was to manage. Nurses were more likely to comment on the child's character, behaviour or development, the emphasis being on the child as an individual. On the other hand, it is widely thought that nursery nurses are too immature and insufficiently well trained to give the children adequate care: to give them a warm, loving relationship and a stimulating environment. The routines imposed by nursery organization are also thought to militate against flexible, responsive care. The quality of the child's experience, the interactions between staff and children, different ways of grouping the children and organizing the day – all these need detailed study. But the task imposed on these young girls, to care for disadvantaged children in a highly structured environment for a long day, does seem onerous.

What about the children's day-to-day life in the two settings? We found day-nursery children played out of doors more but went on fewer outings than minded children; their opportunities for play, in terms of space and equipment, were better. There was more emphasis on routines – for sleep and toilet-training – at the nurseries. Is a child's day at the minder's better than the day at the nursery? Some people allege that life for staff and children at the day nursery is boring. They link this with the low autonomy of the nursery nurse. She may have little responsibility for individual children, few of the ordinary jobs and commitments of ordinary life at home, and an ill-defined set of tasks and goals compared to a nursery-school teacher. She is seen as unsure how to spend the day with the children and so they are relatively aimless, under-occupied and unhappy compared with children at home, at a minder's or in a school. We did not set out to evaluate the children's experiences – to study the detail of the experiences and to judge their worth – but we came away from the two different settings with impressions about how the children were faring. Some of the minded children seemed quiet, inactive or restrained in their activity. There were children who sat quietly all the way through our visit, watching the television, or just sitting with nothing to do. We did not see anything like this at the nurseries. Some nursery groups seemed to go through phases during the day when adherence to routines and time-keeping meant that staff and children waited about – for meals, for a nurse to come back from her lunch, for parents at the end of the day. Other groups seemed to manage better to provide interest and activity for the children all the time. In general there seemed to be more purposeful, happy activity at the nurseries than at minders'. But of course there was in most nursery groups another nurse or student who could look after the children while we talked to a nursery nurse, and this extra adult was not available at the minder's. Indeed the difficulty of making comparable observations was a major reason why we did not attempt a systematic comparison of the children's experiences. In general, we thought that minded children were more likely to be quiet, apathetic and under-occupied than nursery children. It may be indeed that there are aspects of group care that protect the children and perhaps offer them positive benefits.

Jerome Bruner has recently provided an overview of the two studies carried out under his direction by teams in the Oxford Pre-school Research Group: on childminding in Oxfordshire and on nurseries (local authority and private) in London. Though they were methodologically dissimilar, they provide interesting contrasts. In particular, Bruner notes that the nursery researchers found few examples of children who were as subdued as those seen at minders', where many of the children were 'detached and inactive'. Bruner comments on these contrasting impressions and, having discussed some of the shortcomings of nurseries, he concludes that they are to be preferred to minders:

> For all that, the more active, peer-related existence of children in day nurseries seems to keep them from falling into the 'quietness' of mild depression found reported at minders' – in spite of the fact that many of them come from disturbed homes. (Bruner, 1980, Chapter 8).

A most important difference between minding and day nurseries is that minding is inherently much less stable. The child may have to move on, often at short notice, if the minder stops minding, or if minder or mother is dissatisfied. These problems do not arise at the nursery. We found that both minded and nursery children had histories of unstable care at minders'. By a year later, many of the minded children under two (62 per cent) had moved on. But relatively few of the nursery children (32 per cent) had moved, and then in almost all cases because of a change in the family's situation, not because the place was not available or because of dissatisfaction. However, this contrast may not be replicated everywhere. Although in three of the study boroughs children very rarely 'lost' a place, in the fourth, regular reviews of children's 'needs' were made, and many children each year were deemed to be no longer in need of a place. For both mother and child, leaving a day-care place and finding another and starting off at it can be worrying and distressing, and stability was one of the things mothers prized for their children. For most day-nursery mothers getting a day-nursery place meant no more worries about day care – the child was settled until he was five. Even so, there was a different sort of instability for the nursery children, in that many of them were likely to have several nurses looking after them, either concurrently or successively. Again, whether this is an advantage or a disadvantage needs investigation, but on the face of it, it is undesirable.

A further contrast between minding and nurseries concerns the relationship between mothers and caregivers. We found considerable cause for concern about the working relationship between minders and mothers. Some of this was to do with the contractual arrangements; some problems probably arose from national and ethnic differences. Many minders set their own terms and are unlikely to tolerate difficulties for long. On a day-to-day basis, minders and mothers were more likely than nurses and mothers to have a chat about how the child had spent the day. Though nurses and mothers talked to each other, it was often not about the child, and we found there was inconsistent handling of the child, no doubt as a consequence. Some mothers of both minded and nursery children told us they thought it safest policy not to rock the boat by asking too many questions, or by giving their own views on child care. But nursery mothers may well have been less confident as mothers. The offer of a nursery place often carries explicit or implicit denigration of the mother, and this may have accounted for some of them talking little to staff about their child. What was very clear, however, was that almost all the nursery mothers were tremendously pleased and relieved to have a safe, secure place for their child. Virtually none said they would prefer another arrangement, whereas there was much less overall satisfaction among mothers of minded children.

Much work needs to be done on day nurseries, but it seems clear from the study that they do have virtues and that mothers appreciate them. However, since 1968 the DHSS has suggested that some priority children might be placed with minders, with the possibility of the minder's fees being subsidized by the local authority; and in some areas this is now done. The suggestion was made partly as an economy measure, and partly because of the one-to-one relationship supposedly offered at minders'. But there may be grave drawbacks for the children. They are likely to experience frequent changes of placement, and they may suffer from a relatively poor environment, and get relatively little attention from their caregiver. Furthermore, mothers who are already experiencing serious difficulties in their own lives may find it just too difficult to make and keep going a good working relationship with minders, who in turn may be intolerant of them. Even if the minders are hand-picked for quality by the local authority – as sometimes happens – the problem of instability remains. If, as the DHSS also suggests, minded children need education to supplement care at minders', then they will have to be moved when they are three, or divide their day between minder and nursery school or playgroup. So more movement, more instability for the children, will result from patching together different parts of the day-care system. In addition, of course, to remove some children from day nurseries means leaving behind an even greater concentration of children suffering the most serious disabilities and of children at risk. It must be questioned whether this is socially desirable.

Notes

1. The Radical Statistics Race Group's study (1980) is a useful source book, especially on housing and employment. Data on health is sparse (see discussion in the Black Report, 1980, Chapter 2), but growing. Brent Community Health Council (1981) gives a good list of references. Demographic data is given in *Social Trends* (see, for instance, *Social Trends*, 1981, Chart 3:19 for the incidence of lone parenthood in different ethnic groups). Moss (1980) provides data on rates of mothers working by ethnic group.
2. Studies by the Community Relations Commission (1975) and Gregory (1969) – both described in Chapter 3 – show that some ethnic minority groups get a poor service from minders. The CRC also found that black parents were less successful in getting places at day nurseries and nursery schools than white parents. Ferri (1977) found that staff at playgroups were offering a poor service to disadvantaged children and their families, one-third of whom were from ethnic minority backgrounds. Tizard, Mortimore and Burchell (1981) have described the particular problems of increasing parental involvement in nursery schools where parents belong to ethnic minority groups. The parents' expectations of the schools were at variance with teachers' views, staff were ill-informed about the children's background, and would need to show greater willingness to take parents' views into account if parental involvement were to be increased.
3. This was discussed in Chapter 2, where we noted the estimate by the Central Policy Review Staff (1978) that in 1976 24 per cent of under-fives had a working mother; a fifth of these worked full-time and four-fifths part-time. Bone (1977) estimated for 1974 that 26 per cent of under-fives had a working mother, and in a further 22 per cent of cases mothers said they would work if they could find day care for their child.
4. The chapter referred to quotes, for instance, from Michael Young (writing in 1965) on the roles of parents in schools. While he saw fathers as offering skills, such as carpentry or

building, mothers were seen as general dogsbodies who would be available whenever required to help with menial tasks.

5. Patrick Jenkin, then Secretary of State for the Social Services, spoke at the 1979 National Children's Bureau Conference at Bath. Towards the end of his speech he said:

> Some mothers have to go out to work either to make an essential contribution to family finances, but perhaps also for their own fulfilment. There is a need therefore for day-care facilities of a satisfactory standard so as to ensure that children are properly looked after while their mothers are away. I accept that where parents wish to work or have to work there should be facilities for their children. I do not accept that these facilities should be provided free by the State. The State does have a responsibility to provide care for children whose family circumstances, such as poor health, bad social conditions and so on mean that parents are unable to cope . . . For most families however these services are appropriate. If they are made available at public expense too readily, then they can all too easily be seen as the expression of a philosophy which preaches that parents can do what they like and it is the duty of the State to look after the children.

6. There is a similar though less acute problem with nursery nurses, who are sometimes thought to be inadequately trained for the job they are asked to do, and who are typically seen by matrons as needing considerable support and further training. However, at least in a nursery this can be offered by a colleague who works alongside the less experienced nurse and tackles the same problems in her daily work.

7. The National Foster Care Association, founded in 1974, has promoted the view that foster parents should be better paid. They argue that rates of pay have, if anything, declined over the last few years, as a proportion of earnings. The work of the N F C A is described by Cooper (1978, Chapter 2).

8. Detail on schemes to foster 'difficult' children by offering high rates of pay to foster parents is also given by Cooper (1978, Chapter 3).

Chapter Eleven
Improving the Services

The day-care debate

Since the 1960s it has been abundantly clear that day-care policy in this country is hopelessly out of step with the way young families lead their lives. There is a huge gap between provision and demand. Over the years observers have issued a steady stream of demands for a thorough-going reappraisal of the situation and for re-formulation of policy. Demands focused initially on the needs of working mothers (for example, Yudkin, 1967; Hunt, 1968) and these demands were taken up (on paper) by the TUC (1978a). A second kind of campaign became prominent in the 1970s – the demand by feminists for day care as one means towards equal opportunity for women. Two recent summaries of the debate set out the main issues (Challis, 1980; David, 1982).

Government response to the facts and the campaigns has been inflexible. Ineffective measures were taken in 1968 to tighten up childminding legislation and, as we saw in Part I, arguments were produced in the mid-1970s to justify the expansion of the low-cost private market in child care. There has been no change in government policy since then. At present, many politicians and public figures show signs of developing policies which will further restrict choice for families and may lead to difficulties for them. Increasing unemployment has led to demands for women, especially mothers, to go home, and spokesmen for the Conservative party are arguing that more of the costs of providing care for dependents – children, the old, the handicapped and the ill – should be transferred to 'the family' and 'the community'. This in practice means women at home.

Meanwhile as regards day care, there have been many demonstrations of the inadequacy of day-care provision (Mayall and Petrie, 1977; Jackson and

Jackson, 1979; the work of the Oxford Pre-school Research Group). Colleagues at our own research unit have provided rationales for the provision of day care on demand, based on the varying life-styles and wishes of young families in an industrial society (Tizard, Moss and Perry, 1976; Hughes et al, 1980).

At present there is a certain stagnation about the day-care debate in Britain. There is no sign of a crack in government and Civil Service defences. Research money has virtually dried up, so there will be little new empirical evidence for some time to come. Most of what can be said about day care in the context of public policy in this country has been said.

In this report we have tried to move the debate on. We have shown that the day-care system does not meet the criteria governments propose for it. Recommended standards for provision, equipment and child care are not met. Many minders do not provide one-to-one 'motherly' care. Some of the most disadvantaged groups in our society get the poorest deal; day care does not compensate for the disadvantages their children suffer. The findings point to the need for reassessment of day-care policy.

First, we should consider the policy option which is attractive to some people: that it would be better if working parents stayed at home and looked after their children full-time during the early years. This is, after all, a choice which most mothers – but not fathers – make at present. However, it is a choice which has costs in job satisfaction and career prospects, costs which arguably contribute to the unequal position of women in society. (We discuss this point in detail elsewhere: Hughes et al, 1980; Petrie, 1980.) There is a further important point here. Nowadays people think they have a right to take part in ensuring that services, such as health, welfare and education, provide what they want. Increasingly people are taking up that right and asking to be heard. In the case of parents, it is important for full recognition to be given to their sensitivity to their children's needs, their knowledge of what suits their children and the family best. At present day-care services are provided in accordance with various rationing devices, formulated and administered by officials (see Chapter 2). The assumptions are that decisions should be made for families, and that families' life-styles fit neatly into pigeon-holes. Effective forums are needed for discussion and policy-formulation by parents and officials working together to make services more responsive to parents' wishes.

Given a choice, probably many mothers and some fathers would opt for looking after their babies and toddlers themselves. Parents might share the care more equally between them. It may be that in many cases parental care is best for the youngest children. But probably most parents could do with some help, and no one should be forced to be the sole caregiver. If parents are to have a genuine choice about working or child-rearing, then social policy should provide both income replacement and job protection while children are young. Some countries are moving closer to this than others. Kamerman and Kahn (1981, Chapter 2), in their thorough discussion of policies currently being implemented or considered in six countries, find that France, West and East Germany, Hungary and Sweden – all except the United States – have at present an entitlement to income replacement at and after childbirth of between three-and-a-half and nine months, with proposals in some countries to extend it to as long as twelve months. In Britain provision for maternity leave entitlement as originally proposed in the Employment Protection Bill was in line with that in EEC countries, but the entitlement as enacted was for six weeks only. It is possible that pressure will grow for Britain to fall into line with the other EEC countries. Kamerman (1980) argues that overall the trend may be to encourage mothers to stay at home for up to a year with their babies, by lengthening the maternity leave entitlement; and that the best policy option for one- and two-year-olds may be to include them in group-care programmes. A more radical proposal, and one so far implemented only by Sweden (The Swedish Institute, 1979), is to consider both parents as responsible for the child's day care and give both the right to take paid leave after the child's birth, and to work a six-hour day for the first eight years of the child's life. Thus a child might be cared for at different periods of his life and at different times of the day by one or other parent, and he might need non-parental care for at most three or four hours a day. Proposals along these lines need to be considered if the conflicts between parental work and child-rearing are to be solved. They represent, of course, only one possible policy option.

Moss and Fonda (1980) give a useful analysis of current forces likely to influence the way parents divide their time. They point to three broad fields: the changing patterns of employment, and in particular the effects of technological change; the changes taking place in the structure and way of life of young families; and the role of the unions and government in initiating and responding to change. They argue that on balance the trend is likely to be towards greater equality between the sexes, and more varied and flexible sharing of work and child-care roles; but the rate and kind of progress in this direction is debatable.

Improving day care

To return to day care and families who currently choose, or are obliged to use, the available service. What are the possibilities for improvement within the present policy framework? How far does policy need to be changed in order to effect improvements?

This study was concerned with under-twos and our earlier study with two-year-olds. What we have to say here relates mainly to these children – that is, the under-threes. For parents of over-threes the choice is wider, and the situation much better, though not ideal. The DHSS and DES recognize the desirability of group experience and education for these children, and nursery education on demand has been a goal of government policy since the influential Plowden Report (1967). Though the policy is far from being implemented,[1] it remains the ideal for this age-group.[2] Since there have never been enough places in schools and classes to meet demand, the playgroup movement has grown since the mid-1960s, until it is now the largest single kind of provision for over-threes. The need of working mothers for care and education to cover longer than part-time hours has not been recognized by the government departments, although they have urged local authorities to make piecemeal additions to existing provision to provide some care for the children. Extended-day playgroups, nursery schools and classes are one option, and many mothers continue to rely on relatives, neighbours and minders to fill in the beginning and end of the day. As far as government policy is concerned, the sticking point is the refusal of the political parties to recognize the rights of women to work, and the consequent duty of policy-makers to accept what follows: the need for consistent, overall planning to meet the needs of the children. In practice, local authorities are going some way to meet these needs.

However, we are concerned here with under-threes. In order to meet the needs of families with under-threes, two government defences have to be breached. The first is the refusal to reconsider policy towards mothers and fathers with young children, and the balance of work and child-care responsibilities. The second is the unwillingness to give any force in practice to the needs of under-threes for social and intellectual stimulation.

Day-care policy assumes that parents must take all the responsibility for their children's care, except in cases of extreme need. In the absence of local authority provision for all but a handful of children, private day care by minders has been allowed to expand. In Chapter 10 we argued that within that policy framework childminding is not an acceptable service and cannot be improved to an acceptable level. Insufficient money is devoted to it: good child care is expensive. The service has low-level basic resources in terms of premises, equipment and child-care qualifications: childminding would need a massive allocation of resources to lift it to acceptable standards. There is high demand for day-care places and few places available, so there is little incentive to raise standards: parents and local authorities alike will settle for what there is.

Day nurseries represent the other strand of day-care policy. Because the children are deemed to need day care, the local authority takes responsibility for the service and spends (in comparison with minding) a lot on it. For the children and their families the service has some disadvantages, stemming from the idea behind its provision – that the mothers are inadequate.

First, we consider suggestions for improving the services within the present policy framework. Many of these suggestions have a superficial appeal – some have even been put into practice in some areas, and they may be attractive to both central and local government. But they are unlikely to be effective in improving the services. It is important to explain why.

Next we turn to possible changes in public policy towards families with young children.

Possibilities within the present framework

Day nurseries

Information available from other studies on British day nurseries is slight and our own findings do not allow confident generalization; suggestions for improvements can only be tentative and provisional on further studies. But with so little information and discussion about day nurseries it is perhaps useful to air some of the issues raised by the study.

Suggestions for improvements in day nurseries within the present policy framework must take into account the effect this policy has on the service. If we offer a service on the basis that the users are incompetent members of society, we must expect the service to retain signs of this, such as patronizing or inconsiderate behaviour by staff towards parents, and resentment from parents.

Perhaps the most striking thing about day-nursery children is that they are segregated. The children in our study seemed to spend most of their time isolated from local life, and certainly from the activities of ordinary homes: from going shopping, meeting people in the street, helping with the cooking, and so on. These activities provide opportunities for developing understanding of the world, and it is a pity if day-nursery children are shut off from them. Other children, including minded children, probably have more contact with ordinary daily life – though it cannot be assumed that all their caregivers make full use of the opportunities offered for widening the children's knowledge. Of course, day-nursery children tend to have better play-space and better playthings than many other children, certainly than most minded children, and these may provide some compensation. Nevertheless we need to question that day-nursery children should spend their day so differently from most children, remembering that they are already different because they come from disadvantaged backgrounds and they spend their days in the company of similarly disadvantaged children.

The experience of day-nursery children in our study was also different from that of most other children in the kinds and number of relationships they had with adults. At any one time they had several caregivers, because nurses took responsibility for the group rather than for individual children. Over the years children had to adjust to still more staff; they were moved to groups headed by different nurses, nurses themselves moved between groups, and moved quickly in and out of work at nurseries. Current research does not indicate whether having many caregivers is prejudicial to children's welfare or development, although there is some evidence that the longer a caregiver remains with a child, the closer the relationship (Rubenstein et al, 1977; Cummings, 1980). The children had a remarkably large number of caregivers, and in this respect they were treated differently from most children, and in opposition to generally held views about children's capacity for relating to many adults.

Possibly both the discontinuities in relationships and the isolation of the children could be altered by changes in organization and staffing. Some innovations are being made by local authorities and voluntary organizations. One local authority, in cooperation with the Save the Children Fund, has set up a nursery for a small group of children in a terraced house. The aim is to keep the setting as domestic as possible, to maintain high adult – child ratios, and to keep in close contact with the neighbourhood and community. An evaluation of the scheme is being undertaken (personal communication with S C F staff). A community nursery, the Children's Community Centre in Camden, again based in a terraced house, aimed to break down the traditional isolation of nursery children by frequent and regular outings and by involving the children in the day-to-day running of the nursery: helping with jobs about the place, with the shopping and the preparation and serving of meals. Staff aimed to avoid the friendly but detached attitude they observed among some nursery staff and sought more intimate relationships with the children. This meant not only caring for the children as individuals but opening up their own lives to the children so they could experience the adults as real people with joys and sorrows of their own (Hughes et al, 1980).

These examples suggest that it may be easier to start from scratch than to achieve change within existing nurseries, where the constraints of the building and perhaps staff attitudes may stand in the way of re-thinking and reorganization. Where these constraints can be overcome, family grouping seems to give better scope for continuity in the relationship between children and their peers and between children and staff. In nurseries organized into family groups children of all ages are looked after together and there is no segregation of babies, toddlers or older children. Children in these groups stay put throughout their nursery lives and staff can gain experience in caring for children of different ages without changing groups. We know of two local authorities where this is routine and seems to be working well. The employment of men as caregivers (not met in this study but current practice in certain local authorities) would give children a broader range of relationships and supply a masculine element not available for some at home.

Some research evidence suggests ways of providing more personal and less routine experience for the children. Tizard's work (1975) on residential nurseries suggests that allocating small groups of children to individual members of staff, who plan their day and are responsible for most aspects of their care, may improve the children's experience. This strategy increases staff involvement with the children and may well enhance job satisfaction. Although it may be practised elsewhere, it was not evident in the study nurseries.

A possible reason (often put forward) is that under such a regime there is even greater disruption for the child when a nurse leaves. And high staff turnover *is* a problem at day nurseries. The child has little chance of continuous relationships with individual nurses. It may be that radical changes are needed in the nature of nursery nursing. At present girls start training as young as sixteen. Within a few years their plans, hopes and attitudes to work are likely to change. For many reasons girls in their late teens and early twenties are not likely to provide a stable work-force. And as we pointed out earlier, the day nursery offers poor pay, working conditions and prospects compared to other work. It is possible that raising the age of entry for training, encouraging older women to work in nurseries and providing better career prospects, would improve stability of staffing. Men might be attracted too, if conditions and prospects were better. A recent National Nursery Examination Board report on the future of nursery nursing (NNEB, 1981) has suggested that nursery nursing should be developed as a career in its own right, and that there should be a qualification ladder, linked to the education system.

Another point is that mothers should be recognized as important people in the nursery. Mothers and nurses should between them aim for consistent care for the child at home and in the nursery. Most mothers in the study were excluded from consultations with the doctor. Nurseries carried out routines such as toilet-training without telling mothers. Staff were not always available to talk to mothers, did not always know the answer to mothers' questions about what had happened to the child during the day, and were seen by some mothers as unwelcoming and inconsiderate. These problems are recognized,[3] and in some places are being tackled. In our sample, while one nursery seemed to us (and to mothers) to be punitive and hostile to mothers, others were friendly and cooperative. Some nurseries kept a record of the mother's wishes and practices on feeding, toilet-training, and so on, and regularly consulted her. Nevertheless it would seem important for each child to be assigned to an individual nurse. Her task would be to take responsibility for the child's welfare and progress, to keep a diary of the child's activities and progress and to make a point of establishing an easy relationship with the mother so that the child could be regularly discussed between them. On health care at the nursery, it is important that mothers accompany their child to see the doctor, however difficult this may be to arrange. Information passing between mother and doctor, in either direction, should be at first hand, not retailed by a nurse.

Any suggestions for improving the care of children at day nurseries must take into account their implications for staff. The suggestions given here imply that the staff will be willing to organize the day to further good relationships with parents; and staff need more time for this sort of thing. Nurses, and especially matrons, told us how difficult it was to find time for desirable activities. For instance, in some cases regular reviews of children's progress were not carried out. Meetings to consider staff–child relationships and children's progress had to be squeezed into lunch-hours. Helping mothers to feel at home, encouraging them to stay, sometimes teaching them child-care skills – these all take up staff time.

Matrons themselves are increasingly acting as social workers to parents and find it difficult to get through their administrative work as well. Some of the nurseries had no secretarial assistance, and increasingly heavy loads of paperwork had to be absorbed by existing staff. Measures to improve staff morale and motivation, and better staffing levels to allow time and energy for improvements are crucial if the child-care service at day nurseries is to be improved.

These suggestions are fairly modest, but they would almost certainly require greater input of resources than at present. And there would remain great problems, related to the identification of the children as disadvantaged. Some staff at nurseries and in local authorities will argue that the children need protecting from the world, not exposing to it, that the parents cannot be trusted as responsible, that relationships between staff and children must remain distant if these insecure children are not to be further confused. And so on. While children are categorized as 'priority' and the rest, this sort of problem will continue, despite the best efforts of many staff.

Childminding

What scope is there for improving childminding within the present policy framework – that parents are responsible for their children's day care, whether at home or outside, except in cases where they demonstrate their incapacity? Minding within this framework is a private form of care, regulated by the local authority, within the terms of the 1948 law, amended in 1968.

Let us consider first the *availability* of minding places. We found there were not enough places, and mothers could not plan ahead, or choose wisely among such places as there were. Various modest proposals may be made. Local authorities might assess demand for day care in their area, and, if necessary, mount a recruitment campaign for more minders. There may be potential minders, for instance, among mothers with experience and/or training as teachers, social workers, nursery nurses, nurses or playgroup leaders, who might serve as an improved basis for staffing a minding service.

However, those with appropriate qualifications and experience may be difficult to attract. Willmott and Challis (1977) report a poor response to an eighteen-month campaign to recruit suitable minders to care for priority children in a small socially mixed area of Lambeth. Of 36 women who were sufficiently interested to apply, none was currently working in a child-care job and only four had teaching or nursing qualifications. No doubt this reflects the existence of better-paid alternatives, such as home-tutoring or part-time nursing, for well qualified mothers of young children. There are other drawbacks to such a scheme. Well-qualified mothers may have as wide a range of motives as other mothers for returning to work when their children are older, and may have the additional pull of a career to be resumed. They are therefore unlikely to offer a stable service. Secondly, in some local authorities, those needing day care may live in different areas from those willing or competent to give it. We noted earlier that it is important to mothers to have a day-care place reasonably close to home.

There is a particular shortage of minding places for the youngest children. Local authorities might consider promoting childminding as a service for under-threes, while aiming to increase provision at playgroups and nursery schools for over-threes. Extended-day places would be needed to meet the needs of working parents. However, as we found, many minders do not want to take babies, and expansion of this service rests on the willingness of people to come forward for this very demanding and responsible work. There is little reason to suppose that there is a pool of women waiting to be recruited.

One means of improving the service to mothers would be to offer them an advice service. This might conveniently be set in a child health clinic or area social services office; and could be run by part-time workers. For a borough with four area offices, the equivalent of one full-time appointment might be appropriate. The service would provide a clearing-house where mothers could find up-to-date information, and possibly guidance (of a non-judgemental kind) to enable them to make more informed choices. Some of the problems posed by minders' preferences for certain kinds of children might be by-passed or tackled before the mother met the minder. Protecting mothers from racist minders could be an important part of such a service. The service could liaise with the providers of day care, and introduce mothers to them (see page 209 for further discussion). These suggestions are in line with the DHSS/DES Joint Letter (1978, para. 1) which urges maximum coordination of local services, and the use of community resources to improve day care. The disadvantage for the local authority is that it would run the risk of seeming responsible for the standards of minders it merely registered. Local authorities have been slow to set up machinery to help parents, although they have intervened to support minders. Yet to intervene early in mothers' search for day care might do something to assure a better service for some mothers and children.

Secondly, *stability*. We have shown that minding is unstable. Parents may move the child because they are dissatisfied, or because the minder asks the child to leave; parents may prefer other forms of care; minders may stop minding; young families are mobile. There appears to be no way whereby stability can be ensured under the present system, which depends on the use of women who are likely at any time to resume work, who offer a service with widely varying standards of care, and where the child cannot stay on (as at a nursery) if a caregiver leaves. One possible minor measure (adopted by some minders) is to encourage minders to get to know one or two other minded children so that they can take over if necessary. This is formalized in the Danish childminding system.[4]

Thirdly, we come to the central question of standards: *standards for the premises and equipment, and for the minder herself.* We found, as other studies have, wide variations in standards. To date, local authorities have tended to argue that they must register most who apply, in order to attempt to influence the quality of care offered in their area. But this policy results in a disservice to parents, who have no guidelines at all, and no assurance that a registered minder is likely to offer reasonable care. This policy rests too on the questionable assumption that the care offered by minders, once registered, can be improved to acceptable standards by local authority low-cost measures. Minders may not use equipment supplied to them – we have met minders who put loaned toys away 'for best', and would not use a fireguard because it deflected the heat. A minder may refuse to go on a training course, or if she does agree it may make no difference to her attitudes and practice. She may take on more children, including schoolchildren, than she can care for. She may live in housing which cannot be improved, in terms of play-space for the children, whether by low- or high-cost measures.

Under the present system, the local authority could apply more stringent standards for registering applicants. On accommodation, it might specify space per child, height off ground, a safe or separate kitchen. But imposing the sort of standards the DHSS suggests, and we have discussed in this study, would reduce the potential numbers of places available in private homes. In some parts of England housing standards may not present a problem, but in London they certainly do, and they probably do in other inner-city and industrial areas where there is older, cramped and unsafe housing. There appears no means whereby children in these areas can be offered day care in reasonable surroundings at low cost.

As to equipment, we have shown that the list of things a minder requires to provide a good quality service is long and even the 'best' home may not rise to the needs of a varied and changing age-group over time. Minders need child furniture, child transport, toys, baby equipment, safety equipment, a phone. Some minders are likely to be ill-equipped so long as they or the parents bear the costs. We discuss later the costs to local authorities of intervening to equip minders.

Could the local authority intervene to raise standards of care in so far as they depend on the minder's qualities? Applicants might be required to show that they had had previous child-care experience (other than motherhood) or training for child care. Failing that they could be required to take a course of training during their first, probationary year. This might include some discussions and talks, and some practical experience in day-care settings. Full registration would depend on the minder having met these requirements. This sort of proposal is gaining support (by, for instance the National Childminding Association, 1979: Jackson and Jackson, 1979; the Oxford study team, 1980).

There are, of course, dangers in demanding qualifications. Not only may otherwise suitable people be excluded, but the qualifying procedure may not be well enough devised to ensure a uniformly high standard of service from those who go through it. Against this it must be said that there seems little reason to set minding apart as the one child-care service where qualifications are not normally required. It can be argued that minders need better preparation for their work than other child-care staff since they work alone without the support of colleagues. Further, there is now enough research evidence to show that the quality of care at minders' is not uniformly adequate; and it may be more generally recognized that minders' practices, once minders are registered, are difficult to influence. All these considerations provide justification for local authorities to raise their standards as to the fitness of the would-be minder. The local authority could either arrange and monitor suitable training, or provide detailed guidelines for the probationary minder to follow. However, there is no evidence that training courses for minders affect their practices. Indeed one study suggested that a training course had no effect (Jackson and Jackson, 1979, Chapter 12). But this course was a series of meetings. Practical experience in nurseries, playgroups and nursery schools, backed by discussion might be more effective. However, some people would not apply for registration if training were imposed on them, and still others would fail to meet the training requirements.

Lastly under the heading of standards, local authorities could be more rigorous about the number of children at minders'. The study showed that minders who were over-burdened with children offered poorer child care. Local authorities might enforce and monitor DHSS guidelines more closely. School-age children are a major problem here, and it is difficult to see how this problem can be tackled without providing other facilities to care for them before and after school and in the holidays.

Finally, *accountability*. Minders are not accountable to the local authority, or to parents unless minder and parent have agreed on the minder's responsibilities. Both mothers and minders find it difficult initially to have formal discussions and agree on a set of responsibilities. It is possible that both sides might be better satisfied if more care were taken initially with the contractual arrangements. A liaison worker might be of help here. A further step would be for the local authority to insure minders for their work. This would protect minders, children and parents. (See TUC, 1978a; Jackson and Jackson, 1979; National Childminding Association, 1979.)

Raising standards for premises, equipment, child care and numbers of children is desirable, not least in order to meet DHSS recommendations. The central objection is strategic – any effective action by the local authority would be likely to drive many minders out of business, or underground. In the absence of sufficient registered minders, working mothers and fathers would then turn to the unregistered to care for their children. It seems likely indeed that within the present policy framework no measures will increase the number of good quality places at minders'. A similar conclusion was reached by the Oxford research team and their director, Jerome Bruner. They, too, argue for reconsideration of day-care policy 'root and branch'. Meanwhile Bruner (1980) proposes advisory teams of child-care experts to be made available to minding workers; and Bryant, Harris and Newton (1980) suggest modest measures to encourage minders and mothers to cooperate for the benefit of the children. Minders and mothers would, of course, be free to choose whether to fall in with these suggestions.

It is worth pointing in general terms to some of the financial implications of the standards proposed by the Ministry of Health for premises, equipment and child care at minders' (in Circular 37/68). To provide safe housing for children with plenty of space to play, indoors and outdoors requires a high income, a very high one in inner-city areas where much minding takes place. Then to equip a minder with the tools for the job is expensive, both at the outset and recurrently. The Circular's recommendation is that minders should offer care like that given in a good home. To equip a minder initially with the child-care equipment available in a good home, and to maintain that equipment might cost, at today's prices, about £80 per child, per year.[5] And if, as the Circular argues, the minder is to make child care her first and main job during the day, she must not be burdened with the jobs associated with many children, or with her own domestic work. So she must be able to afford to take only two or three children, or charge parents a lot for each. Ideally she needs domestic help too. But minders do not, by and large, have high incomes or spare cash to spend on equipment and domestic help. Generally they are people who hope to supplement a modest household income by their work.

The costs of training minders (even by the short course proposed by the Circular) are also not negligible, though difficult to assess. Much depends on what form the training takes and on what is included in the calculation. Some local authorities have estimated costs as 'nil' or 'absorbed', because staff and buildings used were already costed under different headings (London Council of Social Service, 1977). Shinman (1979) has pointed to the problems of unit cost in her description of drop-in centres, where fluctuating numbers of minders, children, parents and others were involved. But in general, if minders move out of the job at the rate of about one quarter a year, and if there is a shortage of minders, then the recruitment, interviewing and training of minders will occupy a significant part of the time of minding workers. If the successful completion of training (of whatever kind) were considered as a qualification for childminding, the assessment of performance would have to be reasonably systematic. In a borough with a hundred minders, an additional half-time appointment might be needed to cope with the selection and training of new minders.

It is one of the remarkable facts about minding that there has been little recognition by local and central authorities of the costs of providing an adequate service. This is probably, at least in part, because many people assume that minders are voluntary workers, and do not need proper payment. A more important reason may be that people think minders do not need to be well housed or well equipped or trained, since they offer, by virtue of their motherhood, motherly care. However, local authorities have become more aware of the costs of minding since they have begun to use minders for 'priority' children, and to apply higher standards to these minders. The report on the Lambeth salaried minder scheme showed that both minders and the local authority began to see cost as a major issue, and to assess more realistically the costs of domestic child care, especially as regards wear-and-tear, heating, food and equipment (Willmott and Challis, 1977, paras 4.21, 8.8).

Salaried childminding. Some of the problems posed by private childminding have been met by salaried childminding services, established in some countries where the State accepts responsibility for providing day care for the children of working mothers: Sweden, France and Denmark (see Swedish Institute, 1980; Walters, 1977; Wagner and Wagner, 1976; Bang, 1979). It is worth describing salaried minding, because it is one option for this country, within the present policy framework as far as 'priority' children are concerned.

In Denmark, minders ('family day-care mothers') are local authority employees, equipped and supervised by the local authority, which also introduces the parent and child to the family day-care mother.[6] The system is much the same in France and Sweden, and goes some way to tackling the problems we have identified. In particular, local authorities can plan for the day-care needs of their area and can directly recruit staff to meet them. Family day-care mothers may be fairly well satisfied with their job (and so stay in it), since they are paid regularly and reasonably well. They are also supplied with all they need in material terms to offer good care; and there are enough local authority staff to provide a good advice and liaison service. Discrimination against parents can be by-passed or eliminated, and the child has the opportunity to spend a settling-in period before the arrangement is finally made. So great care is taken to make sure that the arrangement gets off to a good start. The service is also accountable: the family day-care mother formally agrees to a list of duties and the local authority can dismiss her if she does not discharge them. Parents have some assurance of minimum standards and may ask the local authority for help if they are not satisfied.

There are, however, some problems with this system. There are said to be difficulties about recruiting enough family day-care mothers, since pay is low compared to an industrial wage (Bang, personal communication). Mothers have to wait for a day-care place, since there is an overall shortage. The standard of care is likely to be lower than in a nursery in terms of accommodation and staff qualifications and the activities available. The service is also relatively unstable. Furthermore, since parents pay a high rate – the same as for a nursery place – they are likely to be dissatisfied. Nevertheless, the scheme shows that the expansion of day-care places can be achieved, though at high cost, by using existing resources (women in their homes) and without the delays and expense of building nurseries.

Modified versions of salaried minding schemes have been established in this country, in order to increase provision for priority children. The most thorough-going example of such a scheme is the Groveway Project (Willmott and Challis, 1977). This includes direct payment of a salary by the local authority for the care of children from the day-nursery waiting list. Pay is on the same scale as that for a trainee nursery nurse and in addition, minders are paid an allowance for each child who attends. Prospective minders must qualify in an introductory course lasting six weeks, and, if accepted, have regular discussion meetings with a local authority tutor. The unique feature of the scheme is that all the minders live within easy walking distance of the Groveway day nursery, and they and the children spend some time there each week. It is thought that the children, minders and nursery staff benefit from this widening of experience. As the authors point out, assessing the cost of the scheme is hazardous, especially over its initial stages when costs per child were abnormally high. However, they calculate the costs per place, per week at £19·27 (1975–76), or about four-fifths of those for a day-nursery place. An additional advantage is that places can be provided relatively quickly.

Various local authorities and voluntary bodies have introduced similar schemes for priority children at minders' over the last few years. Examples for which details are available are in Humberside (Wardell, 1977); Edinburgh (Macauley, 1977); and Hackney (Hackney Sharing Care Scheme, 1980). Such schemes have key features in common. Payment is usually per child, sometimes with a retainer fee; or there may be a basic rate with additions per child. In general, minders are chosen with particular care for the work by a series of interviews; in some cases minders who happen to take on a priority child qualify for inclusion in the scheme. The minder receives some benefits, such as training and/or extra support from the local authority, and also equipment. Local authority staff may operate a liaison system between mothers and minders.

These schemes attempt to increase supervised care for priority children faster and at lower cost than day-nursery places can be provided. They are often considered especially suitable for younger children, for more than one child of the same family, and for children thought to be in need of individual care. They are partly a response to the call in the second half of the 1970s for 'low-cost day care', as well as to the view gaining popularity then, that individual care at minders' had advantages over group care at nurseries. Yet care for priority children in private homes, especially in the absence of day-nursery places in the area, presents problems. Perhaps the most important point is that parents of these children should have some measure of choice. Since their need is great, they should get the best there is – in their opinion. If they prefer a nursery place for their child, one should be available. Also we should perhaps beware of going over wholeheartedly to domestic care. It may be that being with a group, as Bruner suggests, offers protection to children. And we should not underrate the importance of compensating children from disadvantaged backgrounds. They should be offered space, large-scale equipment, the opportunity to interact with various different people. Let us, in fact, keep our options open.

For the generality of children there is of course no prospect at present of salaried childminders. The costs are high. It is no part of day-care policy that local authorities should meet them, in whole or in part and parents could not. Furthermore there is no reason to suppose that enough women in suitable homes would come forward to meet the demand for places. Salaried minding as part of a wide variety of services supervised by the local authority to meet demand – that is another story, and to that inviting prospect we now turn.

Policy changes

We have argued that the private sector is not capable of supplying a service which is both sufficient and of good quality. It is possible that demand for day care could be cut back by measures for parental leave, job protection and income maintenance for families with young children. These steps would be expensive, but so is the alternative of high quality day care. In the absence of such policy – and indeed alongside it, if parental choice is to be maintained – it is necessary to ask how a standard of care which at least meets current D H S S recommendations could be available to all children, so that the very poor service received at present by a substantial minority could be removed. What is important is that those responsible for standards should have the means to bring about improvement. At present, parents are ultimately responsible for the care their children receive, although the local authority is empowered to take some responsibility. It may be maintained that this is as it should be – parents should choose good care for their children (cf. Ministry of Health, 1965); standards and practices may be no worse in some respects at poor minders than in the child's own home; and criteria such as those used in this study are British and middle class and therefore unsuitable for assessing the care of children from the working class or the ethnic minorities (a view put to the authors by an Assistant Director of Social Services).

However, there are reasons for believing that to leave parents with responsibility for adequate standards is not in the child's best interests. First, the parents' ability to choose a good minder depends to some extent on factors which may be outside their control – for example, the willingness of minders to take babies or children belonging to minority groups. It may also depend on their facility in the English language, their knowledge of the day-care system and the information available to them on which to form valid judgements. For some parents, the very fact of registration may continue to lend that 'false official gloss to quite inadequate care for young children' to which Yudkin and Holme drew attention in the early 1960s. However, this study provides evidence that some parents do, over a period of time, become aware that standards are not satisfactory and respond by removing their child.

The claim that some children would do no worse at home than at the minder's may have some truth. Some of the children who lived in overcrowded homes with no garden did no better at their minder's. This bears out Little's statement that in poor, badly housed communities the care given by minders is likely to be equally impoverished. This should not lead to complacency about poor conditions, but alert policy-makers to the deficiencies of current policies. It is because parents are left with ultimate responsibility when they may lack both the power and freedom to exercise it effectively that a substantial minority of children receive poor care. What is more, the local authority is not obliged to take up such responsibility on the parents' behalf. Because of this, the daily experience of the children, especially from working-class families or families from minority groups, is likely to be of a piece with the disadvantages they meet in other aspects of their lives.

To effect improvements a change of public policy is needed so that the maintenance of adequate standards in childminding becomes the *statutory* rather than the discretionary responsibility of local government. We have argued that stringent regulation might produce minders of high quality but inadequate in numbers, with unregistered minders meeting the shortfall. To avoid this it would be necessary to move away from the *protection* of children in private day care, and towards *provision* for children in the public sector. This step would have the further advantage of doing away with the distinction between 'priority' children and the rest as far as child care is concerned.

The best way therefore to ensure the provision of enough high quality day care for under-threes would be to make the local authority statutorily responsible for providing it, whether the services were run privately, voluntarily or by the local authority itself. This is a major recommendation of the Central Policy Review Staff report, *Services for Young Children with Working Mothers* (1978). However, the CPRS proposal is unlikely to be translated into effective action unless there is a centrally coordinated approach to the formulation of policies and expenditure for young children and their families. The CPRS proposes a joint unit to be staffed by DHSS and DES officials. The CPRS is optimistic: it argues that progress towards coordinated working is taking place both centrally and locally. This is a matter of opinion. Local authorities are forming joint committees and implementing joint ventures on a pilot and experimental level, but they face many problems in trying to fuse the two traditions of education and care. To achieve effective and efficient planning and action for young children, it would seem sensible for one central department to be responsible. The proposed services would not centre on priority children and so an exclusive social service interest would no longer be appropriate. The local education authority already provides the greater part of services for children of all ages, and if they took over services for under-threes it might lead to more ordered planning for children as they progressed up the age range. This is not to deny the need for social service and health input. Indeed a local coordinating committee involving all three services would be necessary.

The local authority would be responsible for planning services for the area. It would provide some services directly, and provide secure funding and support for local initiatives. Monitoring and enforcing standards would be a major part of its responsibility. It would be important for the local authority to collaborate fully with parents, who should have the opportunity for involvement in the planning, management and running of services. Local authorities should also be required to take especially careful measures to respond to the wishes of ethnic minority groups, given the particularly severe disadvantages they suffer. In order to achieve provision of reasonable quality across the board, guidelines would be required from the central government department responsible.

Two further issues need mention here. One is training and the other is fees to parents. A unified service, planned to provide for the diverse needs and wishes of families with young children, would offer an opportunity to reform the training of child-care workers. At present, as in every aspect of services for under-fives, there is chaos. There is a variety of trainings – for teaching, playgroup work, nursery nursing and even minding. People cannot easily move from one setting to another and career ladders are short.

Recently, proposals have been made by the National Nursery Campaign (1980) for a training scheme for all child-care workers at pre-school level. The proposals aim for a minimum, nationally accepted qualification, in the interests of providing a reasonable and reliable service. A second aim is for the basic training to serve as a qualification for more advanced studies, and allow workers to transfer from one child-care setting to another. It remains to be seen whether these proposals are accepted by the powerful interests concerned, the unions and government departments. Opposition is likely, since the caring and education professions have long, separate traditions; and the training, pay and status of teachers, nursery nurses, playgroup leaders and childminders have varied greatly. (In fact the NNEB (1981) has already rejected the NNC's proposals.)

On the face of it unified training would have a welcome effect on pre-school provision, including minding. Training courses in the care and education of under-fives might be more sensitive to the wide range of children's needs and interests, than more narrowly focused courses. It might raise the morale of child-care workers by offering them a qualification that allowed them to work in different settings, and so opened up a career in the field. It might help to encourage cooperation between different kinds of pre-school provision. Minding might be seen as an attractive option for a child-care worker when she had young children of her own; and people who started out as minders would benefit from contact with and training with other child-care workers.

What about costs to parents? There have long been calls for services to be provided 'free' to parents. Our present jumble of services makes a variety of charges, based partly on their perceived purposes and partly on historical legacies: education is free, day nurseries are means-tested, childminding fees depend on the play of the market. But if the service is to be based on the principle of parental wishes, access must not be restricted by parents' financial resources, otherwise they are thrown back on an unregulated market, with its variable and often poor standards. A 'free' service at the point of use would be the least restrictive of all, and this is our preferred option. But what is politically acceptable is another question. Investing in young children has never been politically popular in this country. Other European countries have gone for a standard rate for all services, means-tested in some countries. As many commentators have pointed out, it is not a question whether we *can* afford it, but whether we *will*. We realise this is a very large topic to which we cannot do justice here. The point we wish to make is that parents should not be deterred from using services by prohibitive costs.

If local authorities were responsible for providing day care in their area, services might vary according to the needs and wishes of local parents and local circumstances. Family types vary widely: there are lone-parent families, families supported by strong local networks of relatives; families from overseas, or belonging to ethnic minorities; families where parents recognize the mother's right to work and the father's right to be involved in child care; families whose housing is unsatisfactory for bringing up children. These groups may have different needs for their children and different viewpoints. There will be a variety of wishes about the age the child might start, the hours he might attend, what sorts of experiences his day should contain, and how far the parents should contribute by management or direct participation in his care.

Local resources would also determine the kinds of day-care services. In some areas, private high standard childminding might be available, as one choice, and this might suit some families. Salaried childminding is another option. Group care could be extended to under-threes by building on existing resources; providing small groups attached to playgroups and nursery schools and classes. In some areas, parents might wish to run their own community nurseries. In the inner city it would almost certainly be essential to provide some group care, since it is unlikely that there would be enough minders, private or salaried, who met the standards required. We would not want to suggest that any of these options is necessarily better than any other – there is no evidence about this. Both group care and individual care have potential for providing a good service. It is important that both are available in order to meet parents' wishes and so that both are developed to their full potential. We have considered two major policy reforms in this chapter. The first is the underpinning of parental choice to care for children themselves by income replacement and job protection, and the second is the effective regulation and provision of day care by the local authority. Both these measures are costly. They need to be seen against the hidden costs of the present system in which disadvantaged children suffer further deprivation and women's rights to equality cannot be exercised.

Notes

1. In 1979, 44 per cent of four-year-olds, and 18 per cent of three-year-olds were in maintained schools, mainly part-time, compared with the Plowden targets of part-time places for 75 per cent and 35 per cent of the two age-groups, plus 15 per cent full-time places for each age-group (OPCS, 1981; Blackstone and Crispin, 1980).
2. However, policy and goals on nursery education are less clear-cut since the passing of the Education Act, 1980. This converts the duty of education authorities to have regard for providing education for under-fives into a power (Education Act, 1980, Section 24). This measure was introduced in the wake of Oxfordshire's proposal early in 1980 to close its nursery schools as an economy measure. *The Guardian* (8 February 1980) noted that DES lawyers interpreted the relevant clause of the 1944 Education Act to mean that local education authorities had a duty to provide nursery education for those who wanted it for their children.
3. The DHSS has recognized the growing responsibilities of matrons for the welfare of the day-nursery mothers. It has proposed that matrons and their deputies should hold a social work qualification (DHSS/DES, 1978).
4. See note 6.
5. At the outset a minder might need: safety equipment (stair gate, fireguard, cooker-guard) – £50; toys, for an under-two and an over-two – £50; child furniture (high or low chair, cots) and transport (pram, double push-chair) – £75; outdoor equipment (climbing frame, sand-pit, tricycle) – £200; baby equipment (sterilizing equipment, crockery, baby-relaxer, changing mat) – £25. Perhaps a total of £400. Some of these would need to be replaced each year, or different items provided for a different age-group – perhaps £100. If this were spread over five years (a typical work-span for a minder) the cost for equipment would be £800, or £160 per year, per minder, or £80 per child, assuming two children at each minder's. Some of the sturdier items listed might be loaned from local authority stock, thus reducing costs. This calculation omits other running costs – wear and tear on furniture and decoration, heating and phone bills. Assessment of these costs is even more problematic, since usage by the minder's family and by the minded children is difficult to separate out.
6. Under the Danish Family Day Care scheme, women who apply to be family day-care (FDC) mothers are not required to have any formal qualifications, but they are assessed over several interviews, and their premises too are assessed for suitability. The FDC

mother then starts a probationary period of thirteen weeks, with one week's notice on either side. After this time she signs a contract, terminable at one month's notice; she agrees to work a 43½-hour week, normally between 6 am and 6 pm, and may be paid extra if a parent needs a longer week for the child. She may take up to four children under seven years old (the compulsory school age) including her own. In addition she must make and keep contact with one or two other children in this form of care so that she can take them in an emergency or if the other placement ends. She is paid by the local authority per child, and with three children the pay amounts to that for an untrained nursery nurse. The F D C minder's pay is guaranteed if she or the child is ill, and for her annual leave. Some training courses are offered in some areas. The local authority employs staff at the ratio of one to 50 children. Their role is to select, supervise and advise the F D C mothers. They are responsible too for interviewing all mothers wanting day care, and for arranging initial introductory visits by the mother and child to the F D C mothers; at one of these they are present to supervise the making of the formal agreement between the two mothers. They are also responsible for arranging the provision of all equipment needed by the F D C mother to carry out her work. This includes child furniture and transport, baby equipment (including nappies, sterilizing equipment, lotions, furniture), toys and books. They are also responsible for arranging for the health supervision of the children. Mothers pay for this service at the same rate as for nursery care, with a means-tested scale for low-income families. Family day care is thus planned on the principle that it should offer, as far as is practicable in the domestic setting, day care of as high a standard as that offered at nursery centres (Bang, 1979).

Appendices

Appendix A
Numbers of Interviews and Numbers of Children

Interviews

Minding sample:	main sub-sample of minders	66	
	secondary sub-sample	93	159
	mothers	64	
	local authority support staff	4	
Day-nursery sample:	matrons	15	
	nursery nurses	41	
	mothers	40	
	local authority day-care staff	4	
Data obtained 12 months later from:	minders	75	
	matrons	7	

Numbers of children at minders'

0–11 months	49	
12–23 months	108	
2–4·11 years	204	361

including 66 focus children: 0–11 months   27
                        12–23 months   39

Numbers of children at day nurseries

0–11 months	36	
12–23 months	108	
2–4·11 years	590	734

including 44 focus children: 0–11 months   13
                        12–23 months   31

Appendix B
The Childminding Sample and the Weighting

A proportionate stratified random sample of 208 minders was taken from the current list of registered minders supplied by the four boroughs concerned. The strata were the social work areas of each borough. Local authority workers were asked to check the lists in advance (to add the names of newly registered minders and eliminate the names of minders no longer minding in the borough). In three boroughs we selected, as planned, 50 minders into the sample; in the fourth it was necessary to take an extra sample of eight minders because the list initially given provided too few active minders to make up the quota for the sample. The table below shows how we arrived at the 159 minders interviewed for the study.

Table A1: Number of minders interviewed and not interviewed

Borough	1	2	3	4	Totals
Sample number of minders	50	50	50	58	208
Minders who:					
have stopped minding	6	11	2	13	32
have no children at present	1	2	3	3	9
refused interview	3	2	3	0	8
Total number of minders not interviewed	10	15	8	16	49
Total number of minders interviewed	40	35	42	42	159
Total number of minders interviewed as a % of sample number in each borough	80	70	84	72	

Selection of the main sub-sample

The aim was to select into this sample seventeen minders from each borough who were looking after under-twos full-time (six hours or more each day). This was done by working down the randomly ordered list of minders in each social work area, selecting minders caring for an under-two. The target number for each area of a borough was proportionate to the number in the area list. The intention was to obtain, as far as possible, equal numbers of children in two groups: under twelve months, and over twelve months. A long interview and observation was carried out with those minders selected (N – 66). The mother of the focus child was approached and 64 of them interviewed and a parallel observation carried out. Interviews were carried out during the day so that the child could be observed with his minder and then with his mother (since the mothers were at work, most interviews with them were done at weekends). Most of the interviews with mothers (two-thirds) were carried out within one week of the minder interview; almost all the rest within two weeks. In seven cases the interview was shortened, because of language difficulties, and some of these interviews were carried out through an interpreter (a relative).

Those minders not selected into the main sub-sample became the *secondary sub-sample* (N of minders – 93). They were given a short interview, covering some of the topics of the long interview.

The weighting

Two features of the sampling procedure determined the weighting. First, the same number of minders was taken from each borough (except the fourth borough – see above). For the two inner London boroughs the number selected into the sample was about the same proportion (60 per cent and 70 per cent) of the number of registered minders in each borough. For the two outer London boroughs the number selected in each borough represented about one-fifth of the registered minders. Given the uncertainty about the accuracy of local authority lists, it seemed reasonable to ignore the slight variation between the two boroughs in each group.

Secondly, the main sub-sample was a disproportionate stratified random sample with babies and toddlers as the two strata; babies were over- and toddlers were under-represented. This stratification determined the selection of minders to the main sub-sample, the selection of children in the two age-groups, and therefore the selection of mothers.

In these two respects the sampling procedure led to a sample that differed from the target population. In order to restore to the sample the proportions of minders and children in the population from which it was drawn, the data were weighted for analysis. The outer London minders were given a weight of 3·5, and the toddlers a weight of 1·2. Thus where the population of interest is babies and toddlers in all four boroughs, the appropriate weights would be: for babies in inner London – 1·0, for toddlers in inner London – 1·2, for babies in outer London – 1 × 3·5 = 3·5, for toddlers in outer London – 1·2 × 3·5 = 4·2.

In order to present the data in a form that is true to this weighting, findings are given in percentages. The tests were performed on weighted and re-scaled numbers. Where numbers are quoted, this is to give an idea of the size of the group in question, and the numbers used are 'raw' (real) numbers. In a few cases, where the group in question is very small, raw numbers only are given.

Pilot work

The interview schedules with mothers, minders and day-nursery staff were all pre-piloted and piloted (43 pre-pilot and 47 pilot interviews). The observations were also piloted (see Appendix D).

Appendix C
Research Problems

Maintaining the design

The study was designed to investigate childminding and day-nursery provision in each of four boroughs. However, in one borough staff were unwilling for the research to cover their day nurseries, so a fifth borough was approached. Furthermore it was only possible to study a random sample of nurseries in two of the four boroughs. Negotiations for permission to do research on minders and nurseries were time-consuming, and though the research design was maintained for the minding sample, in the end a not so good day-nursery sample was accepted rather than approach more boroughs.

Obtaining the interviews

There was a low refusal rate: only 4 per cent of minders, 3 per cent of mothers of minded children and 9 per cent of mothers with children at day nurseries were unwilling, or too busy, to be interviewed. All nursery staff willingly co-operated. Most interviews with mothers of minded children were carried out within a week of seeing the minder (two-thirds) and almost all the rest within two weeks. It took longer to interview the day-nursery mothers, who were often out in the evenings and weekends. In a few cases the interview had to be delayed because the mother was ill, or had difficulties with housing, relatives, or the day nursery itself. Half the interviews were carried out within two weeks of the interview at the nursery; the rest took longer, and one-fifth took over a month to complete. (This seems worth mentioning as a warning to future researchers of some of the difficulties of research in this area.)

Interviews with non-English-speaking mothers

Nine of the 104 mothers (of minded and nursery children) spoke little or no English. They came from Spain/Portugal (3), Middle Eastern countries (3), India (1), Thailand (1), Greece (1). It was decided to use an interpreter if necessary to obtain basic factual information, but to omit questions requiring detailed answers or answers involving the expression of opinion, since these answers could not reliably have been used alongside those of English-speaking mothers. An elder child or relative was on hand in every case to interpret if required. The disadvantage of this approach is that the study can present little data on some of the problems and attitudes of new immigrants to this country, in particular their satisfactions with their working life and their child-care arrangements. Interviewers conversant with the relevant languages could have been trained to use the interview schedule in the same way as the research team, but this would have been time-consuming and would still have left open the question of how to interpret attitudinal questions.

Appendix D
Observations

Observations were made of the focus child in two situations: with his minder, and at home with his mother; the aim was to study the relationship between the child and his caregivers using the following methods:

1. Where the child was mobile (able to get about by crawling or walking)

An unobtrusive count of his interactions with his mother or minder, was made during the first twenty minutes of the interview. The pre-coded observation categories were *child-initiated* interactions of touch and showing or giving objects; and *adult-initiated* interactions of touch, giving and showing objects, and speech, including admonishment. These interactions were selected for the following reasons:

(a) They were among interactions commonly observed between mothers and children during interviews in the child's home, in the course of earlier studies, and the intention in the present study was to find how far the minder might be a mother-substitute for the minded child.

(b) The categories chosen were not easily missed or misinterpreted, given the situation – an interview in which the interviewer/observer was recording data and so her full attention was not on the minder. The child's or minder's attempts at initiating distal interactions – for example, by smiles, gestures, looking – might easily have escaped observation. Similarly with the child's attempt at initiating interaction with his caregiver, the child's vocalizations were not recorded because of difficulties in interpreting them at this early stage in language development.

Margins along each edge of the interview schedule were set aside for recording interactions. Child-initiated interactions were recorded to the right, and caregiver initiations to the left of the page. The interaction categories were defined as follows:

Caregiver initiations

Speaks. This was an episode of speech, brief or extended, brought to an end by the caregiver stopping talking to the child, and indicating that she was ready to resume the interview: It was recorded 'sp'.

Admonishes. An episode of speech not included in 'sp'. Here the caregiver was using language to try to stop the child from doing something. It was recorded 'adm'.

Object. An episode in which an object was given to the child once, or in which the same object was passed backwards and forwards more than once. Again, the caregiver's successfully resuming the interview indicated the end of the episode. It was recorded 'obj'.

Touch. The caregiver touched the child with her hand. 'Touch' was an action, not continuous contact (which was recorded with child-initiations, defined below). The category included picking the child up, and then putting him down in some other place.

The left-hand column was used also for interactions initiated by the childminder towards her own child. 'A' was used to designate interactions involving her own child for example, 'A sp', and 'X' was used to designate those involving the minded child, for example, 'X sp'.

Child initiations

Object. The same definition as with the caregiver, but this time an interaction initiated by the child.

Touch. The child touched the caregiver with his hand.

Body. The child had more extensive physical contact with the caregiver–sitting on her knee, leaning against her. While this was taking place, there was no recording of any other touch categories, initiated by either the caregiver or the child. The letters 'bod' were recorded, and 'off bod' at the end of the episode.

The right-hand column was used for the childminder's own child, if any, as well as for the minded child. 'A' was used to designate interactions initiated by her own child, and 'X' for the minded child.

In addition, after the interview was over, the interviewer noted whether the child sat on the caregiver's knee at all during the observation time, and whether close bodily contact was maintained for all, about half, some, or none of the twenty minutes.

The number of other adults, if any, present during observation was noted, and whether the focus child, or the minder's own child (a) sat on that person's knee, (b) had any episode of continuous physical contact with her, and (c) engaged in three or more interactions with her (including (a) and (b)). These interactions observations were piloted in the field. Six observations were used for reliability tests in which three interviewer/observers each interviewed and observed twice, and each observed another's interview and observation twice. A correlation of ·94 was obtained for the total number of interactions observed by the three interviewer/observers. No reliability tests were carried out for the separate interaction categories because of the high number of zero scores obtained within categories.

2. Where the child was non-mobile (pre-crawling or walking)

Interactions between the child and his caregiver were observed during a feed. Pre-coded behaviour categories were recorded on an observation schedule as they happened. Two main classes of interaction were recorded: caregiver initiations, and child initiations. The categories were defined as follows:

Caregiver initiations:

Laugh. Defined as an episode of laughter. Recorded: L.

Kiss. The adult kissed the child. Recorded: K.

Sing. An episode of singing. Recorded: S.

Utterance. A word or group of words which contained one idea, question, or piece of information. Included imitation of baby's babble or sounds. Recorded: T.

Exhort. A word or group of words which encourage the child to feed. Recorded: E.

Child initiations:

Babble. An episode of babble. The category includes rasping, coos, and laughs. There is no differentiation between long and short episodes. Recorded: B.

Cry. Intermittent cries or crying/fretting. Recorded: C.

Continuous cry. Continuous crying; the baby does not stop when food is put into his mouth. Recorded: C + .

Except for the category 'Kiss', the behaviours recorded were all vocalizations. 'Kiss' was recorded because it gave evidence of the caregiver's affection. Otherwise, the observation focused on 'utterance' and 'babble'; other categories were recorded only so that they should be distinguished from these. It was hoped, by focusing on language, to find out something further about the relationship between caregiver and child, over and above whether the adult was affectionate. Did the caregiver's behaviour give evidence that she thought the child had language potential? Was she drawn to speak to him? Did the child produce vocalizations in the presence of the adult? Was there any relationship between his babbles and the caregiver's utterances? In the earlier study (Mayall and Petrie, 1977), the children at age two had poor language development. Would observations of the minder's and child's vocalizations during a feed throw any light on this?

The feed observation lasted for ten minutes, or until the feed ended, in which case the duration of the feed was noted. The beginning of the feed was taken to be when the spoon or bottle first approached the baby's mouth. The end of the feed was the point at which the caregiver indicated that the feed was over, either by putting down an empty bottle or plate, or when she gave up urging the child to take more. At the start of the feed, the child's position (for example, on chair or knee) was noted, and the type of feed (bottle or spoon). Any changes in these, and the time at which they occurred, was noted and recorded.

The feed observations were piloted in the field, and with video recordings. An inter-observer reliability study, in which three observers together watched three feeds, obtained correlations of ·97, ·94, ·98 between the three observers for 'utterances', ·97, ·98, ·97 between them for 'babble', and ·26, ·52, and ·55 for 'exhort'.

Other observational data

Other observations concerning the feed, interaction between the caregiver and the mobile child, and the assessment of the minder, were recorded immediately after leaving the premises. These included items such as the number of adults and children present, in case there was any relationship between these and the interaction rate. The *feed observation* included the observer's impressions about how the feed went – for example, if the child cooperated with the feed; if the caregiver's perseverance in feeding the child matched the child's level of cooperation; if she kissed or caressed him; if her manner was warm; and if she ever used a teaching style: giving him information by labelling a quality or object for him. During the last three feeds – those used for reliability tests – there was reasonable agreement between the three observers on each of the items for each of the three feeds.

Items in the *mobile child's observation* also included judgements made by the observer about the caregiver's attitude towards the child – for example, if she spoke coolly to him, or with warmth. This assessment of the relationship between caregiver and child, was derived largely from items in Bettye Caldwell's (1967) Home Inventory. This was appropriate because it has been used with children of different races and classes. In particular, it deals with the observed relationship between a child and its mother or mother-substitute, and it is in this role that the minder's strength has been said to lie. The earlier study provided evidence that this was not the case for two-year-olds. It might, however, prove to be different with younger children. Some of the items are based on easily observed behaviours in the course of the interview. Others depend on the interviewer's judgement, and arise out of what the minder or mother says *to* the child, and *about* the child, in the course of the interview. The items used in the present study were as follows:

Did the caregiver express overt annoyance with, or hostility towards, the child during the visit?

Did she slap him?

Did she scold him?

Did she indicate esteem/praise for his behaviour or manner?

Did her voice convey positive feeling when speaking of the child?

Did her voice convey positive feeling when speaking *to* him?

Did she caress/kiss the child at least once during the visit?

Did she initiate or encourage or advance play during the interview?

In the last eight paired pilot observations, complete agreement was reached between observers on the first three items, and in every case but one on the last five.

Appendix E
Assessment of Minders

Observations were made of various aspects of the minder's care – in particular, her premises and equipment, child-care practice, and relationship with the mothers. Some of these assessments are based on objective circumstances, for example, if heaters were guarded, or whether there was access from the living quarters to an enclosed garden. Others depended on what the minder reported: did she say that she left children unattended while she went out of the house? Still others depended on evaluation based on observation, and/or the minder's report. Was there enough space to play indoors? (This evaluation depended both on where the minder *said* the children spent the day, and on an *evaluation* of the adequacy of the play-space.) Did the observation/interview give evidence of interest in the children, and good child-care practice? The criteria used to make these assessments were reached during the piloting, and as a result of the joint interviews and observations described earlier. Agreement with regard to whether there was sufficient play-space indoors, whether the garden was safe, if the living quarters were warm, and if the children appeared clean, was achieved between observers during the reliability tests. In the case of the other assessment items – were the minder's premises, equipment, and practice, satisfactory – it was decided *not* to carry out reliability tests, but to record assessment items on the observation schedule and to maintain comparability of standards between observers by weekly meetings, at which all the assessments were discussed and agreed. The criteria on which the assessments were based are described in Chapters 5, 7 and 9 which deal respectively with the minder's premises and equipment, the child's day, and the relationship between minders and mothers.

Appendix F
The Children and Their Families, the Minders and the Nursery Nurses

1. The minded children

The sample of 159 minders looked after 361 pre-school children, of whom 41 per cent were under two years old. Most of the under-twos (89 per cent) were minded full-time (30 or more hours a week). It was from this full-time group that the 66 focus children were selected. There were more boys than girls: 55·5 per cent against 44·5 per cent. Their ages ranged from 10 weeks old to 23 months at the time of the first interview with the minder. The age distribution is shown in Table A2.

Table A2: Age of focus children at the time of the first interview (minded and day-nursery children)

	Age in months							
	under 3	3–5	6–8	9–11	12–14	15–17	18–20	21–23
Minded children (%) (N = 64)	2	6	10	11	12	23	22	15
Nursery children (%) (N = 44)	2	0	2	2	28	35	26	2

Seventy-one per cent of the focus children were over one year old. However, most of the children had been looked after by someone other than their mother since they were less than six months old (see Table A3). The mean age of the children when their mother returned to work had been 5·6 months (s.d. 4·1).

Table A3: Age of focus children when their mothers made the first child-care arrangement (minding and day-nursery samples)

| | *Focus child's age at interview* | | | | |
	under 3 months	*3–5 months*	*6–11 months*	*12 months and over*	*N*
Minding sample (%)					
under 12 months	15	49	37	n/a	23
12 months or over	16	37	29	18	37
			no information		4
			Number of children		64
Nursery sample (%)					
under 12 months	18	36	45	n/a	11
12 months or over	21	18	36	25	28
			no information		1
			Number of children		40

Family composition

Most of the children's mothers (56 per cent) were aged under 30 years, and 23 per cent were under 25. The average age was 28 (s.d. 4·8). Most of the focus children were only children (64 per cent); but 26 per cent had one sibling and 10 per cent had two or more. All the focus children but one were the youngest in their family.

Most of the mothers (91 per cent) lived with their husband or cohabitee (referred to throughout as 'father'). But 9 per cent lived with their mother, or with their mother and other relatives or friends.

Where the mothers were born

The sample was divided almost equally between children whose mothers were born in the British Isles (52 per cent) and those born abroad (48 per cent). The second group came from the West Indies (14 per cent), the Indian sub-continent (11 per cent), Europe (11 per cent) and elsewhere (12 per cent). All but one of these had also spent most of their first fifteen years abroad, although some had completed their education in this country. A high proportion of the mothers had been in this country for only a few years: 14 per cent for less than five years, and a further 25 per cent for between five and nine years. However, for 70 per cent of the children, English was their mother's main language.

Mother's qualifications and work

Many of the mothers were well qualified. Twenty-eight per cent had trained for Class I or II work, mostly teaching and nursing, and a further 28 per cent had trained for a Class III non-manual job (mostly secretarial). Only a quarter had neither school-leaving qualifications nor any job training.

Their work reflected their qualifications. All but three were at work and most were in non-manual jobs. Forty per cent were in Class III non-manual work (as secretaries, shop assistants, bank clerks or telephonists); 38 per cent were in professional or managerial work (as accountants, civil service administrators, teachers, nurses or journalists). The smallest group (20 per cent) were in manual work, including 12 per cent in semi-skilled or unskilled work. These mothers worked in hairdressing, as waitresses or in factory work. There was a tendency for the mothers born in the British Isles to be in higher status jobs (RG I or II), but this difference was not statistically significant.

Father's work

Most of the fathers (61 per cent) were in non-manual work, and the biggest group (48 per cent) were in professional or managerial jobs (Class I or II). Two fathers were university students and they have been grouped with the Class II workers. There were no unemployed fathers. There was a strong association between the Class of the mother's and father's work. Where the mother was in Class I or II, 80 per cent of the fathers were also, and almost all (89 per cent) of the mothers in manual work had husbands in manual work. Most of the mother–father pairs (61 per cent) were in non-manual work; only 18 per cent of the pairs were in manual work. So the study sample findings are in tune with national findings, that parents who use minders tend to be in non-manual occupations (see Chapter 2). They are also similar to the findings of the Oxford Study (1980). There 51 per cent of mothers, and of fathers were in Class I or II work or were students; only 21 per cent of mothers and 34 per cent of fathers were in manual work.

Housing

Almost half the families owned their housing, just over a quarter were in council or housing association accommodation, and the rest (26 per cent) were in privately rented housing, furnished or unfurnished, or they lived with relatives, in tied housing, or (in one case) in a squat. Over half the families (56 per cent) lived in a flat or maisonette, one-third (34 per cent) in a house, and the rest in rooms. Three-fifths of the families had a garden of their own, or shared one with others in the house.

A relatively high proportion – 22 per cent – were overcrowded (that is, there were one-and-a-half or more persons per room). And 17 per cent of the families either shared or lacked one or more of the basic amenities: a bath, running hot water, an indoor lavatory, a kitchen.

On all the indicators except overcrowding, the inner London families had poorer housing than the outer London families (see Table 11 on page 91). The privately rented accommodation offered some of the poorest conditions. All the sample families who lived in rooms rather than in self-contained housing, and most of the families with no access to a garden, were in privately rented accommodation.

Two groups of families did worse on housing than the rest. These were families where the mother had been in this country for fewer than five years and those where the mother was under 25 years old.

It should be noted that families who belonged (according to the father's job) to the higher social classes (RG I and II and student) were not better housed than the rest, as to tenure of housing, type of housing, floor level, the presence of a garden and overcrowding. And they were not more likely to live in inner than outer London. Probably this reflects the fact that these were young families not yet established in housing which they owned.

2. The day-nursery children

At the fifteen day nurseries there were 144 children under the age of two years. Forty-four were selected as focus children and information collected about their life at the nursery and further information from 40 of their mothers.

Day-nursery children are among those judged to have a priority claim on day care (see Chapter 2). However, the number of places falls short of the number of children placed on waiting lists. Children may wait a long time for a place, as Table A4 shows.

About a quarter of the children got a place within a month. At the other end of the scale, a fifth of them were on the waiting list for seven or more months. The largest group waited for one to three months.

At the time of the interview the day-nursery children were mostly aged over one year (see Table A2). There were few under-ones at the sample nurseries and so we were unable to select equal groups of children under and over one year (see Chapter 2 for evidence on the general scarcity of under-ones in nurseries.)

Table A4: Length of time children spent on the waiting list for a day-nursery place

	Time spent on the waiting list			
	under 1 month	*1-3 months*	*4-6 months*	*7 months or more*
% of children	25	36	19	19

Range: 0-14 months
Number of children = 36

Table A3 shows how old the child was when his mother first left him in someone else's care. For day-nursery children, this was not, as it was for the minded children, always the same as when the mother went to work. Five of the 40 mothers had not worked since the child was born; and some of the mothers had the child cared for even though they were not at work, because he needed a place for other reasons: for his protection or because his mother was ill. A slightly higher proportion of the nursery children (compared to the minded children) were first placed when they were less than three months old.

As with the minding sample, boys were more highly represented than girls: 62·5 per cent compared with 37·5 per cent.

Family composition
Over two-thirds of the nursery mothers (68 per cent) were lone mothers, and half the mothers lived alone with their children. (By contrast, only 9 per cent of the minded children's mothers were lone mothers.) Nearly half the children had one or more siblings (45 per cent). The average age of the mothers was 26 (s.d. 6·5; range 16 to 43). Three-quarters of them were aged under 30, including five who were under 20 years old.

Where the mothers were born
Three-fifths of the mothers were born in the British Isles, and for 87 per cent their main language was English. Of those brought up abroad (20 per cent), only one had been here less than five years, and the other seven for between five and nine years. This sample was more heavily composed of women who had been born here, or lived here for over ten years, than the minded children's mothers (drawn from much the same areas). Most of those born abroad (eleven of sixteen) came from the West Indies, and none from the

Indian sub-continent (see Chapter 4). By contrast, mothers of minded children came from a wider range of countries.

Mother's qualifications and work

Few of the mothers were well qualified for work. Sixty-eight per cent had no training for a job, 39 per cent had no formal school-leaving qualifications, and 43 per cent had neither training nor qualification. A small proportion, 13 per cent, had a degree. Of those in work (65 per cent) most did Class III non-manual jobs, mostly in offices, or semi- or unskilled manual jobs, in factories, as waitresses, or as cleaners. Forty-five per cent in all were in non-manual work, compared to 78 per cent of the minded children's mothers.

Most of the mothers (88 per cent) had worked at some time since the focus child's birth. Four of the five who had not were mentally or physically ill; the fifth had handicapped twins. But fewer of these mothers, compared to the minded children's mothers, had worked continuously in the same job since the focus child's birth (62 per cent compared to 81 per cent). And nearly a quarter of them (23 per cent compared to only 8 per cent) had moved down in job status since their first child was born.

Fathers

As noted above, only a third of the mothers lived with a husband or cohabitee (13 of 40). All but two of these fathers were in work, one in Class II work, one Class III non-manual work, and the rest in manual work. Altogether there were seven working couples in the sample (18 per cent compared to 79 per cent of the minded children's parents).

Housing

The nursery children's families lived in rather different housing from the minded children's families. Three-quarters of them, compared to half the minded children's families, lived in a flat, and fewer lived in a house. Only 5 per cent of the nursery children lived in houses or flats owned by their parents, compared to 46 per cent of the minded children. But twice as many of them, proportionately, lived in council or housing association accommodation (55 per cent against 28 per cent). This suggests that their housing needs, like their need for a day-nursery place, had been acute, and had been met by the local authority. The same proportion of each group (about a fifth) lived in privately rented accommodation. The rest of the nursery children's families lived with relatives, in tied accommodation, except for one case where the child and his mother lived in a local authority children's home. The fact that many of the nursery children's families lived in council housing, and the household often comprised only one child and his mother, explains why fewer of these households were overcrowded (13 per cent against 22 per cent), or shared or lacked amenities (10 per cent against 17 per cent). But many more of the nursery families lacked a garden (67 per cent against 41 per cent). This is to be expected, since gardens go with houses, and people with children who are buying their housing are likely to choose somewhere with a garden.

The minders and nursery nurses

The figures given here for minders are for the whole sample of 159 minders except where stated. For each topic (age, country of origin, and so on) the data for the 66 minders in the sub-sample is similar. The data under each topic show that the minders and nurses were dissimilar. (Table 2 in Chapter 1 sets out the comparative data.)

Age and family composition
The minders were typically in their thirties, but their ages ranged from 21 to 68 years old. Ten per cent were over 51. None was under 21. The nurses were much younger, typically under the age of 25 (68 per cent) and ranging in age from 18 to 41.

Only six of the 41 nurses had children of their own: two had one child, two had two children and two had three. Half of these children were under five years old. All but one of the minders, on the other hand, were mothers, most commonly with a family of two children. It is notable than a high proportion of the minders (24 per cent) had four or more children, a far higher proportion than in the country at large (OPCS, 1978b). As to the ages of the children, 36 per cent of the minders had pre-school children and 73 per cent school-age children, typically one or two. Most of the minders (78 per cent) had one or more children under the age of sixteen, but a few (18 per cent) had only older, grown-up children.

Country of origin
Most of the minders (78 per cent) were born in the UK or Eire, the rest coming from the West Indies (10 pr cent), Europe (9 per cent), and the Indian sub-continent (4 per cent). The pattern is much the same for where they were brought up. Half the minders were Londoners and 40 per cent thought of themselves as 'local' people. Almost all the nurses (93 per cent)

were born in the UK or Eire, but fewer (37 per cent) were Londoners and 'local' people (34 per cent).

Years in the job
Half the minders had five or more years' experience as minders (49 per cent) including a quarter who had minded for at least ten years. But 37 per cent had minded for under three years. By contrast, none of the nurses had ten years' experience, and most (59 per cent) were in their first two or three years, including a quarter in their first year.

Minders' work history and social class
Most of the minders had been employed before they began minding (92 per cent). Two-thirds of them had worked in non-manual jobs, including one-fifth in Class II jobs (mostly in nursing); the largest group (42 per cent) had worked in Class III non-manual jobs, mainly in shops or offices. The rest of the minders (31 per cent) had worked in manual jobs, mainly as factory workers or cleaners. Only 5 per cent of the sample of minders had previous experience of working with children. More detailed information was collected on the work history of the 66 minders in the main sub-sample. Fourteen per cent of them had done a child-related job at some time in the past (in residential or domestic settings or in hospitals); and there was one nursery nurse, one teacher and one playgroup leader. Some of the 66 minders (18 per cent) had attended a childminder training course run by the local authority. The two groups overlapped (some who had attended a course had also worked with children) and, in all, 27 per cent of the 66 minders had done one or the other or both.

Data was collected on the husbands of the 66 minders in the main sub-sample (89 per cent of the minders had a husband). The husbands were mostly in manual work: 52 per cent in skilled work, and 20 per cent in semi-skilled or unskilled work. Five per cent of them were unemployed. So the minders' households were mainly those of manual workers, if judged by the husband's job. Jobs done by many women, such as clerical or shop work, are classed as Class III non-manual by the Registrar General, and this tends to give women a substantial representation among non-manual workers. The largest group of minders and husbands, viewed as a pair, were classed as manual workers (39 per cent) and the next largest group was where the husband was in manual work and the wife's work had been Class III non-manual (29 per cent). The minders' and mothers' households, therefore, were different in social class terms (see Chapter 9 for discussion).

Nurses' training and work history
Girls are accepted for training as nursery nurses from the age of sixteen. Qualifications for acceptance vary, but may include some GCE O levels. (Three-quarters of NNEB students in 1977, 1978 and 1979 had one or more O levels (NNEB Information Sheet, 1979).) Students follow a two-year National Nursery Examination Board (NNEB) course, during which they spend part of the week attending courses and the rest in day and residential settings for children up to the age of seven. Once qualified, nursery nurses may work in residential or day nurseries, in hospitals, as nannies or in nursery schools and classes. NNEB Annual Statistics for 1979 show that over the years 1976–79, newly qualified students opted consistently more for work in the education service than for work in social service departments (mostly in day nurseries). Increasingly high proportions went to work as private nannies. This may reflect the fact that day-nursery work offers poor conditions of work, compared with other options.

Of the 41 nurses in the study, 88 per cent had NNEB qualifications. Of the rest, one had a residential child-care qualification, one was a sick children's nurse and three had general nursing qualifications. However, all our 44 focus children were in a group with at least one qualified nursery nurse. Sixty-eight per cent of the nurses had done other work before working in a day nursery or training for it; and in 71 per cent of cases this work had been with children – for example, as a nanny or in residential child care.

Appendix G
Summary of Findings

Availability

The data suggested that in the sample boroughs there was an insufficient number of day-care places for under-twos and especially for under-ones. Some mothers had to use unsatisfactory or short-term arrangements; mothers could not easily plan ahead; minders discriminated against some categories of children. Most mothers were using day care at a reasonable distance from home and with hours to suit them, but day-nursery hours were not structured to meet the needs of full-time working mothers.

Stability

Most of the sample under-twos were in their first placement, but some had already had one or more day-care arrangements made for them in the past (32 per cent of minded and 45 per cent of day-nursery children). A year later, most of the minded children, but fewer of the day-nursery children had moved on (62 per cent of minded under-twos, 88 per cent of minded over-twos, and 32 per cent of day-nursery under-twos). Five main causes of instability were identified. First, there is a shortage of satisfactory day-care places. Secondly, minding does not allow for the orderly and gradual placing of children – planning in advance, getting to know the caregiver, settling-in the child. Thirdly, minding does not offer reliable and acceptable standards; mothers remove their child because they are dissatisfied and because they prefer other forms of care. Fourthly, children have to move on when the minder stops minding. Fifthly, the mobility of young families causes some instability for the children. At day nurseries, an additional cause of instability within the nursery is the movement of staff and children from group to group.

Premises and equipment

Most of the inner London minders lived in a flat with no garden; most outer London minders had a house and garden. If one includes those with no garden, then about a third of the minders provided a good setting for child care in terms of space, safety, comfort, hygiene and playthings. And about a third provided a poor setting. An intermediate group did better as to premises than equipment, or vice versa. There was a tendency for children of mothers born abroad and of mothers in manual work to do worse at minders' than others.

Judged by the same criteria, the day-nursery premises were all good or fair (one-third of the rooms did not have direct access to outside play-space), and all the nurseries were well equipped. However, most of the children (65 per cent against 13 per cent of minded children) spent most of their day in one room only, and some staff found the premises or equipment inadequate for the children.

The child's relationships with his caregivers

Compared with the mothers, the minders thought about the child more in terms of management, and for them he presented fewer behaviour problems – he was 'easier' to care for. This may have been because he was, according to our observations, less active than at home with his mother. Most of the children interacted more with their mother than with their minder, in both kinds of observation (during a feed for the babies, and during the interview for the toddlers). They were especially more likely to touch and get close to their mothers. About a quarter of the children (mostly boys) seemed to relate little to their minder, and did not interact with her at all during the observation period. No child behaved like this with his mother. Children tended to interact more with minders who had minded for a relatively short time, or who were less management-oriented and saw the child more as an individual.

Data on the nursery nurses show that they were less management-oriented than the minders. The limited observational data suggest that the interaction rate between nurse and child is more typical of minders than of mothers.

The child's day

Minded children had fewer social contacts than nursery children, but children in both settings had many contacts. Minders and nurses looked after the same number of under-fives, on average 1·3, but if under-twelves are taken into account, minders cared for an average of 4·7 children.

Organization and staffing of the nursery groups varied; but there were broad differences between nursery and minded children's daily experiences. The nursery children played out of doors more, but went out (off the premises) less than the minded children. The nurseries put more emphasis than the minders on toilet-training the child and on letting him feed himself; and more of the nursery children than minded children were given their rest at a routine time.

Assessment of the minders

Half the minders gave no evidence of poor child-care practice, but in nearly a fifth of cases there was serious cause for concern. Using an assessment of the minder's practice (including premises, equipment and child care) we found that just over a quarter were offering a good service; nearly a fifth were offering poor care in one or more respect. Children whose mothers were born abroad and were in lower occupational groups were more likely than the rest to attend poor minders.

Health

The health visitor service was not adequately covering the sample of minded and day-nursery children. In the last six months 45 per cent of minded children had not been seen either at home or at the minder's. Fifty-seven per cent of day-nursery children and 7 per cent of minded children had not been seen at home. However, almost all the minded children (87 per cent) had been taken to the child health clinic in the last six months. Some children, especially those at the day nursery, were seen by health service personnel without their mother. We noted that health service use by under-twos was heavy, and suggested .that recognition should be given to the need for working parents to see to their child's health and welfare requirements.

Accountability

Among day-care services discussed, childminding was found to be the least accountable to the local authority. The standards of care set are low and unreliable. Its responsiveness to parents depends on the contract and working relationship made between each minder and mother. Half the sample minders had had problems with the contract in the past, and half were experiencing contractual problems with the focus child's parents 'now'. A small proportion of mothers (16 per cent) were communicating poorly with the minder about the child, and mothers born abroad were disproportionately highly represented here. There was evidence that a quarter of the minders had a poor relationship with parents. Possible factors leading to unsatisfactory minder–mother relationships were: the poorly defined arrangement; conflicting expectations about what is offered; conflicting life-styles; and attitudes to working mothers.

Standards at the day nursery for staff and premises are controlled by the local authority, and in practice were of a higher and more even standard than at minders'. More of the day-nursery mothers (38 per cent) communicated poorly with staff about their child. It was suggested that mothers, as recipients of a welfare service, might be poorly placed to establish good working relationships with staff. Three further aspects of day-nursery organization and practice may have militated against good communication: most children (84 per cent) were the responsibility of two or more nurses; the nurseries operated a shift system for staff, which reduced their accessibility to mothers; some mothers felt that the nursery was unwelcoming or inconsiderate to parents, or they disliked some aspect of child-care practice at the nursery.

Appendix H
Comments on the Data

The adequacy of the data

As explained in Chapter 1, we obtained our sample through the local authorities. Although minders offer a privately run service, local authorities like to know who is visiting them and for what purpose. For both the minding and day-nursery sample we engaged in lengthy and detailed negotiations to get permission for our study. We were also well aware from our previous study that minders and working mothers, and (we found at the pilot stage) nursery staff, are busy women, with heavy and importunate demands on their time. For all these reasons, we decided to obtain our data mainly from single interviews with these different groups. It may be contended that we would have done better to visit the women on several occasions, so that they would feel fully at ease. A preliminary visit was made to explain the study and to arrange an appointment. But to ask for more than one interview might have been to lose cases through refusals, and when children changed placements. Nor did we feel that the women were ill at ease – child care was a topic on which they were happy to talk. So while we recognize the disadvantages of our approach, we thought it most likely to achieve a good response rate (which it did); and using it we were able to collect data systematically. We used a structured interview schedule which allowed the women to express their views freely. What was said was written down as accurately as possible. Tape-recorders were not used, since we thought their use would be unacceptable to local authority staff and to some of the women.

A second source of data was the observation of what took place during the interview, and an informal inspection of the premises said to be used for and by the children, plus in some cases an additional visit to observe a ten-minute feed. Perhaps a more satisfactory source of data on which to base assessments would have been observations throughout the week of the child's experience and the caregivers' practice. We decided against this because, as suggested above, gaining co-operation at all levels would have been difficult.

The data depend then on what was revealed during a short observation in the course of an interview, and on what minders and nursery staff showed us of the premises. If nothing unsatisfactory was revealed by any of this, then we rated the premises and equipment as satisfactory, and, in the cases of minders only, we rated her child care as satisfactory. It may be that more searching observation might have revealed a greater number of minders and nurseries where standards fell short of the criteria used.

The validity of the criteria

Most of the criteria we used were similar to those given by the Ministry of Health in their guidelines to local authorities (Memorandum to Circular 37/68). So they were the sort of criteria which the local authority child-minding worker might use when inspecting a minder. It cannot be assumed that the aspects of child care we assessed had an important effect on the children's development. An example is the inclusion of toys in the assessment of equipment. Toys are valued in our society almost as a necessary adjunct of childhood. They are recommended for children in day care in the Memorandum, for instance. But we do not know what the outcome of toys, or no toys, is for the child. Watching a curtain fluttering or a television screen may be as useful for him as a mobile toy hung above his cot. Whatever comes to hand may be as interesting as a rattle or soft toy, at a certain age. Furniture may serve the same purpose as the climbing-frame.

When it comes to other criteria, such as safety, or enclosed outdoor play-space, we feel, perhaps, on more solid ground. Nevertheless, it can be said that the criteria used in this study are value-based, rather than outcome-based. We decided not to use tests to measure any of the immediate outcomes for the child of being with a minder, or of any respects of her child care. There were several reasons for this. One was that we did not wish to offend minders. More importantly, the sample was small, and a number of important variables would have to be taken into account when examining test scores: for example, the number of past placements the child had had, his mother's country of origin, the length of time he had been with his present minder, or in day care; and on the minder's side, variables to do with her length of service, previous employment, and so on.

So, as we have indicated, our criteria were based on generally agreed standards of the day. These include what the central government department recommends for day care. We also used as a basis for consideration of minders and day nurseries the standards imposed by the Department of Education and Science for pre-school education. And we have discussed criteria based on what mothers and their young children need from a day-care service.

Generalizing from the data

Childminding

Strictly speaking, generalization can be made only to the four boroughs in North London from which we drew our sample. How confident can we be that our findings would be replicated elsewhere? One approach is to consider what other research studies have found. Another is to look at national figures for, for instance, housing standards, or for the mobility of young families. A third approach is to study integral characteristics of childminding and to deduce from them likelihoods about childminding generally. We have tried to do these three things in the course of our discussion in each chapter, and we will add some comments here.

Research studies on childminding have mostly concentrated on the use of minders by families in urban settings, especially ethnic minorities (for example, Gregory, 1969; Community Relations Commission, 1975). The Jacksons (1979) have provided vivid anecdotal material. The only systematic study in the 1970s, apart from ours, has been the one by the Oxford Pre-school Research Group, which took a random sample from the whole of Oxfordshire. Most studies, except the Oxford one, found cause for concern about housing standards at minders, and all have been uneasy about the quality of care offered.

Some of our findings have been considered in the context of large-scale national collections of data. For instance, Department of Health and Social Security returns show that a quarter of all registered minders are in Greater London, and many others are in our older industrial districts (see Chapter 2). Minders and the children's families share the housing disadvantages of these areas. On the other hand, children in country or new town districts may have adequate play-space both at home and at minders'. On numbers of under-fives, we have pointed to the huge demand for day-care places shown by Bone and the Central Policy Review Staff (see Chapter 2), and the relatively small number of places. The presence of large numbers of children at minders' will presumably vary according to local employment conditions and to the availability of other kinds of day care, but in large towns there is likely to be pressure on minding to accommodate more than the permitted numbers of children. As to the over-fives, Simpson (1980) has indicated the scale of the problem nationally (see Chapter 7). Minders are a major source of help for working mothers of over-fives.

Many of our findings can be related to integral characteristics of childminding. A good deal has been said about this, and the question of standards at minders', and minders' responsiveness to parents has been considered in detail in Chapter 9. Minding is a poorly paid, privately provided service, explicitly promoted as a low-cost solution to the day-care crisis (see Chapter 2). Under these circumstances, where minders cannot afford to spend more money on the children and local authorities do not, the service will remain unreliable and a cause for concern. Chapter 10 discusses minding as a low-cost service in an attempt to provide pointers to why some women choose to childmind, why they give the kind of service we have found, and why local authorities have responded in the way they have.

Nurseries

It is difficult to say how far one can generalize here. As explained in Chapter 1, the sample was not strictly a random one. On the other hand, some features of the nurseries we saw are probably repeated elsewhere. There is little research in the area (see Chapter 3). There were some differences between the sample nurseries in the grouping of children – in family or age groups – and in staff–child ratios. We know that still other patterns of organization exist in other parts of the country. Parry and Archer (1974) found family grouping the most common pattern, but a few nurseries retained a baby room for children up to a year or eighteen months old. They found a staff–child ratio of 1:6·4. This was almost twice as many children per nurse as in the present study, where the focus was on children aged under two years and higher staffing ratios were to be expected. Garland and White (1980) studied three London day nurseries (including one family day-care centre). In spite of age differences, they found similar staff–child ratios to those in this study – 1:4. All three studies found a large proportion of nurses in their earlier twenties or younger. But Parry and Archer found 30 per cent over the age of 35, and they noted that many of the nurses were themselves mothers (unlike our nurses). Possibly these differences are due to different patterns of female employment in different parts of the country.

As to standards for premises and staff qualifications, we can only say that it seems likely that the day-nursery service, paid for as it is out of local authority funds, will maintain reasonably high standards. The relationship of mothers to staff and the amount and kind of participation they have and might have in the care of their child at the nursery, including his health care, clearly need more study. On the face of it, it seems that there are problems; day-nursery families are in receipt of a welfare service, a fact which is likely to make the establishment and continuance of good working relationships between staff and mothers difficult (see Chapter 9).

Bibliography

The bibliography lists works consulted during the study. Not all are referred to in the text. (All publications were published in London unless otherwise noted.)

Abel-Smith, B. and Townsend, P. (1965), *The Poor and the Poorest*. Occasional Papers in Social Administration. No. 17. Bell.

Adams, B. and Conway, J. (1975), *The Social Effects of Living off the Ground*. Housing, Design and Development, Occasional Paper. Department of the Environment.

Ainsworth, M. and Wittig, B. (1969), 'Attachment and exploratory behaviour of one-year-olds in a strange situation', in B.M.Foss (ed.), *Determinants of Infant Behaviour*, Vol.4. Methuen.

Anderson, E.M. and Spain, B. (1977), *The Child with Spina Bifida*. Methuen.

Bain, A. and Barnett, L. (1980), *The Design of a Day-care System in a Nursery Setting for Children Under Five*. Report to the DHSS. Tavistock Institute of Human Relations, 120 Belsize Lane, London NW3.

Bang, B. (1979), 'Public day care in private homes in Denmark', *International Journal of Early Childhood*, Vol. 11, No. 1, pp. 124-30.

Banton, M. (1977), *Rational Choice: a Theory of Racial and Ethnic Relations*. SSRC Research Unit on Ethnic Relations, Working Paper No. 8.

—— (1979), 'It's our country', in R. Miles and A. Phizacklea (eds.), *Racism and Political Action in Britain*. Routledge & Kegan Paul.

Bax, M., Moss, P. and Plewis, I. (1979) *Report on a Thomas Coram Research Unit Social Survey*. Unpublished report to the DHSS.

——, Hart, H. and Jenkins, S. (1980), *The Health Needs of the Pre-school Child*. Report to the DHSS.

—— and Thompson, J. (forthcoming), *Handbook for Health Visitors*.

Becher, A. and McClure, S. (eds.) (1978), *Accountability in Education*. Windsor: NFER-Nelson Publishing.

Belsky, J. and Steinberg, L.D. (1978), 'The effects of day care: a critical review', *Child Development*, Vol. 49, pp. 929-49.

Benn, S.I. and Peters, R.S. (1959), *Social Principles and the Democratic State*. Allen & Unwin.

Bernal, J. (1974), 'Attachment: some problems and possibilities', in M.P.M. Richards (ed.), *The Integration of a Child into a Social World*. Cambridge University Press.

Beveridge Report (1942), *Social Insurance and Allied Services*. Cmnd 6404. HMSO.

Black Report (unpublished) (1980), 'Inequalities in health.' Report of a Research Working Group. DHSS.

Blackstone, T. (1971), *A Fair Start*. Harmondsworth: Allen Lane, The Penguin Press.

—— (1979), 'Parental involvement in education', *Education Policy Bulletin*, Vol. 7, No. 1, Spring, pp. 81-98.

—— and Crispin, A. (1980), 'Education', in D. Blake and P. Ormerod (eds.), *The Economics of Prosperity*. Grant McIntyre.

Blanchard, M. and Main, M. (1979), 'Avoidance of the attachment figure and social emotional adjustment in day-care infants', *Developmental Psychology*, Vol. 15, pp. 455-6.

Blehar, M. (1974), 'Anxious attachment and defensive reactions associated with day care', *Child Development*, Vol. 45, p. 683.

Bone, M. (1977), *Pre-school Children and the Need for Day Care*. HMSO.

Bowlby, J. (1951), *Maternal Care and Child Health*. World Health Organization Monograph. HMSO.

—— (1958), *Can I Leave my Baby?* National Association for Mental Health.

—— (1964), *Child Care and the Growth of Love*. Harmondsworth: Penguin Books.

—— (1971), *Attachment and Loss*. Vol. 1, *Attachment*. Harmondsworth: Penguin Books.

Bradshaw, J. (1972), 'The concept of social need', *New Society*, 30 March, pp. 640-43.

Brent Community Health Council (1981), *Black People and the Health Service*. Brent CHC, Rear Block, 16 High Street, London N W 10.

Bronfenbrenner, U. (1978), *Two Worlds of Childhood*. New York: Pocket Books.

Brookhart, J. and Hock, E. (1976), 'The effects of experimental context and experiential background in infants' behaviour toward their mothers and a stranger', *Child Development*, Vol. 47, pp. 330-40.

Bruce, M. (1961), *The Coming of the Welfare State*. Batsford.

Bruner, J.S. (1974), *The Relevance of Education*. Harmondsworth: Penguin Books.

—— (1980), *Under Five in Britain*. Grant McIntyre.

Bryant, B., Harris, M. and Newton, D. (1980), *Children and Minders*. Grant McIntyre.

Caldwell, B. (1967), 'Descriptive evaluations of child development and of developmental settings', *Pediatrics* (USA), Vol. 40, pp. 46-54.

Carr, J. (1975), *Young Children with Down's Syndrome*. Butterworth.

Central Policy Review Staff (1975), *A Joint Framework for Social Policies*. HMSO.

—— (1978), *Services for Young Children with Working Mothers*. HMSO.

Central Statistical Office (1980), *Social Trends No. 11, 1981 Edition*. HMSO.

Centre for Educational Research and Innovation (1977), *An Approach to the Theme of Children's Rights*. CERI/ECE/77.2. Paris: O E C D.

—— (1980), *Policies for Children: Analytical Report for the Inter-governmental Conference on Policies for Children, March 1980*. CERI/ECE/80.02. Paris: O E C D.

Challis, L. (1980), *The Great Under-fives Muddle: Options for Day-care Policy*. Social Policy and Social Work Group, School of Humanities and Social Sciences, University of Bath.

Clarke, J. (1979), 'Capital and culture: the post-war working class revisited', in J. Clarke (ed.), *Working Class Culture*. Hutchinson.

Clarke-Stewart, A. (1977), *Child Care in the Family*. New York: Academic.

—— (1980), 'Observation and experiment: complementary strategies for studying day care and social development', in S. Kilmer (ed.), *Advances in Early Education and Day Care*. Greenwich CT: J A I Press.

Clift, P., Cleave, S. and Griffin, M. (1980), *The Aims, Role and Deployment of Staff in the Nursery*. Windsor: NFER-Nelson Publishing.

Coleman, J. and Laishley, J. (1978), 'Action research in day nurseries', *Child: Care, Health and Development*, Vol. 4, pp. 156-69.

——, Rothwell, B. and Watt, C. (1975), 'Intervention in a day nursery', *Child: Care, Health and Development*, Vol. 1, pp. 413-19.

Community Relations Commission (1975), *Who Minds*. CRC

Cooper, J.D. (1978), *Patterns of Family Placement*. National Children's Bureau.

Coote, A. and Hewitt, P. (1980), 'Britain's major parties and interest groups', in P. Moss and N. Fonda (eds.), *Work and the Family*. Temple Smith.

Court Report (1976), *Fit for the Future: Report of the Committee on Child Health Services*. Cmnd. 6684. HMSO.

Crowther Report (1959), *15 to 18*. Central Advisory Council for Education. HMSO.

Cummings, E.M. (1980), 'Caregiver stability and day care', *Developmental Psychology*, Vol. 61, pp. 31-7.

Cusden, P.E. (1938), *The English Nursery School*. Kegan Paul, Trench, Trubner.

Daniel, W.W. (1968), *Racial Discrimination in England*. Harmondsworth: Penguin Books.

—— (1980), *Maternity Rights: the Experience of Women*. Policy Studies Institute.

David, M.E. (1978), 'The family-education couple: towards an analysis of the William Tyndale dispute', in G. Littlejohn et al. (eds.), *Power and the State*. Croom Helm.

—— (1980), *The State, the Family and Education*. Routledge & Kegan Paul.

—— (1982), 'Day-care policies and parenting', *Journal of Social Policy*, Vol. 11, Part 1, January, pp. 81-91.

Deakin, N. (1970), *Colour, Class and Citizenship*. Harmondsworth: Penguin Books.

Douglas, J.W.B. and Blomfield, J.M. (1958), *Children Under Five*. Allen & Unwin.

Dunn, J. (1977), *Distress and Comfort*. Fontana/Open Books.

Education, Ministry of (1960), *Circular 8/60*.

—— *(1964), Annual Report*.

Education and Science, Department of (1972), *Education: a Framework for Expansion*. HMSO.

—— (1973), Circular 2/73.

—— (1978), *Annual Statistics*, for 31 December, 1976. Stats. Return No. 24, 1977. DES.

Elliott, J. et al. (1981), *Case Studies in School Accountability*, Vols. I, II and III. Cambridge: Institute of Education.

Employment, Department of (1976), Employment Protection Leaflet, No. 4, *New Rights for the Expectant Mother*. HMSO.

—— (1978), *New Earnings Survey, 1978, Part D*. HMSO.

Engels, F. (1969), *The Condition of the Working Class in England*. Panther (First edition published in Britain, 1892).

Equal Opportunities Commission (1978), *I Want to Work . . . But What About the Kids?* Manchester: E O C.

Federation of Social Insurance Offices, Sweden (1980), *Social Security in Sweden*. FKF 9749 DT 80.02.

Ferguson, S. and Fitzgerald, H. (1954), *Studies in the Social Sciences: History of the Second World War*. HMSO and Longmans Green.

Ferri, E. (1977), *Disadvantaged Families and Playgroups*. Windsor: NFER-Nelson Publishing.

——, Birchall, D., Gingell, V. and Gipps, C. (1981), *Combined Nursery Centres*. National Children's Bureau Series. Macmillan.

Fonda, N. (1980), 'Statutory maternity leave in the U.K.: a case study', in P. Moss and N. Fonda, *Work and the Family*. Temple Smith.

Freud, A. and Burlingham, D. (1973), *Infants without Families, and Reports on the Hampstead Nurseries, 1929-1945*. Hogarth Press (*Infants without Families* first published in 1944).

Garland, C. and White, S. (1980), *Children and Day Nurseries*. Grant McIntyre.

Garvey, C. (1977), *Play*. Fontana/Open Books.

Gaskell, E.C. (1970), *Mary Barton*. Harmondsworth: Penguin Books (first published 1848).

—— (1975), *North and South*. Dent, Everyman pbk. edn. (first published 1855).

Gilroy, D. (1982), 'Informal care – reality behind the rhetoric', *Social Work Service*, No. 30, Summer, pp. 9-18. DHSS.

Gregory, E. (1969), 'Childminding in Paddington', *The Medical Officer*, 5, September, pp. 135-9.

Gronseth, E. (1978), 'Work sharing: a Norwegian example' in R. Rapoport (ed.), *Working Couples*. Routledge & Kegan Paul.

Hackney Sharing Care Scheme (1980), *Hackney Sharing Care Scheme*. From Dr Barnardo's Day Care Centre, Vernon Hall, Hackney Grove, London E 8.

Health, Ministry of, *Annual Reports* for 1920, 1923, 1925, 1936, 1938, 1948, 1951, 1961.

——, *Circulars*: 2535/41, 221/45, 143/48, 5/65, 36/68, 37/68.

Health and Social Security, Department of (1979), *Children's Day-care Facilities at 31 March 1977, England*. A/F77/6. DHSS.

——, with Department of Education and Science (1976), *Local Authority Social Services Letter*, LASSL(76)5. DHSS/DES.

—— (1976), *Low Cost Day-care Provision for the Under-fives*. Papers from a conference held at Sunningdale, 9-10 January, 1976. DHSS/DES.

—— (1978), *Local Authority Social Services Letter*. LASSL (78)1. DHSS/DES.

Hewett, S. (1970), *The Family and the Handicapped Child*. Allen & Unwin.

Hewitt, M. (1958), *Wives and Mothers in Victorian Industry*. Rockcliff (new edn. Greenwood Press, 1976).

Heywood, J.S. (1959), *Children in Care*. Routledge & Kegan Paul.

Hicks, D. (1976), *Primary Health Care*. HMSO.

Hobsbawn, E.H. (1969), *Industry and Empire*. Harmondsworth: Penguin Books.

Holcombe, L. (1973), *Victorian Ladies at Work*. Newton Abbot: David & Charles.

Hood, C. et al. (1970), *Children of West Indian Immigrants*. Institute of Race Relations.

Hughes, M. et al. (1980), *Nurseries Now*. Harmondsworth: Penguin Books.

Hunt, A. (1968), *A Survey of Women's Employment*. HMSO.

—— (1973), *Families and Their Needs*. HMSO.

Imber, V. (1977), *A Classification of the English Personal Social Services Authorities*. DHSS Statistics and Research Series, No. 16. HMSO.

Isaacs, S. (1929), *The Nursery Years*. Routledge.

Jackson, B. (1976), 'Childminding – a breakthrough point in the cycle of deprivation', in *Low Cost Day-care Provision for the Under-fives*. Papers from a conference held at Sunningdale, 9-10 January 1976. DHSS/DES.

—— and Jackson, S. (1979), *Childminder*. Routledge & Kegan Paul.

Jackson, C. (1977), *Equal Opportunities and Childminding*. Speech given at the inaugural meeting of the National Childminding Association, Birmingham. 10 December 1977. EOC, Overseas House, Quay Street, Manchester, M3 3HN.

Jackson, S. (1972), *The Illegal Childminders*. Priority Area Children, Cambridge Educational Development Trust.

Jameson Report (1956), *An Enquiry into Health Visiting: Report of a Working Party on the Field of Work, Training, and Recruitment of Health Visitors*. Ministry of Health.

Jenkin, P. (1979), Speech given at the 1979 National Children's Bureau Conference, Bath, 21 September.

Jephcott, P. et al. (1962), *Married Women Working*. Allen & Unwin.

Kagan, J. et al. (1978), *Infancy: its Place in Human Development*. Cambridge, Massachusetts, and London: Harvard University Press.

Kamerman, S.B. and Kahn, A.J. (eds.) (1978), *Family Policy: Government and Families in Fourteen Countries*. New York: Columbia University Press.

—— (1981), *Child Care, Family Benefits, and Working Parents: a Study in Family Policy*. New York: Columbia University Press.

Kamerman, S. (1980), 'Managing work and family life: a comparative policy overview', in P. Moss and N. Fonda (eds.), *Work and the Family*. Temple Smith.

Kessen, W. (1965), *The Child*. New York: Wiley.

—— (ed.) (1975), *Childhood in China*, New Haven, CT: Yale University Press.

King, R., Raynes, N. and Tizard, J. (1971), *Patterns of Residential Care*. Routledge & Kegan Paul.

Klein, V. (1965), *Britain's Married Women Workers*. Routledge & Kegan Paul.

Kogan, M. (1975), *Institutional Autonomy and Public Accountability*. Paper given to the British Educational Administration Society, University College, Cardiff, 4 October. From Department of Government, Brunel University.

Land, H. (1978), 'Who cares for the family?', *Journal of Social Policy*, Vol. 7, No. 3, July, pp. 257-84.

Laslett, P. (1965), *The World We Have Lost*. Methuen.

Leach, P. (1979), *Who Cares: a New Deal for Mothers*. Harmondsworth: Penguin Books.

Lello, J. (ed.) (1979), *Accountability in Education*. Ward Lock Educational.

Lewis, M. and Weinraub, M. (1974), 'Sex of parents and sex of child: socioemotional development', in R. Richard et al. (eds.), *Sex Differences*. New York: Wiley.

Little, A. (1976), Paper given at Sunningdale Conference. See Health and Social Security, Department of, and Department of Education and Science.

Locker, D. (1981), *Symptoms and Illness*. Tavistock.

London Council of Social Service (1977), *Childminding in London*. LCSS (now London Voluntary Service Council), Chalton Street, London NW1 1JR.

Loring, J. and Burn, G. (eds.) (1975), *The Integration of Handicapped Children in Society*. Routledge & Kegan Paul.

McMillan, M. (1930), *The Nursery School*. Dent.

Macauley, N. (1977), *Information Sheet*, Department of Social Work, Edinburgh Division, Lothian Regional Council.

Mantovani, S. (1977), *Early Childhood Education: Day Care for Children*. CERI/ECE/77.9. Paris: OECD.

Marsh, A. (1976), 'Who hates the blacks?', *New Society*, 23 September, pp. 649–652.

—— (1979), *Women and Shift work*. HMSO.

Marshall, T. (1982), 'Infant care: a day nursery under the microscope',

Social Work Service, No. 32, Winter, pp. 15–31. DHSS.

Mayall, B. and Petrie, P. (1977), *Minder, Mother and Child*. University of London Institute of Education, Studies in Education 5.

Miles, R. and Phizacklea, A. (eds.) (1979), *Racism and Political Action in Britain*. Routledge & Kegan Paul.

Moroney, R.M. (1976), *The Family and the State*. Harlow: Longman.

Moss, P. (1976), 'The current situation', in N. Fonda and P. Moss (eds.), *Mothers in Employment*. Uxbridge: Brunel University.

—— (1980), 'Parents at work', in P. Moss and N. Fonda (eds.), *Work and the Family*. Temple Smith.

Musgrove, F. (1964), *Youth and the Social Order*. Routledge & Kegan Paul.

Myrdal, A. and Klein, V. (1956), *Women's Two Roles*. Routledge & Kegan Paul.

National Childminding Association (1979), *Report of the Working Party Studying the Operation of the Nurseries and Childminders Regulation Act, 1948, as amended by the Health Services and Public Health Act, 1968*. From NCMA, 13 London Road, Bromley, Kent.

—— (1979), *Report of the Working Party on the Training of Childminders*. From NCMA.

National Nursery Campaign (1980), *Integrated Training for Under-fives: Working Party Report*. From Surrey Docks Child-Care Project, Dockland Settlement, Redriff Road, London SE16.

National Nursery Examination Board (NNEB) (1979), *Information Sheet*, October. From NNEB, Argyle House, Euston Road, London NW1.

—— (1981), *A Future for Nursery Nursing*. From NNEB.

National Union of Public Employees (1975), *A Charter for Childminders*. NUPE.

National Union of Teachers (1977), *The Needs of the Under-fives*. NUT.

Newson, J. and Newson, E. (1979), *Toys and Playthings*. Harmondsworth: Penguin Books.

Newsom Report (1963), *Half Our Future*. Central Advisory Council for Education (England). HMSO.

Oakley, A. (1974), *The Sociology of Housework*. Martin Robertson.

Office of Population Censuses and Surveys:

OPCS (1978a), 'One-parent families: numbers and characteristics', in *Population Trends*, 13 September, HMSO.

OPCS (1978b), *Demographic Review for 1977*. Series DR no. 1. HMSO.

OPCS (1979a), *General Household Survey, 1977*. HMSO.

OPCS (1979b), *OPCS Monitor*, GHS FM 1. 79/1. HMSO.

OPCS (1979c), *Mid-1978 Population Estimates of the United Kingdom and*

Great Britain. PP1. 79/5. HMSO.

OPCS (1979d), *Population Projections*, 1977-2017. Series PP2 No. 9. HMSO.

OPCS (1980a), *General Household Survey*, 1978. HMSO.

OPCS (1980b), *OPCS Monitor*. FM 1. 80/2. HMSO.

OPCS (1980c), *Classification of Occupations 1980*. HMSO.

OPCS (1981), *General Household Survey 1979*. HMSO.

Oral History (1977), *Women's History Issue*. Vol. 5, No. 2, Autumn.

Owen, S. (unpublished) (1979), 'The slatternly neighbours; a legislative history provides clues to the nature of childminding in Britain.' Santa Cruz: University of California.

Oxford Study (1980). See Bryant, B., Harris, M. and Newton, D. *Children and Minders*. Grant McIntyre.

Parker, R.A. (1966), *Decision in Child Care*. Allen & Unwin.

Parliamentary Papers: Hansard –

29.10.1945 Vol. 415	Col. 185
12.6.1947 Vol. 438	Col. 1457-1466
28.5.1948 Vol. 451	Col. 513-555
4.8.1965 Vol. 717	Col. 354-5
22.11.1965 Vol. 721	Col. 6
24.4.1967 Vol. 745	Col. 1063-1066
21.12.1971 Vol. 828	Col. 284
8.7.1975 Vol. 895	Col. 499-502

Parry, M. and Archer, H. (1974), *Pre-school Education*. Schools Council Research Studies. Basingstoke: Macmillan Education.

Petrie, P. (1980), 'The effects of different policies in the conflict between working and child-rearing in young families', in *Family Research and Family Policy Pilot Projects under Discussion*. International Colloquium on Family Research 27-29 February 1980. Hanover: Institut för Regionale Bildungsplanang.

Pinchbeck, I. and Hewitt, M. (1973), *Children in English Society*, Vol II. Routledge & Kegan Paul.

Plowden Report (1967), *Children and their Primary Schools*. Central Advisory Council for Education (England). HMSO.

Political and Economic Planning (PEP) (1967), *Report on Racial Discrimination in Britain*. PEP.

Pollak, M. (1972), *Today's Three-year-olds in London*. Heinemann.

Portnoy, F. and Simmons, C. (1978), 'Day care and attachment', *Child Development* Vol. 49, pp. 239-42.

Pre-school Playgroups Association (1978), *Facts and Figures, 1976*. PPA.

Prosser, H. (1978), *Perspectives on Foster Care*. Windsor, NFER Publishing.

Radical Statistics Race Group (1980), *Britain's Black Population*. Published in collaboration with the Runnymede Trust. Heinemann Educational Books.

Rapoport, R., Rapoport, R. and Strelitz, Z. (1977), *Fathers, Mothers and Others*. Routledge & Kegan Paul.

Registrar General)1950), *Statistical Review of England and Wales for the Year 1949*.

—— (1970), *Statistical Review of England and Wales for the Year 1968*.

Rein, M. (1976), *Social Science and Public Policy*. Harmondsworth: Penguin Books.

——, Nutt, T.E. and Weiss, H. (1975), 'Foster family care: myth and reality', in A.L. Schorr (ed.), *Children and Decent People*. Allen & Unwin.

Ricciuti, H.N. (1974), 'Fear and the development of social attachments in the first year of life', in M. Lewis and L. Rosenblu (eds.), *Origins of Fear*. New York: Wiley.

Richmond, A.H. (1973), *Migration and Race Relations in an English City*. Oxford University Press.

Riley, D. (1979), 'War in the nursery', *Feminist Review*, No. 2. pp. 82-107.

Rubenstein, J.L. and Howes, C. (1979), 'Caregiving and infant behaviour in daycare and in homes', *Developmental Psychology*, Vol. 15, pp. 1-24.

——, Pedersen, F.A. and Yarrow, L.J. (1977), 'What happens when mother is away: a comparison of mothers and substitute care-givers', *Developmental Psychology*, Vol. 13, pp. 529-30.

Ruskin, J. (1970), *Sesame and Lilies*. Dent, Everyman's Library edn. (first published 1863).

Russell, B. (1926), *On Education*. Allen & Unwin.

Rutter, M. (1972), *Maternal Deprivation Re-assessed*. Harmondsworth: Penguin Books.

—— (1979), 'Maternal deprivation, 1972-1978: new findings, new concepts, new approaches', *Child Development*, Vol. 50, pp. 283-305.

Ryan, J. (1974), 'Early language development', in M.P.M. Richards (ed.), *The Integration of a Child into a Social World*. Cambridge University Press.

Schaffer, R. (1977), *Mothering*. Fontana/Open Books.

Shinman, S. (1979), *Focus on Childminders*. From Inner London Pre-school Playgroups Association, 314-316 Vauxhall Bridge Road, London SW1V 1AA.

Sinha, R. (1979), *Accountability in Education*. Ward Lock Educational.

Simpson, R. (1980), *Forward from Finer, No. 6: For the Sake of the Children*. National Council for One Parent Families.

Singer, E. (1977), *Women, Children and Child-care Centres*. CERI/ ECE/77.07. Paris: OECD.

Skeffington Report (1969), *People and Planning. Report of the Skeffington Committee on Public Participation in Planning*. HMSO.

Slack, K.M. (1969), *Social Administration and the Citizen*. Michael Joseph.

Sleeman, J.F. (1973), *The Welfare State: its Aims, Benefits and Costs*. Allen & Unwin.

Smelser, N.J. (1974), 'Sociological history: the Industrial Revolution and the British working-class family', in M.W. Flinn and T.C. Smout (eds.), *Essays in Social History*. Oxford: The Clarendon Press.

Smith, P.K. (1979), 'How many people can a young child feel secure with?', *New Society*, 31 May, pp. 504-6.

Spring-Rice, M. (1939), *Working-class Wives*. Harmondsworth: Penguin Books.

Stewart, W.A.C. and McCann, W.P. (1967), *The Educational Innovators*. Macmillan.

Stewart Prince, G. (1967), 'Mental health problems in pre-school West Indian children', *Maternal and Child Care*, Vol. 3, No. 26, June, pp. 483-6.

Stone, L. (1977), *The Family, Sex and Marriage in England 1500-1800*. Weidenfeld & Nicolson.

Stross, B. (1941), *Nursery Education*. Fabian Society Tract, No. 255.

Stroud, C.E. (1967), One hundred mothers', *Maternal and Child Care*, Vol. 3, No. 26, June, pp. 487-90.

Sunningdale Conference (1976). *See* Health and Social Security, Department of, and Department of Education and Science.

Swedish Institute, The (1979), *Current Sweden*, No. 225.

—— (1980), *Fact Sheets on Sweden: Child Care Programme in Sweden*. FS 86 Ohfb. Stockholm: The Swedish Institute.

Swedish Ministry of Health and Social Affairs (1977), *Parental Insurance in Sweden – Some Data*. Stockholm: Ministry of Health and Social Affairs, International Secretariat.

Sylva, K., Roy, C. and Painter, M. (1980), *Childwatching at Playgroup and Nursery School*. Grant McIntyre.

Taylor, G. and Saunders, J.B. (1976), *The Law of Education*. Butterworths.

Taylor Report (1977), *A New Partnership for our Schools: Report of the Committee of Enquiry into the Management and Government of Schools*, HMSO.

Thayer, P. (1976), 'Childminding and day care', *Social Work Service*, No. 10, July, pp. 45-51.

Thompson, E.P. (1968), *The Making of the English Working Class*. Harmondsworth: Penguin Books.

Titmuss, P.M. (1950), *Problems of Social Policy: History of the Second World War*, HMSO.

Titmuss, R.M. (1963), 'The position of women', in *Essays on the Welfare State*. Unwin University Books.

—— (1970), *The Gift Relationship*. Allen & Unwin.

Tizard, B. (1975), 'Varieties of residential experience' in J. Tizard (ed.), *Varieties of Residential Experience*. Routledge & Kegan Paul.

—— and Hodges, J. (1978), 'The effect of early institutional rearing on the development of eight-year-old children', *Journal of Child Psychology and Psychiatry*, Vol. 19, No. 2, April, pp. 99-117.

——, Carmichael, H., Hughes, M. and Pinkerton, G. (1980), 'Four-year-olds talking to mothers and teachers', in L.A. Hersov and M. Berger (eds.), *Language and Language Disorders in Childhood*. Oxford: Pergamon Press.

——, Mortimore, J. and Burchell, B. (1981), *Involving Parents in Nursery and Infants Schools*. Grant McIntyre.

Tizard, J. (1975), 'The future place of the handicapped in society', in J. Loring and G. Burn (eds.), *The Integration of Handicapped Children in Society*. Routledge & Kegan Paul.

——, Moss, P. and Perry, J. (1976), *All Our Children*. Temple Smith.

—— (1977), *Day Care for Young Children*. CERI/ECE/77.10. Paris: OECD.

Trades Union Congress (TUC) (1978a), *The Under-fives; Report of a TUC Working Party*. TUC.

—— (1978b), *Homeworking: A TUC Statement*. TUC.

Uttley, A. (1976), 'Field toys', in J.S. Bruner and A. Jolly and K. Sylva (eds.), *Play: its Role in Development and Evolution*. Harmondsworth: Penguin Books.

Uttley, S. (1980), 'The welfare exchange reconsidered', *Journal of Social Policy*, Vol. 9, Part 2, April, pp. 187-206.

Van der Eyken, W. (1977), *The Pre-school Years*. 4th edn. Harmondsworth: Penguin Books.

Vaughn, B. et al. (1980), 'The relationship between out-of-home care and the quality of infant-mother attachment in an economically disadvantaged population', *Child Development*, Vol. 51, pp. 1203-14.

Wagner, M. and Wagner, M. (1976), *The Danish National Child-care*

System. Colorado, USA: Westview Press.

Walters, P.A. (unpublished) (1977), 'A short note on day-care provisions and policy in France'. Paper submitted to the EOC Working Party on Day-Care.

Wardell, R.D. (1977), 'Day fostering in Humberside', *Social Work Service*, May, pp. 39-41.

Warnock Report (1978), *Special Educational Needs: the Report of the Committee of Enquiry into the Education of Handicapped Children and Young People*. HMSO.

Whitbread, N. (1972), *The Evolution of the Nursery-infant School*. Routledge & Kegan Paul.

Wilkin, D. (1979), *Caring for the Mentally Handicapped Child*. Croom Helm.

Willmott, P. and Challis, L. (1977), *The Groveway Project: an Experiment in Salaried Childminding*. Department of the Environment.

Wilson, E. (1977), *Women and the Welfare State*. Tavistock.

Wood, K. (1976), 'Childminding 1975', *Social Work Service*, December, pp. 42-5.

Young, Sir G. (1980), Speech given at the Annual Study Seminar of the National Association of Nursery Matrons, Bournemouth, 22 January.

Young, M. and Willmott, P. (1973), *The Symmetrical Family*. Routledge & Kegan Paul.

Yudkin, S. (1967), *0-5, A Report on the Care of Pre-school Children*. Allen & Unwin.

—— and Holme, A. (1963), *Working Mothers and their Children*. Michael Joseph.

List of Figures and Tables

Figure

Tables

Author Index[1]

[1] Includes authors of works in the bibliography, other people referred to in the text and organisations.

Subject Index